Orby Shipley

Preparation for Death

Orby Shipley

Preparation for Death

ISBN/EAN: 9783742814722

Manufactured in Europe, USA, Canada, Australia, Japa

Cover: Foto ©Andreas Hilbeck / pixelio.de

Manufactured and distributed by brebook publishing software
(www.brebook.com)

Orby Shipley

Preparation for Death

ASCETIC LIBRARY

VOL. II.

Preparation for Death

RIVINGTONS

London	... ...	*Waterloo Place*
Oxford	... ...	*High Street*
Cambridge	... ...	*Trinity Street*

Preparation for Death

TRANSLATED FROM THE ITALIAN OF

ALFONSO, BISHOP OF S. AGATHA

EDITED BY THE

REV. ORBY SHIPLEY, M.A.

RIVINGTONS

London, Oxford, and Cambridge

1868

Preface

THE object of the present Treatise is expressed by a passage which is to be met with in one of the Epistles of S. Fulgentius, on the subject of prayer: "*Compunction of soul* excites an *affection* for prayer; humble *prayer* obtains the Divine help. Compunction of soul, leads it to regard its wounds; but prayer, earnestly demands the medicine for its healing. And who is sufficient for these things? For who can pray as he ought, unless the Divine Physician Himself pours into the heart the beginning of spiritual desire."

It will be seen that the following Manual of Devotion consists of a series of chapters or instructions upon important points of Christian teaching, which are called "Considerations." These Considerations are written for the purpose of pricking or of wounding the conscience, it may be in many points, that so it may be thoroughly aroused and awakened; of exciting, that is, *compunction of the soul*, real remorse of conscience for past as well as for present coldness and dryness. It must be a very hard heart, indeed, which is not moved by these "Considerations," so touchingly simple are they, so plain, and so wholly true. They deal with such doctrines and facts as have an universal application, which admit of no dispute, and which are always confirmed by some passage from Holy Scripture. It must be allowed, on all hands, that it is necessary for the soul to be aroused to feel its own needs, to regard its own wounds, that so it may be directed to a source whence these needs can be supplied, and these wounds be healed. One great aim of this Treatise, is to arouse, as well as to direct the mind, to lead it to consider its own wants, and to seek by prayer to have those wants supplied. The book is essentially a guide to prayer. It represents, from its beginning to its end, the continual outpouring of heart before God; an outpouring that is ofttimes expressed in the very same words which imply, at the same time, a new phase of thought. These several repetitions are not to be regarded as tokens of intellectual inferiority, but as so many developments of a plan, which is both carefully laid down and accurately carried out under a seeming carelessness of expression.

Regarded as a Manual of Mental Prayer, each of these

"Considerations" has a technical and special signification. They treat of life and death, of the value of time, of the mercy of God, of the habit of sin, of the general and particular judgments, of the love of God, of the Holy Communion, and of kindred subjects equally important. The "Consideration," as here used, implies far more than a mere inquiry. Its equivalents, the Italian *Considerazione*, and the Latin *Consideratio*, do not fully express its particular meaning in this Treatise, where it stands for a reflectional meditation. It calls into play the exercise of the memory, which puts together all the circumstances of the subject under notice; it excites the imagination, which represents, as in a picture, all such circumstances, bringing them vividly before the mind's eye; and, lastly, it urges the will so to fix and detain these things in the soul, that, by its own effort, it may unite itself with the will of God, so that God's will and the will of man may become one.

S. Thomas Aquinas defines Consideration to be "an act of the intellect, and of the beholding the truth of a proposition," (Sum. 22[æ], Q. liii. 4); to be, moreover, principally related to the judgment. As one of the three divisions of prayer, properly so called, these Considerations must also be considered as reflections, as reasonings of the mind upon definite subjects, either for its perfect conviction of some vital truth, or for its persuasion to the formation of some holy resolution. The chief end of all such reflection, must be the bringing the soul into communion with God; but this cannot be effected by the intellect alone. Man is not united to God through the mind only, but chiefly through the heart; the "*Consideration*" must pass onwards into an "*Affection*," which forms another leading division of mental prayer; where the action of the former ends, that of the latter begins.

Let us apply these "Considerations" to one or two of the subjects which are treated of in the present Treatise.

At the first thought of *Death*, we are all naturally inclined to fear it, but the "Consideration" upon death (c. viii.) tends to remove this fear, since it brings death before us, Firstly, as "the end of our labours;" of that toil by which we are prepared for our eternal rest. Secondly, as the "consummation of our victory" over sin and weakness; the struggle has been a sore one; the battle has been hardly fought, but it has been won at last. Thirdly, as the "gate of life;" therefore the death of the Saints is called a birth-day, a day in which they are born to that other and blessed life which can never end. These are the three "*Points*" in the "Consideration" upon Death which disarms it of its terrors.

Again, are we sorely troubled by our struggles with self-will? We find a "Consideration" on conformity to the will of God (c. xxxiv.), the "First Point" of which indicates the connection between perfect resignation to God's will and perfect love towards His Person. The "Second Point" shows that nothing comes amiss of earthly sorrow and humiliation, not even martyrdom itself, if all things be submitted to His Divine will. The "Third Point" explains that peace of soul which fills a heart whose every desire is in conformity to God's will. Let come what may, I wish for it, "because God wills it."

Perhaps, with its cares and pleasures, the world is occupying too large a portion of our time and thoughts. The "Consideration" upon its vanity (c. xiii.) will teach us, in the *first* place, to care chiefly for those things which we can carry away with us after death, to endeavour to gain eternal possessions. In the *second* place, to weigh the things of time against those of eternity, and to mark their lightness. In the *third* place, to contrast time with eternity, and so to become "rich toward God." Each Consideration opens up three *points* for meditation, and to each of these is added an "Affection" and a "Prayer."

The "Considerations" employ the mind, the "Affections" excite the heart; they awake in us those emotions by which it seeks to unite itself with God. It is that *affectus orationis* of which S. Fulgentius makes mention. The affection is kindled by consideration, and the consideration is supplemented by the affection; neither can afford to be separated the one from the other. Whilst the "Consideration" sets forth death as the end of toil, the "Affection" urges the soul to anticipate it, to ask heaven of Jesus, not that it may enjoy itself the more, but that it may love Him the more. The former bids us look at the consummation of our victory, the latter expresses such love, that it longs quickly to die, if such be the will of Jesus. Better far to die, and so to be delivered from the danger of losing grace, and from the fear of love ever growing cold.

The "Affections" to the three points of the Consideration upon the will of God lament over the times when God's will was not followed. They desire from henceforth that His will shall reign perfectly in the heart. And lastly, they express an earnest cleaving to Him who laid down His will for our sakes. "I give thee my will, my liberty, my all." With Affections our author has joined "Prayers." It would have been more conformable to the ordinary divisions of prayer had he substituted "*Resoluzioni*" for the "*Preghiere;*" for, indeed, as is but natural, the "*affection*" in the present book passes into a "*resolution;*" the prayer is more of a resolve than a petition. It is generally a firm resolve which is made in prayer either to renounce some things for God's glory, or to perform or suffer other things for the same end. The "spiritual desire," "*spiritalis desiderium*," of S. Fulgentius expresses itself in the form of spiritual resolution.

This brief explanation of the plan upon which this book has been written, naturally leads to some suggestions as to its use.

And, firstly, it may be remarked, that only one Consideration should be read at the same time. In many cases one point even, with its "Affections and Prayers," will afford sufficient employment both for the head and heart. It must be remembered that the book is intended to be suggestive merely, not final or ample. It presents a skeleton which the devout reader is to clothe with flesh and blood, and animate with the life of his own spirit. It is an outline, the details of the picture being left to the reader to complete.

Secondly, it will be found most profitable, after having fixed the "Consideration" upon which the meditation is to be made, to read, first of all, its title, and the initial text of Holy Scripture, and for the reader to try to form a meditation for himself; after which he can compare his own thoughts with those of the book, noting carefully in what they agree, in what they differ, and how far they mutually minister to each other.

Thirdly, it must be remembered, that the Treatise is but a means to an end, and that end is gained, when the attention is arrested, and the heart is moved. Let the book be then closed, and let a certain time of quiet be given to the mind, during which it may do its sufficient work in the soul.

It is, moreover, believed that this book may be made of no small value to many as a help for the preparation of sermons. Its fulness of application of Holy Scripture is very great, and many of its quotations from the Fathers are both striking and apposite; and many a parish Priest, with but small time for reading at his disposal, may often find in one point only of a Consideration the hint and outline of a whole sermon.

Take, for instance, the first point of Consideration xiv. It is reducible to the following heads:—I. General considerations. 1. The moral inequalities in the government of this world, and the need which these imply for another life. 2. This earth is not man's country; his earthly home is but an inn. 3. The folly of those who spend their substance in buying possessions in a land which is not theirs. II. The heavenly home for the faithful. 1. Beauties of heaven. 2. In it is the fulness of desire. 3. It is an ocean of delight, and an existence of continual joy. 4. Its enduring nature. III. The dreadful home of the lost. 1. It will be a place of straitness and confinement. 2. A place of destitution, forsaken by all, forsaken by God. 3. A home of your own choice. 4. A state of endless pain. But several of the points are richer in material than the one to which reference has been made.

With regard to the translation, it is sufficient to observe that the Italian is rendered into as literal English as the differences of idiom between the two languages would admit. In some cases it may be feared that the English has been made to give way somewhat too much—an error on the safe side; so uncertain and unsatisfactory is a loose paraphrastic style of translation. A few omissions are made. Two Considerations are rejected as unsuitable for our present use. The repetition of the same anecdote is avoided. A few irrelevant miracles or stories do not appear. Occasionally a reading from the Apocryphal has been replaced by one from the Canonical Scriptures. And in all things, that *spiritual edification* which was the one object of the author in writing this book, has not been lost sight of in the preparation of this English edition. But while acknowledging gladly, how useful the present and kindred books are for this end, it is well ever to remember the statement of that same Saint whose words have formed the beginning and text of these remarks. "Œdificatio spiritualis, nunquam oportunius petitur, quam ab ipso Christi Corpore (quod est Ecclesia) in Sacramento Panis et Calicis Ipsum Christi Corpus et Sanguis offertur." (S. Fulg. De Miss S. Spt., c. xi.)

All Saints, A.D. 1868.

Contents

CONSIDERATION PAGE

PREPARATION FOR DEATH

CONSIDERATION I

Description of one who has Departed this Life

"Dust thou art, and unto dust shalt thou return." Gen. iii. 19.

FIRST POINT.

CONSIDER that thou art dust, and unto dust thou must return. The day will come when thou must die, and be placed in a grave where "the worms" shall "cover thee." (Isa. xiv. 11.) The same fate awaits all, both nobles and plebeians, both princes and vassals. Directly the soul shall leave the body, with the last gasp, it will go into eternity, and the body will return to its dust. "When Thou takest away their breath they die, and are turned again to their dust." (Ps. civ. 29.)

Imagine to yourself a person, whose soul has just departed. Behold that pale corpse, which is still upon the bed, the head fallen upon the breast; the hair dishevelled and bathed in the sweat of death; the eyes sunken; the cheeks hollow; the face of ashy paleness; the tongue and the lips of a leaden hue; the body cold and heavy. Those who see it grow pale and tremble. How many there are who, upon seeing a relation or friend in this condition, have changed their life, and have left the world!

But still more dreadful is it when the body begins to decay. A few hours or days will hardly have passed ere it will become offensive. The windows will have to be opened; incense will have to be burned—nay, it must be sent in haste to the church to be buried, that the whole house be not infected. Behold to what that proud, that voluptuous man is reduced? In life he was the favourite, the one who was sought after in society; now he makes all those who look upon him shudder. His relations hasten to have him removed from the house, and men are hired to bear him, shut up in a coffin, to his grave. He was once famous for his great talent—for his great politeness—for his courteous behaviour, and for his facetiousness; but now that he is dead, his memory will soon pass away, "their memorial is perished with them." (Ps. ix. 6.)

Upon hearing the news of his death, some people say he was of great dignity—others, that he left his family well-provided for; some grieve because he had done them good, and others rejoice because they derive some benefit from his death. Within a short time, however, he is spoken of by no one. And his nearest relations, even from the hour of his death, will not hear him mentioned, lest their grief should be renewed. When the visits of condolence are made, other things form the subject of conversation; and if any one by chance alludes to the departed one, the relations immediately exclaim, "In kindness, do not mention him to me."

You must consider that what you have done at the death of your friends and relations, others will do at your death. Those who are living, enter upon the stage of life, to occupy the wealth and the position of the dead, and little or no esteem is paid to the dead, and very little mention is ever made of them. Your relations will at first mourn for you for some days, but they will soon be consoled with that share of property which will fall to them, so that they will shortly rejoice because of your death, and in the same room in which your soul has gone forth, to be judged by Jesus Christ, they will dance and eat, laugh and play, as they did before; and your soul, where will it be then?

Affections and Prayers.

O Jesus, my Redeemer, I thank Thee that Thou didst not let me die when I was in disgrace with Thee. During how many of the past years have I not deserved to be cast into hell? If I had died on such a day, or on such a night, what would have become of me for all eternity? I thank Thee for this, O my God. I accept my death as a satisfaction for my sins; and I accept it in whatever manner it may please Thee to send it to me. But since Thou hast waited for me until now, wait for me yet a little longer. "Let me alone, that I may take comfort a little." (Job x. 20.) Give me time to weep over the offences which I have committed against Thee, before Thou comest to judge me.

I will no longer resist Thy sweet voice that calls me. Perhaps these words which I have just read may be the last call for me. I confess that I do not deserve pity, for Thou hast so often pardoned me; and I, ungrateful one that I am, have again offended Thee; but "a broken and contrite heart, O God, shalt Thou not despise." (Ps. li. 17.) O Lord, since Thou wilt not despise a broken and contrite heart, look upon a traitor, who being repentant, flees unto Thee. "Cast me not away from Thy presence." (Ps. li. 11.) In mercy, do not cast me from Thee, for Thou hast said, "Him that cometh to me I will in no wise cast out." (S. John vi. 37.) It is true that I have offended Thee more than many others, because I have been favoured by Thee with light and grace; but the blood which Thou hast shed for me gives me courage, and gives me pardon, if only I repent. Yes, O my Sovereign Good, I do repent with my whole heart for having despised Thee. Pardon me, and give me grace to love Thee for the time to come. I have offended Thee too many times already. I will not spend the life that remains to me, O my Jesus, in giving Thee offence, but I will spend it ever weeping over the displeasure I have caused Thee, and in loving Thee with all my heart, Thou, O God, who art so worthy of infinite love.

SECOND POINT.

In order more clearly to see what indeed thou art, my Christian soul, S. John Chrysostom observes, "Go to a sepulchre, contemplate dust, ashes, worms, and sigh." See how that corpse becomes at first yellow, and then black. Afterwards there is seen upon the body a white and unpleasant mould. Then there issues forth a foul and corrupt matter, which sinks into the ground. In that corruption many worms are generated, which feed upon the flesh. The rats then come to feast upon the body, some on the outside, others entering into the mouth and bowels. The cheeks, the lips, and the hair fall in pieces; the ribs are the first to become bare of flesh, then the arms and the legs. The worms after having consumed the flesh eat each other, and, in the end, nothing remains of that body but a fetid skeleton, which, in course of time, is divided, the bones being separated, and the head falling from the body: they "become like the chaff of the summer threshing-floors, and the wind carried them away," (Dan. ii. 35.) Behold, then, what man is—a little dust upon a threshing-floor, which is carried away by the wind.

Behold that nobleman, who was considered to be the life and soul of society, where is he? Go into his room, he is not there; if you look into his bed, it belongs to another; his clothes, his arms, others have already taken and divided them. If you wish to see him, you must seek for him in that grave where he is changed into all that is unpleasant, and into fleshless bones. O my God, that that body fed with so many delicacies, clothed with so much pomp, attended by so many servants, should be reduced to this! O ye saints, ye, who for the love of that God whom ye loved alone, upon this earth, knew how to mortify your bodies;—and now your bones are kept and prized as sacred relics in golden shrines; and your souls which are beatified, rejoice in the presence of God, waiting for the final Day, when your bodies even, will again become the companions of your souls in glory, as they were once the companions of your souls, in bearing the cross of this world. This is the true love of the body, so to burden it with mortifications here, that it may be happy in eternity; and to deny it those pleasures here which would render it unhappy in eternity.

Affections and Prayers.

Behold, therefore, O my God, to what my body will become reduced, through which I have so often offended Thee, it will be reduced even to worms and corruption. But this does not grieve me, O my God, nay, it rather cheers me, for this my flesh to become putrid and consumed, which made me lose Thee, O my Sovereign Good. But it does grieve me very much, to think that I should have taken so much delight in those wretched pleasures which have so often displeased Thee. But I will not distrust Thy mercy. Thou hast waited for me to give me pardon. "Therefore will the Lord wait that He may be gracious unto you." (Isa. xxx. 18.) And Thou wilt pardon me if I repent. Yes, Thou wilt, for I do repent with all my heart for having despised Thee, O God of infinite goodness. I will repeat to Thee as did S. Catherine of Genoa, "No more sins, O my Jesus, no more sins." No, I will no longer abuse Thy patience; neither will I wait to embrace Thee until the hour of death. O my Crucified Love, now will I embrace Thee, now will I commend my soul into Thy keeping. "Into Thy hands I commend my spirit." My soul has been many years in this world without loving Thee; give me light and strength to love Thee during the life that remains to me. I will not wait until the hour of death to love Thee; from this moment, I will love Thee, and embrace Thee, and unite myself to Thee, and I promise never more to leave Thee.

THIRD POINT.

My brother, in this description of death, thou seest thyself, and that, which one day thou wilt be, "Dust thou art, and unto dust shalt thou return." Reflect, for in a few years, nay, perhaps in a few months, and even days, thou wilt become a mass of corruption and worms. By thinking upon this, Job became a saint, "I have said to corruption, Thou art my father, to the worm, Thou art my brother and sister." (Job xvii. 14.)

Everything must have an end; and if, when the hour of death

arrives, thy soul is lost, everything will be lost for thee. S. Lawrence Justinian says, "Consider thyself as dead already, since thou knowest thou must die. If now the hour of thy death were approaching, what is there of good, that thou wouldst not like to have done? Now, that thou art living, reflect, that one day thou must die. Bonaventure observes, that in order to guide the vessel aright, the pilot must place himself at the helm: even so must a man, if he wishes to lead a holy life, reflect that death is ever nigh. Therefore, S. Bernard observes, "Look upon the sins of youth, and blush; look on the sins of manhood, and weep; look upon the present evil habits of thy life, and tremble, and hasten to make amends."

When Camillus de Lellis beheld the graves of the dead, he said within himself, "If all these dead bodies could come back again to life, what would they not do to gain eternal life? and I, who have now the opportunity—what am I doing for my soul?" Yet it was humility on the part of this saint which caused him to say this. But perhaps, my brother, thou mightst with reason fear, lest thou shouldst be like that barren fig-tree, concerning which our blessed Lord said, "Behold these three years I come seeking fruit on this fig-tree, and find none." (S. Luke xiii. 7.) Thou, who for many more years than three hast been living in this world, what fruit hast thou yielded? Take care, remarks S. Bernard, for the Lord does not require flowers only, but seeks for fruit also; that is to say, not only good desires and resolutions, but also good works. Therefore, take care to make good use of the time which God in His mercy grants to you; do not wait until "time shall be no longer" to desire to do good—when it shall be said unto you: "Time shall be no longer, depart." Make haste, it is now almost time to leave the world; make haste, what is done, is done.

Affections and Prayers.

Look upon me, O my God, for I am that tree which for so many years deserved to hear these words, "Cut it down, why cumbereth it the ground?" (S. Luke xiii. 7;) yes, because during the many years that I have been in the world, I have yielded no other fruit than the briars and thorns of sin. But Thou, O Lord, dost not wish me to despair. Thou hast said to all those that seek Thee, that they shall find Thee. "Seek and ye shall find." I do seek Thee, my God, and I do desire Thy grace. I am indeed sorry for all the sins I have committed against Thee. I would grieve even to death because of them. During the past years, I have often fled from Thee; but now I value Thy friendship more than all the kingdoms of the world. I will no longer resist Thy calls. Thou dost wish me to be Thine alone. I yield myself wholly to Thee, without any reserve. Thou didst give Thyself entirely for me, upon the Cross; now I give myself entirely to Thee.

Thou hast said: "If ye shall ask anything in my name, I will do it." (S. John xiv. 14.) My Jesus, I trust in this Thy great promise, and in Thy name; and through Thy merits I seek of Thee Thy grace and Thy holy love. Let Thy grace and Thy most holy love abound in my soul, where sin did once abound. I thank Thee greatly, for having given me the Spirit to make this prayer to Thee. Whilst Thou dost inspire me to pray, it is a sign that Thou wilt graciously hear me. Hear me, O my Jesus, and give me a great love towards Thee, and give me a great desire to please Thee, and then the strength to follow the desire.

CONSIDERATION II

All Ends with Death

"An end, the end is come." Ezek. vii. 2.

First Point.

BY the worldly, those only are considered happy who enjoy the things of this world, its pleasures, its riches, its pomps; but death puts an end to all these joys of earth, "For what is your life? it is even a vapour that appeareth for a little time." (S. James iv. 14.) The vapours which arise from the earth, sometimes when raised in the air and clothed with the light of the sun, cause a beautiful appearance; but how long does it last? It vanishes with a little wind. Behold that great man, who to-day is courted, feared, and almost adored; to-morrow, when he is dead, he will be despised, reviled, and scorned. When death comes, all must be left. The brother of that great servant of God, Thomas à Kempis, boasted of having made a beautiful house; but a friend told him one day that there was one great defect. What is it? he demanded. "The defect," replied the other, "is, that you have had a door made in it." "Indeed!" exclaimed he; "is the door a defect?" "Yes," replied the friend, "because one day you will have to be carried out of that door dead, and thus will you have to leave your house and all that is in it."

Death, in short, despoils man of all the things in this world. What a sad sight it is to see a prince carried forth from his palace, never more to enter it, and to see others take possession of his furniture, his money, and of all his other goods! He is left in the grave with a garment on that will scarcely cover his body. There is no one now to prize and to flatter him; neither are there any who take account of his last commands. Saladin, who acquired many kingdoms in Asia, when dying, said, that when his body was taken to be buried, a man should go before it, with his shirt suspended to a pole, crying, "This is all that Saladin carries to the grave."

When the body of that prince is shut up in the grave, the flesh will soon fall off, and his skeleton will no longer be distinguished from other skeletons. S. Basil crys, "Contemplate the sepulchre, and see whether you can distinguish who was the servant and who was the lord."

Diogenes was one day observed by Alexander the Great to be anxiously seeking for something amidst certain skulls. "What dost thou seek?" inquired Alexander, with curiosity. "I am seeking," he replied, "the skull of thy father, King Philip, and I cannot distinguish it; if thou canst find it, show it to me." In this world, men are born of unequal rank, but after death all will be equal, observes Seneca. And Horace said, that death makes the spade equal to the sceptre.

Finally, when death comes, "the end comes;" everything is ended, and everything must be left, and nothing is taken to the grave, of all the things of this world.

Affections and Prayers.

Since, my dear Lord, Thou dost grant me understanding to know, that all that the world esteems, is but vanity and foolishness, give me strength to leave all its allurements before death may come to snatch me from them. Alas! wretched me, how often, because of the miserable pleasures and possessions of this world, have I not offended, and lost Thee. O Thou Infinite Good, O my Jesus, O my Heavenly Physician, look upon my poor miserable soul, and upon the heavy wounds I have made with my sins, and do Thou have mercy upon me. "If Thou wilt Thou canst make me clean." I know Thou wilt make me clean; but in order to cleanse me, Thou desirest that I should repent of all the injuries I have done Thee. I do indeed repent of them with my whole heart; heal me, therefore, now that Thou canst do so. "Heal my soul, for I have sinned against Thee." (Ps. xli. 4.) I have often been forgetful of Thee, but Thou hast never been forgetful of me; and now make me feel that Thou wilt also forget those offences which I have committed against Thee, if only I abhor them. "If the wicked will turn from all his sins that he hath committed . . . . he shall surely live, he shall not die." (Ezek. xviii. 21.) I do, indeed, detest them, and hate them above every other evil. Forget Thou, O my Redeemer, the sins I have committed against Thee. In future, I would rather lose all, even life itself, than Thy grace. And of what use are all the world's treasures to me without Thy grace?

Ah, help me! for Thou knowest how weak I am. Satan will never cease to tempt me; he is now preparing to assault me, in order to make me his slave once more. No, my Jesus, I know Thou wilt not abandon me. I wish to be the slave of Thy love from this day forth. Thou alone art my Lord; Thou hast created me, Thou hast redeemed me, Thou hast loved me beyond all others; Thou alone deservest to be loved; Thee only will I love.

Second Point.

Philip II., King of Spain, being near death, called his son to him, and casting aside his royal robe, and showing him his breast, which was all gnawed by worms, said to him, "Prince, see how we die, and see how all the grandeur of this world is finished." Theodoret spoke truly when he said, that "death fears neither riches nor guards, nor the purple; rottenness follows, and health fails." So that every one who dies, although he may be a prince, takes nothing with him to the grave; all the glory remains upon the bed where he died. "For he shall carry nothing away with him when he dieth: neither shall his pomp follow him." (Ps. xlix. 17.)

S. Antoninus relates, that when Alexander the Great was dead, a certain philosopher, exclaiming, said, "Behold he who was treading upon the earth yesterday, now by that same earth is possessed. Yesterday, the whole earth was not enough for him, now, he lies in about seven spans thereof. Yesterday, he conducted his armies over the earth, and now he is taken by a few men to be put under the earth." But rather let us listen to God, when He says: "Why is earth and ashes proud?" (Ecclus. x. 9.) Man, dost thou not see, that thou art nothing but dust and ashes; and of what, therefore, art thou proud? Why, therefore, dost thou spend thy years, and thy thoughts, in seeking to make thyself great in this world? Death will soon come, and then all thy grandeur will come to an end, and also all thy designs. "And then all his thoughts perish." (Ps. cxlvi. 3.)

Oh how much happier was the death of S. Paul the hermit, who lived sixty years shut up in a cave, than the death of Nero, who was emperor of Rome? How much happier was the death of Felix, a Capuchin lay brother, than the death of Henry VIII., who lived in royal splendour, but who was the enemy of God? But we must consider, that these holy men, in order to die such a happy death, gave up everything—their country, the hopes and pleasures which the world offered them; and they embraced a life which was poor and despised. They buried their lives in this world, so that they might not be buried when dead, in hell. But how can the worldly, who are living in sin—in worldly pleasure, in dangerous occasions—how can they, I repeat, hope to die a happy death? God now threatens those who are living in sin, that when they are on the bed of death they will seek Him, but they will not find Him. "Ye shall seek me and shall not find me." (S. John vii. 34.) God says, that that will be the time for vengeance, but not for mercy. "To me belongeth vengeance and recompence." (Deut. xxxii. 35.) Reason tells us the same; for at the hour of death, a worldly man will find his mind fail him; his heart dark and hardened, because of his evil habits; his temptations will be very strong; how can he, who in life has been wont to yield to sin and to let sin conquer him—how can such an one, I say, ever expect to be able to resist temptation at the hour of death? An all-powerful Divine grace is then needed to change his heart; but will God give him this Divine grace? Has he deserved it, during the unholy life he has led? And does he deserve it now, that he is dying? And yet this is a question concerning his eternal happiness or his eternal misery. How is it then that he who thinks upon this, and believes in the truths of faith, does not give up everything, so as to give himself entirely to God, who, according to our works, so will He judge us?

Affections and Prayers.

Ah, Lord, how many nights have I, wretched one that I am, laid me down to sleep at enmity with Thee? O God, what a wretched state was my soul then in! It was hated by Thee, and it did not mind Thy hatred. Once I was condemned to hell, the sentence only remained to be executed. But Thou, my God, hast never ceased to seek me, and to invite me to pardon. But who is it who can assure me that I am pardoned now? Must I live, my Jesus, in this fear until the time shall come for me to be judged? But the grief that I feel at having offended Thee; the desire which I have to love Thee; and much more, Thy great compassion, my loved Redeemer; make me hope to remain in Thy blessed favour. I am very sorry for having offended Thee, O Thou Sovereign Good, and I love Thee beyond all things. I have resolved to lose all rather than lose Thy grace and Thy holy love. Thou desirest that heart which seeks Thee to rejoice. "Let the heart of them rejoice that seek the Lord." (1 Chron. xvi. 10.) O Lord, I detest my offences against Thee; give me courage and confidence; do not reproach me with my ingratitude, for I am very conscious of it; I detest it. Thou hast said, "I have no pleasure in the death of the wicked; but that the wicked turn from his way and live." (Ezek. xxxiii. 11.) Yes, my God, I will leave all and be converted to Thee. I seek Thee; I desire Thee; and I love Thee more than all things. Give me Thy holy love, and I ask for nothing more.

THIRD POINT.

David likened the happiness of this present life to a dream, when one awakens. "Yea even like as a dream, when one awaketh." (Ps. lxxiii. 19.) A certain author observes, "In a dream the senses being at rest, great things appear, and are not, and quickly vanish away." The goods of this world appear great, but in truth they are nothing; like sleep, they last but a short time, and then they all vanish away. This thought—namely, that all things end with death—made S. Francis Borgia give himself up entirely to God. This saint was obliged to accompany the body of the Empress Isabella to Granada. When the coffin was opened, all those present fled, because of the dreadful sight and smell; but S. Francis, led by Divine light, remained to contemplate, in that body, the vanity of the world; and looking upon it, he said, "Art thou then my empress? Art thou that great one to whom so many great ones bowed the knee? O my mistress, Isabella, where is now thy majesty and thy beauty?" "Even thus," he concluded within himself, "do the grandeurs and the crowns of this world end. From this day forward I will therefore serve a Master Who can never die!" Therefore, from that time he gave himself entirely to the love ot Jesus crucified; and then he formed this resolution, that if his wife should die he would become a religious, which resolution he afterwards fulfilled by entering the Society of Jesus.

Truly, then, did one disabused of the world write these words on a skull: *Cogitanti vilescunt omnia.* It is impossible for him who thinks upon death to love the world, and therefore are there so many unhappy lovers of this world; because they do not think upon death. "O ye sons of men, how long will ye blaspheme mine honour: and have such pleasure in vanity, and seek after leasing?" (Ps. iv. 2.) O miserable children of Adam, the Holy Spirit warns us; why therefore do you not drive away from your hearts that affection for the world which causes you to love vanity and deceit? That which happened to your forefathers will one day happen to you; they, at one time were living in the same houses, and many slept upon the same beds that you do now; but now they are no more: the same will happen to you.

Therefore, my brother, give thyself now to God, before death shall come to Thee. "Whatsoever thy hand findeth to do, do it with thy might." (Eccles. ix. 10.) Whatsoever thou canst do to-day do it, and wait not until to-morrow, because this day will pass away, and will never return, and to-morrow death might overtake you, so that you would then be able to do nothing at

misc
beli
to gi
so w

lai
wr
an
hel
G
B
M
m
T
T
re
o
ai
g
T
L
T
wi
T
bu
Y
T
Gi

I
whe

CONSIDERATION III

The Shortness of Life

"For what is your life? It is even a vapour, that appeareth for a little time."
S. James iv. 14.

First Point.

WHAT is your life? It is like unto a vapour, which is dispersed by a breath of wind, and is no more. All know that they must die; but the mistake that so many make is that they imagine that death is so far off, that it will never overtake them. But no; for Job warns us that the life of man is short: "Man is of few days. . . . . He cometh forth like a flower, and is cut down." (Job xiv. 1, 2.) The Lord commanded Isaias to preach this same truth: "Cry," He said to him, "All flesh is grass . . . . The grass withereth, the flower fadeth." (Isa. xl. 6, 7.) The life of man is like the life of a blade of grass; death comes, the blade is dried up, and behold life is finished, and the flower of all grandeur and of all earthly possessions is cut down.

"My days are swifter than a post." (Job ix. 25.) Death comes to meet us more quickly than a messenger, and we at every moment run towards death. At every step we take, at every breath we draw, we approach death. During the time I write, observes S. Jerome, I am approaching death. "For we must needs die, and are as water spilt on the ground, which cannot be gathered up again." (2 Sam. xiv. 14.) Thou seest how the stream flows to the sea; and these running waters, [illegible] never return again; thus, my brother, do thy days f all. Quickly remove yourself from all that separates, or that may separate you from God. Let us now give up all our love for this world's goods, before death takes them away from us by force. "Blessed are the dead which die in the Lord." (Rev. xiv. 13.) Blessed are those, who, when dying, are found dead to the affection of this world. By such as these, death is not feared—it is desired, it is joyfully embraced; for instead of separating them from all that they love, it then unites them to their Sovereign Good, Who is alone loved by them, and Who will make them blessed for evermore.

Affections and Prayers.

My dear Redeemer, I indeed thank Thee for having waited for me. What would have become of me if I had died when I was far from Thee? For ever blessed be Thy mercy, and Thy patience, which Thou hast exercised towards me, during the many years that are past. I thank Thee for the light and grace with which Thou dost now assist me. At one time I did not love Thee, and then I cared little for being loved by Thee. Now I love Thee with all my heart, and now I have no greater grief, than what I feel, for having once displeased a God so gracious. This grief torments me, but the torment is sweet, because this grief gives me confidence that Thou hast indeed pardoned me. My sweet Saviour, would that I had died over and over again, rather than once even, to have given Thee offence. I tremble and fear, lest at any time I should ever again displease Thee. Ah, rather let me die a most painful death, than that I should ever again lose Thy grace. Once I was the slave of hell, but now I am Thy servant, O God of my soul. Thou hast said that Thou wilt love those who love Thee. I love them that love me. I do love Thee, therefore Thou art mine, and I am Thine. I might lose Thee at some time, but this is the grace that I seek, namely, that it would be better for me to die, than to lose Thee again. Thou hast given me so many graces that I have not asked Thee for, therefore I cannot fear that Thou wilt fail to grant me this grace, for which I am now asking Thee. Never again let me lose Thee; give me Thy holy love, and nothing more can I desire.

CONSIDERATION III

The Shortness of Life

"For what is your life? It is even a vapour, that appeareth for a little time."
S. James iv. 14.

FIRST POINT.

WHAT is your life? It is like unto a vapour, which is dispersed by a breath of wind, and is no more. All know that they must die; but the mistake that so many make is, that they imagine that death is so far off, that it will never overtake them. But no; for Job warns us that the life of man is short: "Man is of few days. . . . . He cometh forth like a flower, and is cut down." (Job xiv. 1, 2.) The Lord commanded Isaiah to preach this same truth: "Cry," He said to him, "All flesh is grass. . . . . The grass withereth, the flower fadeth." (Isa. xl. 6, 7.) The life of man is like the life of a blade of grass; death comes, the blade is dried up, and behold life is finished, and the flower of all grandeur and of all earthly possessions is cut down.

"My days are swifter than a post." (Job ix. 25.) Death comes to meet us more quickly than a messenger, and we at every moment run towards death. At every step we take, at every breath we draw, we approach death. During the time I write, observes S. Jerome, I am approaching death. "For we must needs die, and are as water spilt on the ground, which cannot be gathered up again." (2 Sam. xiv. 14.) Thou seest how that stream flows to the sea; and these running waters, they will never return again; thus, my brother, do thy days pass, and thou drawest near to death: so do thy pleasures pass—thy amusements, pomps, praises, acclamations—and what remains? "The graves are ready for me." (Job xvii. 1.) We shall be cast into a grave, and there we shall have to lie deprived of everything. At the moment of death the remembrance of all the delights enjoyed in life, of all the honours we have acquired, will only serve to increase the grief and the mistrust that we shall feel as to obtaining eternal salvation. The miserable wordly one will then exclaim, Alas! my house, my gardens, that furniture, those paintings, those garments, within a short time will no longer be mine! "The graves are ready for me."

Alas! for at that time no earthly possession will be regarded except with sorrow, by him who has loved it with such devotedness. And this grief will only serve to place the salvation of the soul in greater danger; for we know that those people who are so fond of the world, at the time of death, will only permit their infirmities, the physicians who are to be called in, and the remedies which may relieve them, to be discussed; and when the condition of their souls is spoken of, they immediately grow weary, and desire that they may be left to repose, because they have a headache, and they cannot bear the noise of conversation; and when sometimes they answer, they get confused, neither do they know what to say. Even so do those die who think but little upon death.

Affections and Prayers.

Ah, my God and Lord of infinite greatness, I blush to appear before Thee. How often have I esteemed Thy friendship of less moment than a base pleasure, a passion of anger, a little earth, a vain whim, a vapour? I adore and kiss Thy holy wounds, which I, nevertheless, have inflicted on Thee by my sins, but, through which, however, I hope for pardon and salvation. Make me to feel, O my Jesus, the grievous wrong I have done Thee in leaving Thee—Thou Who art the Fountain of all good—to drink of waters which are putrid and poisonous. What do I now feel, because of all my many offences against Thee, except remorse of conscience and fruits for hell? "Father, ... I am no more worthy to be called Thy son." (S. Luke xv. 21.) My

Father, do not cast me from Thee. It is true that I do not deserve Thy love, that I may become Thy son; but Thou hast died to give me pardon. Thou hast said, "Turn ye unto me, . . . and I will turn unto you." (Zach. i. 3.) I leave every gratification, I renounce all the pleasures that the world can give me, and I turn to Thee. Pardon me through that Blood which Thou hast shed for me, for I repent with all my heart, for all the offences which I have done against Thee. I repent, for I love Thee beyond all other things. I am not worthy to love Thee, but Thou art indeed worthy to be loved; let me love Thee, do not turn from me, let that heart which once neglected Thee now love Thee. Thou didst not leave me to die, when I was living in sin, in order that I might come to love Thee; yes, I do indeed desire to love Thee during the remainder of my life, and I would love none but Thee. Help me, give me holy perseverance, and Thy most holy love.

SECOND POINT.

King Hezekiah wept and said, "I have cut off like a weaver my life; . . . from day even to night wilt Thou make an end of me." (Isa. xxxviii. 12.) Oh! how many who are busy weaving, that is, planning and executing their worldly designs, which they have undertaken with such care, are overtaken by death, which cuts off all. At the hour of death, all the glory of everything that is worldly vanishes away, applause, amusements, pomps, and grandeur. Great secret of death! which makes us see that which the lovers of the world do not see. Fortunes which have been envied, the grandest dignities, the proudest triumphs, lose all their splendour when they are reviewed from the bed of death. The notions of certain false happiness, which we have formed in our own minds, these are changed into exceeding great indignation, against our own folly. The black and gloomy shadow of death covers and obscures all dignities even though they be royal.

Our passions, now make the things of this earth appear different from what they really are; death unveils them, and makes us see what in truth they are—nothing but smoke, dust, vanity, and misery. O my God! of what avail are riches, possessions, and kingdoms in death, when nothing is needed but a coffin, and a simple robe to cover the body? Of what avail are honours, when nothing remains of them but a funeral train and a pompous burial, which will assist the soul in no way if it be lost? Of what avail is beauty, if nothing remains of it but worms, corruption, and horror, even before death, and afterwards—nothing but a little foul dust?

"He hath made me also a byword of the people." (Job xvii. 6.) That rich man dies, that minister, that captain, and then he will be spoken of everywhere; if he has led a wicked life, he will become a byword of the people, and he will serve as a warning to others, being an example of the vanity of the world, and also an example of Divine justice. In the grave his ashes will be mingled with the ashes of the poor. "The small and great are there." (Job iii. 19.) Of what use has the beautiful form of his body been to him, if now he is only a mass of corruption? What has the authority he possessed availed him, if his body is now thrown into a grave to corrupt, and his soul has been cast into hell to burn? Oh! what misery to be the object of these sad reflections to others, instead of making them for his own profit. Let us, therefore, be persuaded that the proper time for satisfying the stings of a remorseful conscience, is during the time of life, and not at the hour of death. Let us hasten now to do that which at that time we shall not be able to do. "The time is short." All things quickly pass away and end—therefore, let us so act, that all we do, may serve towards obtaining our eternal salvation.

Affections and Prayers.

O God of my soul, O Infinite Goodness, have mercy upon me, who have so often offended Thee. I did indeed know that by sinning I should lose Thy grace, and I did not mind losing it; but teach me what I can do to regain it. If Thou desirest that I should repent of my sins, I do repent with my whole heart; I would even like to die for grief at having once sinned. If it is Thy wish that I should hope for pardon from Thee, I do truly hope for it, through the merits of Thy blood. If Thou desirest that I should love Thee above all things, I will leave all; I will renounce all the joys and the riches which the world can give me; and I will love Thee beyond all other things, O my most adorable Saviour. If Thou willest that I should demand graces of Thee, I ask for these two—that Thou wilt never let me offend Thee more, and that Thou wilt make me to love Thee, and then do with me whatsoever Thou wilt.

THIRD POINT.

Therefore, is it not folly for the short and paltry pleasures of this brief life to incur the risk of dying a miserable death? and with that death to begin a wretched eternity? Oh, of how much importance is that last moment, that last gasp, that last closing of the scene! It is an eternity either of every joy, or of every pain that is at stake—a life for ever happy or for ever miserable. Let us think that Jesus Christ was willing to die a bitter and cruel death, in order to obtain for us a peaceful and happy death. For this end He calls us so many times; He gives us so many lights; He admonishes us with so many threats, that we may be induced to spend that last moment in the grace of God.

Even the Pagan Antisthenes, when he was asked what was the greatest blessing in this world, answered, "A happy death." And what ought a Christian to say, who knows by faith, that from the moment of death, eternity begins; so that in that moment he lays hold of one of the two wheels which draws with it, either eternal happiness or eternal suffering? If there were two tickets in a lottery, upon which hell might be written on one, and heaven on the other, with what care would you not try to draw out that one, upon which Paradise was written? O God, how must those unhappy wretches tremble who are condemned to throw the die upon which their life or death depends! What fear will be yours when you will find yourself near to that last moment; when you will say, "Upon this moment, which is drawing so near, depends my eternal life or death! Now, it is to be decided whether I shall be for ever blessed or for ever miserable." S. Bernardine, of Sienna, tells of a certain prince who when dying, in great terror, exclaimed, "I have many lands and palaces in this world; but if I should die during this night, I know not what lodging will be mine."

My brother, if thou believest that thou hast to die, and that there is an eternity, and that once only thou canst die, so that if thou once makest a mistake, the mistake will be for ever without any hope of remedy—why is it that thou dost not begin, from this moment in which you read these words, to do all that liest in thy power to secure for thyself a happy death? S. Andrew Avellino said tremblingly, "Who knows what will be my lot in the life to come? Whether I shall be saved or condemned to eternal death?" S. Louis Bertrand also trembled so much that he was unable to take rest because of this thought which would suggest itself to him, "Who knows whether thou wilt be lost?" And thou, who has committed so many sins, dost thou not tremble? Be quick and make amends in time; resolve to give thyself indeed to God, and begin, at least from this time, a life the remembrance of which may not grieve, but may fill thee with joy at the hour of death. Give thyself to prayer, frequent the Sacraments, quit dangerous occasions, and if necessary, leave even the world, so that thou mayest secure to thyself an eternal salvation; and understand, that to secure this eternal life no precaution can be too great.

Affections and Prayers.

O my dear Saviour, how much am I not indebted to Thee! How couldst Thou bestow so many favours upon one so ungrateful; upon such a traitor as I have been to Thee? Thou hast created me, and in creating me Thou didst foresee all the offences that I should commit against Thee. Thou didst redeem me by dying for me, and even then Thou didst know of all the ingratitude I should show towards Thee. When I was placed in this world, I turned away from Thee, and thus was I dead indeed in sin, until Thou with Thy grace didst restore me to life. I was blind, and Thou didst enlighten me. I had lost Thee, and Thou didst enable me to find Thee. I was Thy enemy, and Thou didst make me Thy friend. O God of mercy, grant me to feel how deeply I am indebted to Thee, and make me mourn over my offences against Thee. Avenge Thyself upon me by making me very sorry for my sins; but do not punish me by depriving me of Thy grace and of Thy love. O Eternal Father, I detest and abhor more than any other evil, the offences I have committed against Thee. Have mercy upon me, for the love of Jesus Christ. Behold Thy Son upon the Cross. "His Blood be upon me." May that Divine Blood flow down and wash my soul. O King of my heart, "Thy kingdom come." I am resolved to drive away every affection that is not felt for Thee. I love Thee more than anything; come and reign alone in my soul. Let me love Thee, and let me love Thee only. I would please Thee as much as it is possible for me to do; and I would give Thee entire satisfaction during the life that remains to me. Bless, O my Father, this my desire, and give me grace ever to be one with Thee. I consecrate all my affections to Thee, and from this day forward I would be Thine alone, Who art my Treasure, my Peace, my Hope, my Love, my All; and all this I hope for through the merits of Thy dear Son.

CONSIDERATION IV

The Certainty of Death

"It is appointed unto men once to die." Heb. ix. 27.

First Point.

THE sentence of death is written against all men; thou art man, thou hast to die. S. Augustine observes that "our good things and our evil things are uncertain—death alone is certain." It is uncertain, whether that new-born infant will be poor or rich, whether it will have good or bad health, whether it will die young or old—but it is quite certain that it will have to die. Every noble, every monarch, will be cut off by death. And when death arrives, there is no strength able to resist it. Fire may be resisted, water may be resisted, the sword may be resisted, the power of princes may be resisted, but when death comes there is no power able to resist that. Belluacensis relates that a certain king of France whose last moment was fast approaching, exclaimed, "Behold that I, with all my power, am unable to make death wait one more hour for me!" When the end of life is indeed come, not even for one moment can it be deferred. "Thou hast appointed his bounds, that he cannot pass." (Job xiv. 5.)

Should you therefore live, dear reader, for all the years that you hope to, still one day must come, and one hour of that day, which will be the last for you. For me who am now writing, and for you who will read this little book, there is a day, and there is a moment decreed, in which I shall no longer write, neither will you read. "What man is he that liveth and shall not see death?" (Ps. cxxxix. 47.) The sentence is passed. There has never been a man so foolish as to flatter himself he will not have to die. That which happened to your ancestors will also happen to you. Of all those, who, at the beginning of the last century were living in your country, behold not one of them remains. Even the princes, the kings of the world, have passed away; nothing remains of them but a marble mausoleum with a grand inscription, which now serves to warn us that a little dust confined within the tomb is all that remains of the grand ones of this world. S. Bernard asks, "Tell me where are the lovers of the world?" and he replies, "Nothing remains of them save ashes and worms."

Therefore, we must endeavour to obtain, not that happiness which has an end, but that which is eternal, for our souls are eternal; for of what use would it be to be happy, (even were it possible for true happiness to be felt by that soul which is at enmity with God) I repeat, to be happy in this life, if in the life to come you must be unhappy for all eternity? You have built that house to your satisfaction, but you must reflect and think, that soon you will have to leave it, to remain corrupting in a tomb. You have obtained that dignity which renders you superior to others; but death will soon come, and will make you lower than the lowest peasant on the earth.

Affections and Prayers.

Alas, wretched one that I am, who for so many years have only offended Thee, O God of my soul. Alas, that those years have already passed away, and perchance death is drawing nigh, and I feel my conscience troubled and filled with remorse. Oh, that I had ever served Thee my Lord! How foolish have I not been, to have lived so many years, and instead of trying to fit myself for the other world, I have laden myself with debts to the Divine Justice. My dear Redeemer, give me light and strength now to make my reckoning sure with Thee. Death for me, perhaps, now stands nigh at hand. I should like to prepare myself for that great moment in which my everlasting happiness, or unhappiness depends. I thank Thee for having waited so long for me; and since Thou dost give me time to atone for what I have done amiss, look upon me, O my God, and tell me what I must do for Thee. Dost Thou wish me to grieve over the offences I have committed against Thee? I do grieve over them—they do displease me very much indeed. Dost Thou wish me to spend the years and days which may remain to me, in loving Thee? Yes; then I will do so. O God, during the years that are past, many times have I desired to do this, but my desires have afterwards proved failures. No, my Jesus, I will no longer be ungrateful for the many favours Thou hast bestowed upon me. If now, at least, I do not try to love Thee, how shall I be able when the hour of death approaches to hope for pardon in Paradise? Behold now I do really firmly resolve to place myself in Thy service. But Thou must give me strength, Thou must not abandon me. But Thou didst not abandon me when I offended Thee, therefore do I indeed greatly hope for Thy gracious assistance, now that I have resolved to leave all, in order to please Thee. Accept me, therefore, and love me, O God, Thou who art worthy of infinite love. Accept the traitor, who being now repentant, embraces Thy feet, and loves Thee, and asks Thee for mercy. I love Thee, O my Jesus, I love Thee with all my heart, I love Thee much more than I love myself. Behold I am Thine alone. Dispose of me, and all that is mine, as it may please Thee; give me perseverance in obeying Thee; give me Thy love, and then do with me as Thou wilt.

Second Point.

"It is appointed." It is, therefore, quite certain that we are all condemned to die. S. Cyprian says that we are all born with the halter round our neck, and we approach nearer to death at every step we take. My brother, as your name has one day been entered in the register of baptism, so it will one day be entered in the register of deaths. As you now speak of your forefathers, even so will your descendants speak of you. As you have often heard the death-bell toll for others, even so will others hear it toll for you.

But what would you say, if you were to see a condemned man

going to the scaffold jesting, laughing, looking about him, thinking only of plays, festivities, and amusements? And are not you advancing on the road to death? And of what are you thinking? Look into that grave, and see your friends and your relations upon whom justice has already been executed. What fear do those feel who are condemned to die, when they behold their companions suspended on the gallows, and dead! Behold, then, those corpses, each one of which repeats to you, "Yesterday for me, and to-day for thee." (Ecclus. xxxviii. 23.) The portraits of those of your friends even, say the same to you, as do their memoranda-books, their houses, their beds, and even the clothes they have left behind them.

What greater folly, therefore, can there be than to know we must die, and that after death an eternity of joy or an eternity of pain awaits us; to know that upon that moment our eternal happiness or our eternal unhappiness depends, and yet not to care to make our reckoning sure, and to use all the means we can, to make our death a happy one. We pity all those who die suddenly, and who are not prepared for death; and why, therefore, do we not strive to be ever prepared to die, because the same sudden death may happen to us? But sooner or later, either with warning or without it—whether we think it or whether we do not think it, we shall have to die; and at every hour, at every moment, we approach nearer to our gallows—even to that last illness, which will be the cause of our death.

At every age the houses, the streets, and the cities, are again inhabited by fresh people, and the old inhabitants are borne to the grave—their last resting-place. As the days of life are for ever finished for these, so will the time come in which neither I nor you, nor any of those who are now living, will be any more living upon this earth. Our "memorial is perished with us." (Ps. ix. 6.) We shall all then be living in eternity, which will be for us either an eternity of endless joy, or an eternity of endless woe. There is no middle way; this is certain, and is an article of faith—that either one lot or the other will be ours.

Affections and Prayers.

My beloved Redeemer, I should not have the courage thus to

appear before Thee, did I not behold Thee hanging upon that Cross, wounded, derided, and dead for me. My ingratitude has been great, but Thy mercy has been still greater. My sins have been very great, but Thy merits are greater. Thy wounds, Thy blood, Thy death, are my hope. I deserved hell from the moment I committed my first sin; how many times afterwards have I not again offended Thee; and not only hast Thou preserved my life, but with so much pity and so much love, Thou hast offered me pardon and peace; how, therefore, can I fear being driven from Thee, now that I love Thee, and now that I have no other desire than Thy blessed favour. Yes, I love Thee with all my heart, my dearest Lord, and I desire nothing else than to love Thee. I love Thee, and am very sorry for having scorned Thee, not so much because I have rendered myself worthy of hell, as for having offended Thee, my God. Who hast loved me so much. Take me to Thy bosom, O my Jesus, and add mercy to mercy. Let me never more be ungrateful to Thee, and change my heart entirely. Grant that my heart, which at one time esteemed Thy love of no account, and which has so often exchanged it for the miserable gratifications of this world, may be wholly Thine; and grant that it may burn in continual flames of love for Thee. I hope to come to Paradise, there to love Thee for ever; I cannot hope for a place there, among the innocent; my place will be amongst the penitent; but amidst those I will love Thee more than the innocent. For the glory of Thy name, let a sinner be seen by heaven to burn with a great love for Thee—a sinner who has so often offended Thee. I resolve, from this day forward, to be Thine only, and to think of nothing but of loving Thee. Assist me with Thy light and with Thy grace, that strength may be given to me to fulfil this my desire, which Thou Thyself hast given me through Thy love.

Third Point.

Death is certain. But, O God, many Christians already know this; they believe it, they see it; how then can they live so forgetful of death as if they would never have to die? If after this life there were neither a heaven nor a hell, could they think less of it than they do now? And it is on this account that they lead such wicked lives. My brother, if you wish to lead a proper life, endeavour to live during the days which may remain to thee, keeping death ever in view. "O death, thy judgment is good." (Ecclus. xli. 3.) Oh how well does he who judges of things and regulates his actions act; who judges and regulates them, with death ever in view. The memory of death makes us lose all the affection which we feel for things that are earthly. "Let the end of this life be thought upon, and there will be nothing in this world to be loved," observes S. Lawrence Justinian. "For all that is in the world: the lust of the flesh, and the lust of the eyes, and the pride of life." (1 S. John ii. 16.) All the pleasures of the world may be reduced to the pleasures of sense, the pleasures of riches and honours; but he who thinks that within a short time he will be reduced to ashes, and that he will be food for worms under the earth, despises all the pleasures the world can give him.

And the saints, indeed, who have kept death ever in view, have despised all the goods of this world. To keep death ever in view, S. Charles Borromeo kept a skull upon a little table, so that he might continually contemplate it. Cardinal Baronius had these words inscribed upon his ring: "Remember death!" The Venerable Father Juvenal Ancina, Bishop of Saluzzo, had this motto written on a skull, "What thou art I was once; what I am thou wilt be." Another saint, a hermit, being asked when dying why he was so rejoiced, answered, "I have kept death ever before my eyes, and therefore, now that it is come, I see nothing new in it."

What folly would it not be for a traveller, if when travelling, he were only to think of making himself great in that country through which he only has to pass, without minding the being reduced to live miserably in that country where he will have to spend his whole life? And is he not foolish, who seeks his happiness in this world, where he has to remain but a few days, and who by so doing, runs the risk of being unhappy in the world to come, where he will have to remain for ever?

He who possesses anything that is borrowed does not place

his affections on it, knowing, as he does, that within a short time he will have to restore it. All the goods of this world are but given to us as a loan; it is indeed foolish to place our affections on them, being obliged within so short a time to leave them. Death will come and deprive us of all. All the gains and the riches of this world will end in a dying gasp, a funeral, and a descent into the grave. The house which you have built, within a short time you will have to give up to some one else. The tomb will be the place where your body will have to dwell until the day of judgment, and from the tomb your body will have to pass either to heaven or to hell, whither your soul will have gone before.

Affections and Prayers.

Therefore, will all be finished for me in death? I shall find nothing else, O my God, than that little which I have done through my love for Thee. And what am I waiting for? Am I waiting until death shall come and find me miserable and defiled with sin as I am now? If I were now to die, I should die restlessly, and should be very dissatisfied with my past life. No, my Jesus, I do not wish to die so dissatisfied. I thank Thee that Thou hast given me time to mourn over my sins, and to love Thee. I will begin from this moment. But, above all things, I grieve for having offended Thee, O my Sovereign Good; but I love Thee more than anything, more than my life itself. I yield myself entirely to Thee; my Jesus, from this hour I attach myself wholly to Thee. I would press Thee to my heart; and from this moment I deliver my soul into Thy keeping. "Into Thy hands I commend my spirit." I will not wait to give my soul into Thy keeping until the time shall come when it shall be commanded to leave this world with that summons, "Go forth, O Christian soul." I will not wait until that moment arrives to beg Thee to save me. "O Jesus, be a Jesus to me." Save me now, O my Saviour, by giving me Thy pardon, and by giving me the grace of Thy holy love. If this consideration which I have this day read should be the last warning which Thou shouldst give me, and the last mercy thou shouldst show me, then stretch forth Thy hand and take from me all my indifference; give me fervour; grant that I may obey Thee with great love in all that Thou mayst require of me. Eternal Father, for the love of Jesus Christ give me holy perseverance, and the grace to love Thee, and to love Thee, and Thee only, during the life that may yet remain to me.

CONSIDERATION V

The Uncertainty of the Hour of Death

"Be ye therefore ready also: for the Son of man cometh at an hour when ye think not." S. Luke xii. 40.

FIRST POINT.

IT is certain that we must all die, but it is uncertain when. The author, who styles himself Idiota, observes, "Nothing is more certain than death, but nothing is more uncertain than the hour of death."

My brother, already is the year, the month, the day, the hour, and even the moment fixed, in which both you and I will have to leave this earth, and to enter upon eternity; but this time is not known by us. Therefore, that we may ever be prepared, the Apostle tells us that death will come "as a thief in the night." (1 Thess. v. 2.) Our Blessed Lord tells us to be watchful, for when least we expect it, He will come to judge us. (S. Luke xii. 40.) S. Gregory observes, that God, for our good, keeps the hour of our death hidden from us, so that we may ever be found prepared for death.

Since, therefore, at any time, and in any place, death may deprive us of life, S. Bernard remarks, that at every time, and in every place, we must stand awaiting it, if we would die a happy death and be saved.

Every one knows that he or she must die, but the mistake that so many make, is to imagine that death is so far off, that they, as it were, lose sight of it. Even old men, who are most infirm, and people who are very sickly, flatter themselves that they have at least three or four years more to live. But, on the contrary, I say, how many have we not known during our life-time, who have died suddenly; some sitting, some walking, and some lying upon their beds? And certainly none of those who have died thus suddenly, ever thought to die in that way, or upon that day upon which they died. And, moreover, I say, how many who have this year passed on to another life, and who have died from some slight illness, never for once imagined that their days were this year to come to an end. Few indeed are the deaths which do not happen unexpectedly. Therefore, dear Christian brother, when the devil tempts you to sin, saying, that to-morrow, after the sin has been committed, you will go to confession; answer him in this manner, "And how do I not know that to-day may not be the last of my days upon earth?" If that hour or that moment in which I sinned against God were to be the last for me, so that there would be no time to implore forgiveness for it, what would become of me in eternity? To how many poor sinners has it not happened, that in the same moment in which they have been yielding to some wicked passion, death has overtaken them suddenly, and they have been cast into hell? "As the fishes that are taken in an evil net, so are the sons of men snared in an evil time." (Eccles. ix. 12.) The "evil time" is precisely that, in which the sinner actually offends God. The devil tells you that it will not happen in this way with you; but you ought to say, if it should happen, thus—what will become of me for all eternity?

Affections and Prayers.

Dear Lord, the place where I ought now to be, is not here where I now am—but in hell, where I have deserved to be so many times, because of my many transgressions. "Hell is my house." But S. Peter tells us, that "the Lord . . . . is long-suffering to us-ward, not willing that any should perish, but that all should come to repentance." (1 S. Pet. iii. 9.) Therefore it is, that Thou hast had so much patience with me, and hast waited so long for me, because Thou didst not wish me to be lost, but Thou didst wish me to come to repentance. Yes, my God, I come to Thee, I cast myself at Thy feet, I crave for mercy. "Have mercy upon me, O God, after Thy great goodness." O Lord, great and extraordinary mercy is needed for me, because I have offended Thee, although Thou hast blessed me with Thy light. Many are the sinners who have offended Thee but they have not had the light which Thou hast graciously given to me. And yet for all that, still Thou dost command me to repent of my sins, and I hope for pardon from Thee. Yes, my dear Redeemer, I repent with all my heart for having offended Thee, and I look for pardon through the merits of Thy Passion. Thou, my Jesus, being innocent, was willing to die like a guilty one upon the cross, and to shed all Thy Blood to wash awav my sins. "O Blood of the Innocent, wash away the sins of the penitent." O Eternal Father, pardon me, for the love of Jesus Christ, listen to the prayers that He makes for me, now that He is interceding for me, and making Himself my Advocate. But it is not sufficient for me to be pardoned. O God, Thou who art worthy of infinite love, I want the grace to love Thee. I do love Thee, O my Sovereign Good, and I offer Thee from henceforth my soul, my body, my will, and my liberty. From this time I will avoid, not only grave offences, but also slight ones. I will fly from all dangerous occasions. "Lead us not into temptation." Deliver me, for the love of Jesus Christ, from these occasions in which I might chance to offend Thee. "But deliver us from evil." Deliver me from sin, and then punish me as Thou wilt. I accept all the infirmities, griefs, and losses which it may please Thee to send me, there is nothing that I mind, if I do not lose Thy grace, and Thy love. Thou dost promise to give me whatsoever I ask, "Ask and it shall be given you." I ask Thee for these two graces, holy perseverance, and the grace to love Thee.

Second Point.

The Lord does not wish us to be lost, therefore He never ceases to warn us to change our habit of life, bv threatening to punish us. "If a man will not turn, He will whet His sword," (Ps. vii. 13.) "Behold," He says in another place, "how many, because they would not leave off sinning when they were least expecting it, and were living in peace, thinking to live for many long years, have been surprised by death, which has suddenly come upon them." "For when they shall say peace and safety, then sudden destruction cometh upon them." (1 Thess. v. 3.) Likewise He says: "Except ye repent, ye shall all likewise perish." (S. Luke xiii. 3.) Why, therefore, does He give us so many warnings before He sends the punishment if He does not wish that we should amend our lives, and so avoid dying an unhappy death. S. Augustine well observes that he who says to thee "Take care," wishes thee no ill.

It is therefore necessary to prepare our account before the day of reckoning may arrive. My Christian brother, if before this night arrives you should die, and your eternal welfare should be decided, what do you think? Would your reckoning be right; or would you not indeed be rather willing to give anything to obtain from God one year, one month, or at least one day more? And wherefore, now that God does give you this time, do you not seek to make your conscience free from everything? Is it because you cannot think this day can be the last for you? "Delay not to be converted to the Lord, and defer it not from day to day. For His wrath shall come on a sudden, and in the time of vengeance He will destroy thee." (Ecclus. v. 8, 9.) If you wish to be saved, my brother, sin must be left; therefore, as a day will come when you must leave it, why do you not leave it now? inquires S. Augustine. Perhaps you are expecting death; but for those who are obstinate, death is not the time for pardon, but for vengeance. "In the time of vengeance He will destroy thee." (Ecclus. v. 9.)

When some one owes you a large sum of money, you immediately take the precaution to provide yourself with a written security, saying to yourself, "Who knows what may happen?" And why do you not use the same precaution concerning your immortal soul, which is of much more importance than the large sum of money? Why do you not say of your soul, "Who knows what may happen?" If you were to lose that money, you would not lose everything; and even if in losing it you should lose all your patrimony, still you would have the hope of regaining it. But if in death you should lose your soul, then indeed would you lose all, and there would be no hope of ever again rescuing it. You are so diligent in keeping an account of your money, lest by chance any should be lost if a sudden death were to befall you; and if death should come upon you unawares, while you are at enmity with God, what would become of your soul for all eternity?

Affections and Prayers.

Ah, my Redeemer, Thou hast shed all Thy Blood. Thou hast given Thy life to save my soul, and I have so often lost it, hoping in Thy mercy; and in this way have I so often made use of Thy great goodness, for what? to offend Thee more. For this, I did deserve that Thou shouldst suddenly deprive me of life, and then send me to everlasting punishment. I have as it were been striving with Thee; but Thou hast striven, by showing mercy towards me, and I by offending Thee; Thou by seeking me, and I by flying from Thee; Thou by giving me time to implore pardon for all the offences committed against Thee, and I by using that time to add offence to offence. Gracious Lord, make me feel the great wrong I have done against Thee, and make me feel that it is my greatest duty to love Thee. Ah, my Jesus, how couldst Thou love me so much, Thou who didst seek me so many times when I strove to drive Thee from me? How couldst Thou show so many favours to one who has so often given Thee offence? From all this I feel how desirous Thou art for me not to be lost. I repent with all my heart for having offended Thee, O God of infinite goodness. Ah, receive this ungrateful sheep who returns repentant to Thy feet; receive it, and bind it to Thy shoulders, so that it may never more stray from Thee. No, I will never more fly from Thee. I would love Thee, I would be Thine, and if only I am Thine I am content with every pain, for what greater pain can I feel, than to live without Thy grace, separated from Thee, Who art my God, Who hast created me, and my God Who has died for me? Ah, hateful sins, what have you done? You have made me displease my dear Saviour, Who hast loved me so much. Ah, my Jesus, as Thou hast died for me, even so ought I to die for Thee. Thou didst die for love of me, and I ought to die of grief for having so much displeased Thee.

I accept death when and in what manner it may please Thee to send it to me; but until now I have not loved Thee, or I have not loved Thee enough; it is not thus that I would die. Oh grant me a little more time, so that I may indeed love Thee before I die. Therefore, change my heart, wound it, inflame it with Thy holy love. Grant this, through that exceeding love which made Thee die for me. I love Thee with all my soul, and I am indeed desirous to love Thee. Never let me lose Thee more. Give me holy perseverance, and give me Thy most holy love.

Third Point.

"Be ye ready." The Lord does not say that we must prepare ourselves when death comes upon us, but that death, when it comes, must find us prepared. When death comes, as it will do, in as it were a great tempest and confusion, it will be almost impossible to give ease to a troubled conscience. Even thus does reason argue. But God warns us by saying that He will not then come to give pardon, but to avenge the scorn which the wicked have shown concerning His favours. "Vengeance is Mine; I will repay, saith the Lord." (Rom. xii. 19.)

S. Augustine observes that this will be a just punishment for that one who, when able, has not wished to be saved, and who, when willing to be saved, will not be able. But some will say, "Perhaps even then it will be possible for me to be converted and live." But would you throw yourself into a well, saying, Perhaps even though I throw myself in, I may live and not die? O God! what a thing is this, that sin should so darken the mind as to make it lose even reason. When men speak of the body, they speak like wise men; but when they speak of the soul, they speak like fools.

My brother, perhaps this point that you are now reading may be the last warning that God may send you. Let us hasten to prepare for death, so that it may not overtake us being unprepared. S. Augustine says that God keeps the last day of our lives secret from us, so that at any, and every day, we may be prepared to die. S. Paul teaches us that it is not only necessary to work out our salvation with fear, but even with trembling. "Work out your own salvation with fear and trembling." (Phil. ii. 12.) S. Antoninus tells us of a certain king of Sicily who, in order to make one of his subjects understand the fear in which he occupied the throne, made him sit at table with a sword suspended by a slender thread over his head, so that being thus situated, he could hardly eat any food. We are all standing in the same danger, for at any moment the sword of death may fall upon us, upon which our eternal salvation depends.

It is indeed a question of eternity. "If the tree fall toward the south or toward the north, in the place where the tree falleth there it shall be." (Eccles. xi. 3.) If when death comes, it should find us in the grace of God, Oh, what joy will it be for the soul then to exclaim, "I have secured all things, never again can I lose God; I shall be happy for ever." But, on the contrary, if when death comes it should find the soul in a state of sin, with what despair will it then cry out, "Thus have I sinned, and my sin can never be reclaimed for all eternity." Oh, wherefore did I err? and my sin will never be pardoned throughout all eternity! This fear made the venerable Father Avila, when the announcement was brought to him that he was dying, cry out and say, "Oh that I had a little more time to prepare myself for death!" This fear also made the Abbot Agathe exclaim, although he died after many years of repentance, "What will become of me; for who can understand the judgments of God?" S. Arsenius also trembled when the hour of death arrived, and being asked why he was in such fear, answered, "This fear is not new to me, I have felt it all my life." Especially did holy Job tremble, saying, "What then shall I do when God riseth up? and when He visiteth, what shall I answer Him?" (Job xxxi. 14.)

Affections and Prayers.

Ah, my God, there is no one who has ever loved me as Thou hast loved me? and yet there is no one whom I have ever displeased more than I have displeased Thee. My only hope is in Thy Blood, O my Jesus. Eternal Father, look not upon my sins, but look upon the blessed wounds of Jesus Christ; look upon thy well-beloved Son, Who is grieving for me, and beseeching Thee to pardon me. I am very sorry, O my Creator, for having displeased Thee; it grieves me more than any other evil that I have done. Thou didst create me to love Thee, and I have been living as if Thou hadst created me to offend Thee. For the love of Jesus Christ pardon me, and give me grace to love Thee. At one time I resisted Thy will; now I will no longer resist it; I will do all that Thou dost command me. Thou dost wish me to detest all the offences which I have committed against Thee. I do indeed detest them with all my heart. Thou dost command me to resolve never more to offend Thee; then I do indeed resolve to lose my life rather than to lose Thy grace. Thou dost wish me to love Thee with my whole heart, then indeed I will love Thee with all my heart, and will love none other than Thee; and Thou shalt be, from this day forth, my only loved one, my only love. Thou dost command me to have holy perseverance, but it is from Thee alone that I can hope to obtain it. For the love of Jesus Christ, let me ever be faithful to Thee; and that I may always say to Thee with S. Bonaventure, "My beloved is one, my love is one." No, I do not want my life to be spent any longer in giving Thee even the slightest offence. I would spend it only in weeping over the displeasure I have given Thee, and in loving Thee.

CONSIDERATION VI

The Death of the Sinner

"Destruction cometh; and they shall seek peace, and there shall be none. Mischief shall come upon mischief." Ezek. vii. 25, 26.

FIRST POINT.

IT is now that sinners try, as far as they can, to drive away the memory and the thought of death, and thus to find peace, although they never will do so, by leading a life of sin; but when in the agonies of death, they must enter into eternity when "destruction cometh; and they shall seek peace, and there shall be none;" then they will try to fly from the stings of their troubled consciences; they will seek peace, but what peace can a soul find which is laden with sin, which bites it like so many vipers? What peace, knowing that in so short a time it will have to appear before Jesus Christ the Judge, whose law and friendship, until that moment, it has esteemed of so little worth? "Mischief shall come upon mischief." The intelligence that the sinner has just received, that he is dying, the thought that he must bid farewell to everything in this world, the stings of a troubled conscience, the time that is for ever lost, the time that he is now in want of, the severity of the Divine Judge, the miserable eternity which awaits all sinners—the thought of all these things will come upon him in terrible confusion, which will greatly trouble his mind and increase his apprehensions, and thus confused, and being filled with fear, the soul of the dying man will pass into the other life. Abraham, to whom great praise is due, hoped in God against all human hope, believing in the Divine promise, "who against hope believed in hope." But sinners, with great demerit, and who are the cause of their own ruin, falsely hope, not only against hope, but even against faith, whilst they pay no attention whatever to the warning which God gives to those who are obstinate. They dread an unhappy death, but they have no fear in leading a wicked life. But who is able to assure them, that their death will not suddenly be caused by a thunderbolt, by an apoplectic fit, or by the bursting of a blood-vessel? And even should they have time, when they are dying, to be converted, who can assure them, that their conversion will then be a true one? S. Augustine had to strive against his evil habits for twelve years, in order to overcome them. How then will one, who is dying, who has ever had a conscience stained with sin, who will be tormented with pain, with dreadful feelings in the head, and who will be in the confusion of death, how will he, then, I repeat, be possibly able to be truly converted? I say truly, because at that time the saying and promising will be of no use, it will be necessary to say and to promise from the depth of the heart. O God, into what terror will not the miserable sufferer be thrown, whose conscience, when remorseful, has been blighted, when he finds himself oppressed by his sins, and by the fears of the coming judgment, by the thought of hell and of eternity? Into what dreadful confusion will not these thoughts throw him, when he finds that his memory is failing him, his mind becoming darkened, and his body overcome with the pains of death which is already fast approaching? He will confess, he will promise, he will weep, he will cry to God for mercy, but without knowing what he is doing; and in that tempest of agitation, of remorse, of anguish, and of fear, his soul will pass into the other world. "The people shall be troubled at midnight and pass away." (Job xxxiv. 20.) It is well said by an author, that the prayers, the tears, and the promises of a dying sinner, are like the tears and promises of a man who finds himself assailed by his enemy, who puts a dagger to his throat to take away his life. He who lies down on his bed, and whose soul passes from it to eternity, is indeed a wretched man, if he lies down in the great displeasure of Almighty God.

Affections and Prayers.

The wounds of Jesus are my only hope. I should despair of pardon for my sins, did I not look upon you, ye fountains of pity and of mercy, through which my God has shed all His Blood to wash my soul from the many sins which it has committed. I adore you, O ye holy wounds, and in you confide. I detest and abhor those unworthy pleasures through which I have displeased my dear Redeemer, and through which I have lost His holy friendship. Looking then upon you, my hopes are raised, and therefore I turn my affections towards you. My beloved Jesus, it is only right that all men should love Thee, and that they should love Thee with their whole heart. But I have so often offended Thee, and counted Thy holy love of no moment; and yet, notwithstanding all my shortcomings, Thou hast borne with me so long, and hast so often offered me pardon. Ah, my Saviour, never more let me offend Thee, and by so doing lose my soul for ever. O God! what dreadful pain it would give me to see Thy dear Blood, and to remember Thy many mercies which Thou hast shown to me, if I should ever be cast into everlasting punishment. I love Thee now, and I would love Thee for ever. Give me holy perseverance. Take away from my heart every love that is not Thine, and establish in me a real desire and resolution to love Thee alone. Thou Who art my Sovereign Good, may I do this from henceforth and for ever.

Second Point.

The agonies of the dying sinner will not be one agony only, but they will be many. It will be one agony to be tormented by the devil. When the hour of death comes, that dreadful enemy uses all his strength to ruin that soul which is on the point of launching into eternity. The devil knows that at that hour, there is but little time to gain that soul, and that if it is lost to him then, it will be lost for ever. "The devil is come down unto you, having great wrath, because he knoweth that he hath but a short time." (Rev. xii. 12.) There will not only be one devil, but many devils, who will surround the dying man, who will do all that lies in their power to gain his soul. "Their houses shall be full of doleful creatures." (Isa. xiii. 21.) One will say, "Fear not, thou wilt soon be well." Another will say, "How is it that thou, who for so many years hast been deaf to the voice of God, canst expect Him now to show thee mercy?" And another, "How canst thou now remedy those evils that are done, and the reputations thou hast ruined?" And another, "Dost thou not see that thy confessions have been of no avail, without true grief; without any intention to do better for the future? How then canst thou now repair the evil which is done?"

Besides all this, the dying man will behold himself surrounded by his sins: "Evil shall hunt the wicked person to overthrow him." (Ps. cxl. 11.) S. Bernard observes that these sins, like so many watchful guards, shall hold him in their grasp, and shall say to him, "We are thy works; we will not leave thee; we will go with thy soul to the other world, and with it present ourselves to the Eternal Judge." Then the dying man will want to rid himself of these enemies; but to get rid of them it would be necessary to hate them; it would be necessary for his heart to become converted to God. Whereas his mind is darkened, and his heart is hardened. "A hard heart shall fear evil at the last; and he that loveth danger shall perish in it." (Ecclus. iii. 27.) S. Bernard says, that that heart which has been so obstinate in sin during life, will use every means to free itself when dying from this state of condemnation, but will be unable to do so; and being oppressed with its own wickedness, will pass from life in this state. Until the hour of death arrived, the sinner always loved sin; he has also loved the danger of his own damnation; very justly therefore will the Lord allow him to perish in that peril in which he has loved to live until the time of his death. S. Augustine believes, that "he who is left by sin before he himself leaves it, at the hour of death will hardly dislike it as much as he ought, because whatever he does at that time will be done through necessity."

Miserable indeed is that sinner who is so hardened that he resists the voice of God when He calls him! "His heart is as firm as a stone; yea, as hard as a piece of the nether millstone." (Job xli. 24.) Instead of yielding and being softened by the voice of God, he becomes more hardened; even as the anvil is hardened by the strokes of the hammer. As a punishment for all this, he will find himself in the same obstinate frame of mind at the hour of death, although he may be on the point of passing into eternity. "A hard heart shall fear evil at the last." Sinners, saith the Lord, "have turned their back unto me, and not their face: but in the time of their trouble they will say, Arise, and save us. But where are thy gods that thou hast made thee? let them arise, if they can save thee." (Jer. ii. 27, 28.) The miserable sinners when dying will fly unto God, and God will say to them, "Now you can come to me. Call upon creatures to help you, for they have been your gods." Even thus will the Lord answer those who at that time seek Him, because they will not seek Him with any sincere wish to become converted. S. Jerome has said, that he fully believes, and has learnt from experience, that he who has led a wicked life until the hour of death, will never be happy when the hour of death arrives.

Affections and Prayers.

My dear Saviour, help me, and do not abandon me, for I see my soul all wounded with my sins; my passions do violence to me, and my evil habits oppress me. I throw myself at Thy feet; have mercy upon me, and deliver me from all my evil passions. "In Thee, O Lord, have I put my trust: let me never be put to confusion." (Ps. lxxi. 1.) Do not permit a soul that trusts in Thee to be lost. I repent of having offended Thee, O God of Infinite Goodness; I have done evil, and I confess it. I wish to amend, at any price. But unless Thou dost assist me with Thy grace, I am lost. Receive, O my Jesus, this rebellious one, who has displeased Thee so much. Remember that Thou didst spend Thy Blood and Thy Life for me. Through the merits, therefore, of Thy Passion and of Thy Death, receive me into Thy arms, and give me holy perseverance. I was almost lost, but Thou didst call me; behold, I will no longer resist; I consecrate myself to Thee; bind me to Thy love, and never more allow me to lose myself by again losing Thy grace. Do not, my Jesus, allow it.

THIRD POINT.

It is a marvellous thing that God does nothing but threaten sinners with an unhappy death: "Then shall they call upon me, but I will not answer." (Prov. i. 28.) "Will God hear his cry when trouble cometh upon him?" (Job xxvii. 9.) "I also will laugh at your calamity; I will mock." (Prov. i. 26.) God laughs when He will not show mercy. "To Me belongeth vengeance and recompense; their foot shall slide in due time." (Deut. xxxii. 35.) In many other places God threatens the same, and yet sinners live in peace, and are as secure, as if God had certainly promised to give them pardon when dying, and after death, to give them Paradise. It is quite true that, in whatever hour the sinner is converted, God has promised to pardon him; but He has not said that the sinner shall be converted in death. On the contrary, He has often declared that he who lives in sin shall die in sin: "Ye . . . . shall die in your sins." (S. John viii. 21.) He has said in another place that he who seeks Him in death shall not find Him. "Ye shall seek me, and shall not find me." (S. John vii. 34.) Therefore, it is indeed necessary to seek God when He can be found. "Seek ye the Lord while He may be found." (Isa. lv. 6.) Yes, because there will be a time when He will no longer be found. Poor sinners—poor blind ones—who put off their conversion until the hour of their death, when there will be no more time to be converted! Oleaster well says, that "the wicked will never have learned to do well save when there is no time in which to do it." God wishes all men to be saved; but He will punish those who are obstinate in their sins.

If some miserable sinner living in sin should be seized with an apoplectic fit, and thus be deprived of his senses, what pity all those would feel who would see him die thus, without the Sacraments, and without any sign of repentance! and, on the contrary, what great joy would not every one experience, if this poor sinner should recover from his fit, seek for absolution, and become repentant? But is not he indeed mad who, having time to repent, continues in a state of sin, or else returns to sin, and so places himself in danger of being surprised by death, at the same time that he is perhaps committing sin? It is very fearful to see any one die suddenly, and yet so many put themselves in danger of dying thus, and in danger of dying in sin. "A just weight and balance are the Lord's." (Prov. xvi. 11.) We do not take any account of the favours which the Lord bestows upon us; but the Lord takes the account and measures them; and when He sees them despised up to a certain point, He allows the sinner to remain in his sin, and in this state to die. Miserable indeed is that one who defers his repentance until the day of his death. S. Augustine remarks that "the repentance which is demanded of the infirm is infirm." S. Jerome says, that amongst a hundred thousand sinners who remain in a state of sin until the day of their death, hardly one will be saved. S. Vincent Ferrer declares that it would be a greater miracle for one who has lived in habitual sin all his life to be saved, than it would be to raise one who is dead, to life. What sorrow or what repentance could be felt at the hour of death by him who until that time, has loved sin? Bellarmine tells us that, having gone to assist a dying person, and having exhorted him to make one act of contrition, the dying one answered that he did not understand what contrition meant. Bellarmine tried to explain to him, but the sick one said, "I do not understand you, father; I am not capable of these things." And thus he died, "leaving clear signs of his condemnation." S. Augustine observes that it will be a just punishment to that sinner who has been unmindful of God during his life, to be unmindful of himself in death. The apostle warns us, saying, "Be not deceived; God is not mocked: for whatsoever a man soweth, that shall he also reap: for he that soweth to his flesh, shall of the flesh reap corruption." (Gal. vi. 7, 8.) It would indeed be mocking God for any one to live, despising his love, and then to reap a reward and everlasting glory; but "God is not mocked." That which is sown in this life, shall be reaped in the next. He who loves the forbidden pleasures of this life, shall reap corruption, misery, and eternal death in the life to come.

Christian brother, what is said for others is also said for you. Tell me, if you were now at the point of death, despaired of by the doctors, and already in great pain, would you not pray to God to grant you one more month, one more week, in order to make your conscience clear in His sight? But God does give you that time now. Return thanks to Him, and quickly try to atone for the evil you have done, and use every means to be found in a state of grace whenever death shall come, because then there will be no time to atone for past evils.

Affections and Prayers.

Ah, my God, and who is there who would have had so much patience with me as Thou hast! If Thy goodness were not infinite, I should cease to hope for pardon. But I have to do with a God who died to pardon and to save me. Thou dost command me to hope, and I will hope. If my sins affright and condemn me, Thy merits and Thy promises give me courage. Thou hast promised the life of Thy grace to him who returns to Thee, "Turn yourselves and live ye." (Ezek. xviii. 32.) Thou hast promised to embrace him who turns to Thee. "Turn ye unto Me, ... and I will turn unto you." (Zec. i. 3.) Thou hast said that Thou wilt not despise him who humbles himself and repents. "A broken and contrite heart, O God, shalt Thou not despise." (Ps. ci. 17.) Behold, O Lord, I return and come to Thee; I confess myself worthy of condemnation, and I repent of having offended Thee. I sincerely promise never more to offend Thee willingly, and I would wish to love Thee for evermore. Ah, do not allow me to be any more ungrateful towards such goodness. Eternal Father, through the merits of the obedience of Thy Son Jesus Christ, Who died in obedience to Thy will, let me obey Thee in all things until death. I love Thee, O Thou Highest Good, and because of the love I bear for Thee, I would obey Thee in all things. Give me holy perseverance, Thy holy love, and I ask for nothing more.

CONSIDERATION VII

Sentiments of One who has Reflected little upon Death

"Set thine house in order: for thou shalt die and not live." Isa. xxxviii. 1.

First Point.

IMAGINE yourself at the bed-side of some sick person, to whom a few hours of life alone remain. Poor creature, see how much he is overcome with pain, with fainting fits, with suffocation, with want of breath, with cold perspirations, with weakness of the brain, that he can scarcely hear, understand, or speak. But the greatest misery he endures is, that he feels death is approaching, and instead of thinking about his soul, and of making his reckoning sure, he thinks alone about his physicians, and the remedies which can be applied to free him from the disease, and from the pains which are killing him. S. Laurence Justinian, speaking of people who are thus dying, observes that "Nothing, save themselves, suffices to occupy their thoughts." His relations and friends should, at least, warn him of the dangerous state in which he is; but no, there is not one amongst them who has the courage to tell him that he is dying, and instead of advising him to take the Holy Sacrament, all refuse to tell him, lest they should give him offence by so doing. O my God from this moment, I indeed thank Thee that when I am dying Thou wilt allow me to be assisted by the dear brothers of my congregation, whose only interest will then be my eternal salvation, and who will all endeavour, as far as they can, to make my death a glorious one But although they do not warn him that death is approaching, nevertheless, the sick man, seeing the family in such confusion, the number of doctors who are so busily talking, the many and numberless remedies that are tried, is filled with terror and confusion, and amidst the continued attacks of fear, remorse, and distrust, says within himself, "Alas! perhaps the end of my days is already come." What then will be the feelings of the dying man when he is told that he is dying? "Set thine house in order: for thou shalt die and not live." With what fear, will he not be told that his illness is mortal, that he must make his peace with God, and receive the Blessed Sacrament, and bid farewell to the world? What! he exclaims, must I leave the world, and all I possess, that house, that villa, those relations, friends, conversations, games, and amusements? He is told that he must, for already is the lawyer come, and then he has to sign this document, "I bequeath, I bequeath." And what does he take away with him? Nothing, except what he is covered with, which, within a very short time will decay with him in the grave.

Oh what grief and sadness will the dying man feel, when he sees the tears of his household, and the silence of his friends who keep silence, not having the heart to speak in his presence! But the greatest punishment that he will have to bear, will be the dreadful stings of conscience which in that tempest, as it were, will be felt so much more, because of the corrupt life which he has led, up to the hour of his death—notwithstanding the seasonable advice of his spiritual fathers, and the many resolutions made, which have been either never performed or else entirely neglected. He will then exclaim, "O wretched one that I am, God has granted me so many lights, I have had so much time to make my conscience clear in his sight, and yet I have not done it; and at length death has overtaken me! What would it have cost me to fly from that occasion to sin, to keep myself from that friendship, and to avail myself of confession? And even though it should have cost me much, nevertheless I ought to have done everything I could, to save my immortal soul which was all-important. Oh, that I had carried that good resolution into practice. Oh, that I had continued as I began. Then indeed should I be happy now! But I did not do it, and now there is no time. The feelings of dying men, such as I have described, who have been during life so forgetful of their conscience, resemble the feelings of those who are for ever lost, who, when in hell, lament over their sins as being the cause of their punishment, but they lament without finding any relief or remedy.

Affections and Prayers.

O Lord, if at this moment the news of my approaching death were to be brought to me, such would be my sentiments of grief. But I thank Thee for giving me this light and this time to amend. No, my God, I do not wish to fly again from Thee; it is so many times that Thou hast sought me. Justly indeed ought I now to fear, lest, if I do not return to Thee again and come to Thee, Thou wilt altogether abandon me. Thou didst give me a heart to love Thee, but I have put it to so bad a use; I have loved the creature, but I have not loved Thee, Who art my Creator and my Redeemer, and Who didst give Thy life for me! Instead of loving Thee, Oh, how many times have I not displeased Thee, and turned away from following Thee! I was fully aware that in committing that sin, I should displease Thee, and yet I did commit it. My Jesus, I am truly sorry for it; I mourn over it with all my heart: I would indeed become changed. I renounce all the pleasures of the world, so that I may love, and please Thee, O God of my soul. Thou hast given me so many proofs of Thy love, that I should wish to give Thee some proofs of my love before I die. From this time I will accept every infirmity, and every cross, every scorn, and every vexation, that I must receive from men—only give me strength to endure the same in peace, for I wish to endure them all to gain Thy love. I love Thee, O Infinite Goodness, more than anything, only give me more love, and holy perseverance.

Second Point.

Oh, how clearly, when the hour of death arrives, do the truths of faith make themselves felt, only to add greater torment to that dying man who has lived a wicked life, and particularly if he is one who has been consecrated to God, and so has had much opportunity of serving Him, much time, many good examples, and much inspiration. O God, with what grief will he then reflect and say, "I once admonished others, and afterwards have committed more grievous sin than they. I once left the world, and afterwards have become more attached to its pleasures, vanities, and love." With what remorse will he then reflect upon the light which he has received from God, such as would have changed a heathen into a saint! With what remorse will he then recall to mind that he had despised the practices of piety in others as weakness of mind, and had praised certain worldly maxims of self-esteem and self-love; such as not liking other people to take precedence of us, to avoid suffering, and to enjoy every pleasure which may present itself.

"The desire of the ungodly shall perish." (Ps. cxii. 10.) When the hour of death arrives, how much will the time which we waste now be coveted? S. Gregory tells us in his Dialogues, of a certain rich man, named Chrysantius, who had led a very wicked life, and who, when the hour of death came, cried out against the devils who visibly appeared to him to seize him, "Give me time, give me until to-morrow." And these answered him, saying, "O fool, dost thou now seek time? Thou hast had so much and wasted it, and spent it in sin; and now dost thou ask for it? Now there is no more time for thee." The wretched man continued to cry and to implore help. A son of his, whose name was Massimo, and who was a monk, was with him, to whom the dying man said, "My son, help me; Massimo, my son, help me." And in the meantime, throwing himself from one side of the bed to the other, and thus agitated, and with cries of despair, he breathed forth his wretched soul. Alas, that these foolish ones should so love their folly in life, but should put off until the hour of death to open their eyes to their folly, and then confess that they have been so unwise! For at that time it only serves to increase the difficulties which they feel in trying to atone for the sins which they have committed; and dying in this frame of mind, the salvation of their souls is very doubtful. My brother, perhaps whilst reading this you are saying to yourself, "Yes, it is very doubtful." But if it is so doubtful, your folly and your misfortune is much greater still—if, as you know and understand these truths in life, you do not try during life to make amends for past sins. These words, even, which you have just read, would be a sword of sorrow for you in death.

Arise, therefore, for as there is time to avoid a death so frightful, hasten to make amends for the past, and wait not until there will be no fit time for reparation. Wait not for another month, another week. It may be that this light which God now grants to you in mercy, may be the last light and the last call for you. It is foolish, indeed, not to wish to think upon death, which is absolutely certain, and on which eternity depends; but it is greater folly to think upon it, and not to prepare for it. Make those reflections and resolutions now, which you would make if you were dying now with profit, but at that time very uselessly; now in the hope of being saved, but at that time in great fear, lest you should not be saved. A gentleman of the court of Charles XI., when leaving court, being asked by the emperor for what reason he was leaving, answered, that in order to be saved it is necessary that some interval should elapse between the time of repentance from a sinful life and the hour of death, so that a period of repentance may be passed through.

Affections and Prayers.

No, my God, I will no longer abuse Thy mercy. I thank Thee for the light which Thou art now giving me, and I promise Thee to change my life, to amend my life. I can see plainly that Thou wilt not bear with me much longer. And shall I wait until Thou wilt be constrained to condemn me to everlasting death? or until Thou wilt give me up to a life utterly lost, which would be a greater punishment to me than death itself? Look upon me at Thy feet; receive me into Thy favour. I know I do not deserve it; but Thou hast said that "the wickedness of the wicked, he shall not fall thereby in the day that he turneth from his wickedness." (Ezek. xxxiii. 12.) If, therefore, my Jesus, in the time that is past, I have offended Thy infinite Goodness, now I repent with all my heart, and I hope for pardon from Thee. With S. Anselm, I will say to Thee, "Suffer not my soul to be lost through its sins, for Thou hast redeemed it with Thy

Blood." Look not upon my ingratitude, look only upon that love which caused Thee to die for me. If I have lost Thy grace, Thou hast not lost the power to give it back to me. Have pity therefore upon me, my dear Redeemer. Pardon me, and give me the grace to love Thee; whilst I, from this day forward, promise to love none other than Thee. Thou hast chosen me from amongst so many of Thy creatures to love Thee; therefore I choose Thee, O my Sovereign Good, to love Thee above every other thing. Thou dost go before me with Thy Cross—I will not cease to follow Thee with that cross which Thou dost give me to carry. I embrace every mortification and every trouble which may come to me from Thee. It is enough that I am not deprived of Thy grace, for with that I am indeed content.

Third Point.

To the dying man, who during life has been forgetful concerning his soul's good, there will be thorns in everything that presents itself to him. There will be a thorn in the memory of pleasures that are past—a thorn in the remembrance of rivalries overcome, and of pomps displayed—a thorn in the friends who will come to see him, with everything that they bring back to his memory—a thorn in the spiritual fathers, who by turns will assist him—a thorn in the last Sacraments which he will receive.

The poor sufferer will then exclaim, "O fool that I have been! I ought to have become a saint, with all the lights, and opportunities, which God granted to me; I ought to have led a life of happiness, in the favour of God; and now, what is remaining to me of the many years that are past, except torments, distrust, fears, stings of conscience, and an account which I shall have to render up to God? And it is indeed doubtful whether my soul will be saved." And when will he say all this? Not until the oil in his lamp is nearly consumed, and the scene of this world is about to close upon him for ever—not until he has both eternities in view: the one an eternity of everlasting joy; the other an eternity of everlasting woe—not until the time is approaching for that last gasp, upon which depends his everlasting blessedness, or his everlasting despair—even as long as

God is God. What would he not then give, to have one more year, one more month, or at least one more week, with a clear head? For suffering then, as he will do, with distraction of the head, oppression at the chest, and failing breath, he will be able to do nothing; he will not be able to reflect, nor to employ his mind in doing one good action; he finds himself shut up as it were in a dark pit of confusion, where he can imagine nothing else but that there is a great ruin hanging over him from which he feels himself unable to flee away. Therefore he will long for time; but it will be said to him, "*Proficiscere*," depart, make haste, put your accounts in order as best you can, during the short time which remains to you, and depart; for dost thou not know that death neither waits for, nor respects any one?

Oh what terror will it then be for him to think and to say, "I am alive this morning; very likely this evening I shall be dead! To-day I am lying in this room; perhaps to-morrow I may be in my grave! And where will my soul be?" When he feels the cold sweat of death coming upon him—when he hears his relations go from the room, never more to return during his life—when his sight begins to grow dim and his eyes become darkened—but what will be the use of understanding these truths then, when the time for profiting by the understanding, is past?

Affections and Prayers.

Ah, my God, Thou dost not wish me to die; but Thou desirest that I should be converted and live. I thank Thee for having waited for me until now, and I thank Thee for the light which Thou art now giving me. I know the error I have committed in neglecting Thy friendship, the vile and miserable pleasures through which I have accounted Thee of so little value. I repent and I grieve with all my heart, for having done Thee so grievous a wrong. Ah, do not cease, in the life which may remain to me, to assist me with Thy light and Thy grace, so that I may know how to do that which I must do, in order to amend my life. Of what use will it be for me to understand this truth, when the time for reparation will be taken from me? "Deliver not up to beasts the souls that trust in Thee." When the devil shall tempt me again to offend Thee, I beseech Thee, my Jesus, through the merits of Thy Passion, to stretch forth Thy hand and to deliver me from falling into sin, and from again remaining a slave of the enemy. Grant, that then I may ever flee unto Thee, and that I may never cease to entreat Thy protection as long as the temptation may last. Thy Blood is my hope, and Thy Goodness is my love. I love Thee, my God. Thou Who art worthy of infinite love, grant that I may ever love Thee. Let me know from what things I must separate myself so that I may be Thine alone, for I would be Thine alone; but do Thou give me the strength to fulfil the same.

CONSIDERATION VIII

The Death of the Just

"Right dear in the sight of the Lord is the death of his saints." Ps. cxvi. 13.

First Point.

WHEN we view death according to the senses, it terrifies and affrights us, but when we view it with the eye of faith, it consoles us and makes us desire it. It appears terrible to sinners, but lovely and very precious to saints. S. Bernard tells us, that "death is precious as the end of labours, the consummation of victory, the gate of life." "The end of labour," yes, truly, does death put an end to our labours and toil. "Man that is born of a woman is of few days, and full of trouble." (Job xiv. 1.)

Behold what our life is; it is short, it is full of misery, infirmities, fears, and passions. The worldly, who desire a long life, what do they seek, observes Seneca, but a longer time of suffering? If we continue to live, do we not continue to suffer?—as S. Augustine himself remarks. Yes, indeed, because, according to S. Ambrose, our present life was not given to us for repose, but for work, and by that work to make ourselves worthy of eternal life. When God, as Tertullian justly observes, shortens the life of any one, He shortens his suffering. Hence it is, that although death was given to man as a punishment for sin, yet, notwithstanding this, the miseries of this life are such, as S. Ambrose remarks, that death would appear to be given to us rather as a relief than a punishment. God calls those who die in His grace blessed, because their labours are finished, and they go to their rest. "Blessed are the dead which die in the Lord from henceforth : Yea, saith the Spirit, that they may rest from their labours." (Rev. xiv. 13.)

The torments which afflict the sinners, when dying, do not trouble the saints. "The souls of the just are in the hand of God, and the torment of death shall not touch them." (Wisd. iii. 1.) The saints do not grieve when they hear that *Proficiscere* which terrifies the worldly so much. The saints are not troubled when they have to leave their worldly goods, for they have kept their hearts severed from them. They go about ever repeating to themselves, "God is the strength of my heart, and my portion for ever." (Ps. lxxiii. 25.)

Blessed are you, writes the Apostle to his disciples, who have been stripped of all your earthly possessions, for the sake of Jesus Christ. "Ye . . . . took joyfully the spoiling of your goods, knowing in yourselves that ye have in Heaven a better and an enduring substance." (Heb. x. 34.) They do not grieve at leaving the honours, because they always detested them, and reckoned them, as they indeed are, nothing but smoke and vanity ; they esteemed loving God, and being loved by God, their only honour. They do not grieve at leaving their relations, because they have only loved them in God ; when dying, they commend them to that Heavenly Father, who loves them more than they, and trusting to be saved, they hope to be able to help them more, when they are in Paradise, than while on this earth. Finally, what they have ever said in life, "My God and my all," they repeat, with greater consolation and tenderness, when dying.

He, therefore, who dies loving God, is not tormented by the fears which death brings with it ; but, on the contrary, he is pleased with them, thinking that his life is now ended, and that there is no more time to suffer for God, and to offer Him any more proofs of his love. Then, lovingly and peacefully, he gives Him these last moments of his life, and consoles himself in uniting the sacrifice of his death with the sacrifice which Jesus Christ once offered for him on the cross to His eternal Father. And thus he joyfully expires, saying, "I will lay me down in peace and take my rest." (Ps. iv. 9.) Oh, what peace to die, given up to and reposing in the arms of Jesus Christ, Who has loved us even unto death, and was willing to endure a cruel death, to obtain a sweet and peaceful death for us.

Affections and Prayers.

O my beloved Jesus, Who, to obtain a happy death for me, wast willing to die a death so bitter upon Calvary, when shall I behold Thee? The first time that I shall see Thee it will be as my Judge, in that same place in which I shall breathe forth my soul. And then what shall I say to Thee? What wilt Thou say to me? I will not wait until that time to think what I shall say. I will think now. I will say to Thee, My dear Redeemer, Thou art the same Who hast died for me. At one time I did offend Thee, I was ungrateful to Thee, and I did not deserve Thy pardon; but afterwards, being assisted by Thy grace, I repented, and during the remainder of my life, I have mourned because of my sins, and Thou hast pardoned me. Pardon me once more, now that I am at Thy feet, and do Thou Thyself give me a general absolution for my sins. I did not deserve to love Thee any more, for having despised Thy love; but Thou in Thy mercy hast drawn my heart to Thee, and if it has not loved Thee as Thou ought to be loved, at least, it has loved Thee above all other things, giving up everything in order to please Thee. Now what wilt Thou say to me? I can see, that Paradise and possessing Thee in Thy kingdom, is a blessing too great for me, but I cannot trust myself to live far from Thee, especially now, that Thou hast once let me see Thy beautiful and lovely face. Therefore, I seek to live in Paradise, not that I may be happy there, but that I may love Thee more.

And now, my beloved Judge, raise Thy hand and bless me, and tell me that I am Thine, and that Thou wilt be mine for ever. I would ever love Thee, do Thou ever love me. Have mercy upon a soul that loves Thee with all its strength, and longs to see Thee, so as to love Thee more.

Even thus do I hope, O my Jesus, do I hope then to speak to Thee. In the meantime, I pray Thee to grant me grace so to live, that when dying, I may say to Thee that which I have just thought. Give me holy perseverance, and give me Thy love.

SECOND POINT.

"And God shall wipe away all tears from their eyes; and there shall be no more death." (Rev. xxi. 4.) Therefore, in death the Lord will wipe away from the eyes of His servants the tears which they have shed, living as they do in trouble, in fears, in dangers, and in battles with hell. What can be greater consolation to a soul that has loved God when death is announced, than the thought, that soon it will be freed from the many dangers that there are in this life of offending God, from the many stings of conscience, and from the temptations of the devil. This present life is a continual warfare with hell, in which we are in constant danger of losing our souls, and then our God. S. Ambrose tell us, that upon this earth we are ever walking amidst the snares of the enemy who lies in wait to rob us of the life of grace. It was this danger which caused S. Peter of Alcantara to say when dying to a religious who, when assisting him, touched him, "My brother, keep away from me, because I am still living and am yet in danger of being eternally lost!" It was this danger also that caused S. Teresa to be consoled each time that she heard the clock strike, rejoicing that another hour of warfare was passed, for she said, "At any moment of my life I may sin, and by doing so I may lose God." Therefore it is, that the saints are so rejoiced when death is announced to them, knowing, as they do, that very soon their battles and their dangers will be ended, and that they, within a very short time, will reach that happy state when they will no longer be able to lose God.

It is related in the lives of the Fathers, that once when an aged Father was dying in Scythia, he laughed when the others wept; on being asked why he laughed, he answered, "Wherefore do you weep, knowing, as you do, that I am going to my rest?" Likewise, Catherine of Sienna, when she was dying, said, "Rejoice with me, for I am leaving this world of sorrows, and I am going to a place of rest." S. Cyprian observes, that if some one were living in a house, the walls of which were falling down, and the floors and roof were shaking, so that everything was threatening ruin, would not such an one be very desirous to quit that house? In this life, all things are threatening ruin to the soul, the world, hell, the passions, the rebellious senses; these all draw us on to sin and to everlasting death. The apostle exclaims, "Who shall deliver me from the body of this death?" (Rom vii. 34.) Oh, what joy will the soul feel when it hears those words, "Come with Me from Lebanon, My spouse, with Me from Lebanon .... from the lions' dens." (Sol. Song iv. 8.) Come, my spouse, come from the place of tears, and from the dens of lions that are seeking to devour thee, and to make thee lose the Divine grace. Therefore S. Paul desiring death, said that Jesus Christ was his only life; and therefore, he thought that to die was his greatest gain, since, in dying, he obtained that life which has no end. "For me to live is Christ, and to die is gain." (Phil. i. 21.)

It is a great favour which God grants to that soul that is in a state of grace to take it from this world, where, at any time, it may become changed, and may lose the friendship of God! "He was taken away lest wickedness should alter his understanding." (Wisd. iv. 11.) Happy in this life is he who is united to God; but, like the sailor, who cannot be called safe until he has arrived in port, and is escaped from the tempest: even so, a soul cannot be called fully happy until it has departed this life in the favour of God.

Now, if it causes joy to the sailor when, after many dangers, he has almost safely arrived in port, how much more shall not he rejoice who is just on the point of securing eternal salvation?

Besides, in this life it is impossible to live without committing sin, at least venial sin: "For a just man falleth seven times." (Prov. xxiv. 16.) He who is leaving this life, ceases to give offence to God. S. Ambrose asks, "What is death but the sepulchre of vice!" It is even this that makes death so desirable to the lovers of God. With this the venerable Vincent Carafia consoled himself when dying, by saying, "When I cease to live, I shall cease to offend God." And S. Ambrose also said, "Wherefore do we desire this life, in which the longer any one lives the greater will be the burden of sins with which he is laden."

He who dies in the grace of God, is placed in a state in which he cannot, neither does he know how, to offend God. "The dead know not how to sin," remarks the same saint. Therefore the Lord praises the dead, more than any man living, although he may be a saint. "Wherefore I praised the dead which are already dead, more than the living." (Eccles. iv. 2.) A certain good man ordered, that he, who should come to announce his death to him, should say, "Rejoice, because the time is come when thou shalt no more offend God."

Affections and Prayers.

"Into Thy hands I commend my spirit, for Thou hast redeemed me, O Lord, Thou God of truth." (Ps. xxxi. 5.) Ah, my sweet Redeemer, where should I have now been if Thou hadst allowed me to die when I was living far from Thee? I should now be in hell where I could never love Thee more. I thank Thee for not having abandoned me, and for having granted me so many graces to win my heart to Thee. I am very sorry for having offended Thee. I love Thee above all things. I pray Thee ever to make me more sensible of the evil I have committed in despising Thee, and of the love which Thy Infinite Goodness deserves. I love Thee, and I would like soon to die—if it be Thy holy will, in order to be freed from the danger of ever losing Thy holy grace, and to be sure of loving Thee for ever in eternity. Ah, during the years that may remain to me of my life give me strength, my beloved Jesus, to do something for Thee before death shall overtake me. Give me strength to withstand the temptations and passions, and especially against that passion which for the past time has most caused me to displease Thee. Give me patience in infirmity, and under the wrongs that I may receive from men. I now pardon, through Thy love, all who may have despised me, and I pray Thee to give them those graces which they may desire. Give me strength to be more diligent in avoiding even venial sins, concerning which I know that I am negligent. Help me, my Saviour, I hope for all things because of Thy merits.

THIRD POINT.

Not only is death the end of our labours, but it is even the gate of life, as S. Bernard observes. He who wishes to enter in, and see God, must pass through this gate. "This is the gate of the Lord; the righteous shall enter into it." (Ps. cxviii. 20.) S. Jerome called out to death, and said, "Open to me, my sister." My sister, death, if thou dost not open the door, I cannot go in to enjoy my Lord. S. Charles Borromeo, having a painting in his house which represented a skeleton with a scythe in the hand, called for the painter, and ordered him to erase the scythe, and to paint a golden key; desiring by this, that the wish for death should ever be kindled in his heart, for death is that key which must open the gate of heaven for us to see God.

S. John Chrysostom observes, that if a king had prepared an apartment in his palace for some one, but for some time desired that person to live in a hovel, how much would he not desire to leave the hovel, and to go to the palace? The soul during this life being in the body, is as it were in a prison, from which she must pass to enter into the kingdom of heaven; therefore David prayed, saying, "Bring my soul out of prison." (Ps. cxlii. 9.) And the holy Simeon, when he had the Infant Jesus in his arms, sought for no other favour than death, so as to be freed from the prison of this life, "Lord, now lettest Thou Thy servant depart in peace." (S. Luke ii. 29.) S. Ambrose also says, "he seeks, as if he were held by necessity, to be dismissed." The Apostle also desired the same grace when he said, "having a desire to depart, and to be with Christ," (Phil. i. 23.)

What joy the cup-bearer of Pharaoh felt when he heard from Joseph, that he should soon be released from prison, and should return to his post! And a soul that loves God, does it not rejoice when it hears that within a short time it will be released from the prison of this world, and will go to enjoy God? "Whilst we are at home in the body, we are absent from the Lord." (2 Cor. v. 6.) Whilst we are united to the body, we are far from the sight of God; as it were in a foreign land, and far from our own country; and therefore S. Bruno remarks, that our death ought not to be called death, but life. Hence the death of the saints is called their birth-day; yes, because when they die they are borne to that blessed life which will never have an end. S. Athanasius observes, that "the just die not, but are translated." To the just death is no other than the transition to eternal life. "O beautiful death," says S. Augustine, "and who is he that does not long for thee, seeing that thou art the end of all work—the end of toil, and the beginning of eternal rest?" Therefore the saint earnestly prayed, saying, "May I die, O Lord, that I may see Thee."

S. Cyprian observes, that death must indeed be feared by the sinner, because he will pass from a temporal to an eternal death. "Let him fear to die who shall pass to the second death;" but he who is in the grace of God, does not fear death, because he will pass from death to an eternal life. In the life of S. John the Almoner it is related, that a certain rich man recommended his only son to the saint, and gave him much alms, so that the saint might obtain a long life for his son from God; but the son soon afterwards died. As the father was grieving over the death of his son, God sent an angel to him, who said, "Thou didst seek a long life for thy son; know that he is now enjoying it eternally in Paradise." This is the grace that Jesus Christ obtained for us, as it was promised in Hosea, "O death, I will be thy plague." (Hos. xiii. 14.) Jesus, in dying for us, made our death to become life. When Pionius the martyr was being borne to the scaffold, he was asked by those who led him, "How it was he could go so joyfully to death?" The saint made answer, "You deceive yourselves; I go not to death, but to life." Even thus was the youthful S. Symphorian encouraged by his mother when the time of his martyrdom drew nigh, "O my son, life is not taken away from thee; it is exchanged for a better."

Affections and Prayers.

O God of my soul, for the time past I have dishonoured Thee, in turning away from Thee; but Thy Son has honoured Thee in sacrificing His life to Thee upon the Cross. Through the honour done to Thee by Thy dearly beloved Son, forgive the dishonour that I have done Thee. I am very sorry, O my Sovereign Good, for having offended Thee; and I promise from this day forward to love none other but Thee. I hope for my salvation from Thee. Whatever I have now that is good, is all of Thy mercy; I know that I receive it all from Thee: "By the grace of God I am what I am." (1 Cor. xv. 10.) If during the time past I have dishonoured Thee, I hope to honour Thee for ever in eternity in blessing Thee for Thy mercy. I feel a great desire to love Thee; but Thou givest me the desire; and I thank Thee for it, O Jesus, my Love. Continue, Oh, continue to help me, as Thou hast already done; for I hope from this day forward to be Thine, and Thine alone. I renounce all worldly pleasures; for what greater pleasure can I have than pleasing Thee, my Lord, Who art so lovely, and Who hast loved me so much? I only seek for love, O my God; and I hope ever to seek it from Thee; until dying in Thy love, I shall reach the kingdom of love, where, without asking any more for it, I shall be filled with love, and I shall never for one moment cease to love Thee, with all my strength, for ever in eternity.

CONSIDERATION IX

The Peace that a Just Man feels when Dying

"The souls of the just are in the hands of God, and the torment of death shall not touch them. In the sight of the unwise they seemed to die, ... but they are in peace." Wisd. iii. 1-3.

First Point.

"THE souls of the just are in the hand of God." If God holds the souls of the just in His hand, who is it that can pluck them out of it? It is true that hell never ceases to tempt and to insult the saints, even when they are dying; but God never ceases to assist them; and when, as S. Ambrose observes, His faithful servants are placed in more danger, then does He give them more help.

When the servant of Elisha saw the city surrounded by enemies, he was affrighted; but the saint encouraged him, saying, "Fear not, for they that be with us are more than they that be with them." (2 Kings vi. 16.) And Elisha then prayed, and the young man's eyes were opened, and he saw an army of angels sent by God to defend them. The devil will indeed come to tempt the dying man, but his guardian angel will also come to comfort him. S. Michael, who is appointed by God to defend His faithful servants in this their last combat with hell; but above all, Jesus Christ will come to keep this His penitent and innocent sheep for whose salvation He once gave up His life. He will give thy soul that confidence and strength which in such a combat it will stand in need of, so that He will exclaim with all courage, "Lord, be Thou my helper." (Ps. xxx. 10.) "The Lord is my light and my salvation, whom then shall I fear?" (Ps. xxvii. 1.) God, as Origen observes, cares much more about our eternal salvation than the devil does about our eternal ruin; because God loves us much more than the devil hates us.

God is faithful, observes the apostle, and will not suffer us to be tempted above that we are able. (1 Cor. x. 13.) But you will say, "Many saints have died in great fear concerning their eternal salvation." I answer, that few are the examples of those who, having led a holy life, have afterwards died in great fear. Belluacensis observes, that the Lord permits this in some saints, in order to purge them when dying from some defect. Besides, do we not read that almost all God's servants have died with a smile upon their lips? To all, the Divine Judgment gives fear of death; but where sinners pass from fear to desperation, the saints pass to assurance. S. Antoninus narrates that S. Bernard being ill, was tempted to fear, but thinking upon the merits of Jesus Christ, he dismissed every fear, saying, "My merits are Thy wounds." S. Hilarion at first was afraid, but afterwards he said, rejoicing, "Go forth, my soul, of what art thou afraid? For well nigh seventy years thou hast served Christ, and dost thou now fear death?" As if he wished to say, my soul, what dost thou fear after having served a God Who is faithful, and Who will never abandon him who has been faithful to Him in life? Father Joseph Scamacca being asked if he felt he was dying with confidence, answered, "What! have I been serving Mahomet all my life, that I should now doubt the goodness of my God as to whether He may wish me to be saved?"

If the thought of having once offended God at any time should torment us in death, we know that the Lord has promised to remember no more the sins of the penitent. "If the wicked will turn from all his sins that he hath committed, ... they shall not be mentioned unto Him." (Ezek. xviii. 21, 22.) But some will say, how can we be sure that God has pardoned us? S. Basil even, asks this question, and replies, "If we can say, I hate and abominate my sin;—because he who hates sin, may rest secure that God has pardoned him already." The heart of man cannot exist without love ; it either loves the creature, or it loves God; if it does not love the creature, then it loves God. And who is it that loves God? Even he who keeps His commandments. "He that hath My commandments, and keepeth them, he it is that loveth Me." (S. John xiv. 21.) He therefore who dies, observing God's commands, dies loving God ; and he that loves God shall not fear : for "perfect love casteth out fear." (1 S. John iv. 18.)

Affections and Prayers.

Ah, my Jesus, when will that day come when I shall be able to say, "My God, never more shall I be able to lose Thee?" When will that day come, when I shall see Thee face to face, and shall rest secure of loving Thee with all my strength for all eternity? Ah, my Sovereign Good, my only love, as long as I live I shall stand in danger of offending Thee, and of losing Thy blessed grace! There was once an unhappy time when I loved Thee not, and when I despised Thy love; but now I repent with all my heart, and hope that Thou hast already pardoned me ; for now I love Thee with all my heart, and I desire to do all I can, to love Thee, and to please Thee ; but I am still in danger of not loving Thee, and of again turning away from Thee. Ah, my Jesus, my Life, my Treasure, do not permit me to do this. Rather than allow this dreadful misfortune to befall me, let me now die the most painful death it may please Thee to send me. I am content with it, and I pray for it. Eternal Father, for the love of Jesus Christ, give me not over to this great ruin. Punish me as Thou wilt, I deserve it, and I accept it ; but deliver me from the punishment of ever beholding myself deprived of Thy grace and of Thy love. My Jesus, for Thine own sake have mercy upon me.

SECOND POINT.

"The souls of the just are in the hand of God ; and the torment of death shall not touch them. In the sight of the unwise they seemed to die, ... but they are in peace." (Wisd. iii. 1–3.) It seems in the sight of the unwise that the servants of God die with sorrow, and unwillingly, even as the worldly do ;

but no, for God knows well how to comfort His children when they are dying; and amidst the pains of their death, He makes them feel a certain incomparable sweetness, as a foretaste of that Paradise, which within a short time He will bestow upon them. Like those who die in sin, who even upon their death-bed experience certain foretastes of hell, such as remorse, fear, and despair; so on the contrary do the saints, by the acts of love which at that time they often make towards God, by the desire and by the hope that is in them, of very soon enjoying God, begin even before death to feel that peace which they will afterwards fully enjoy in heaven. Death to the saints is not a punishment, but a reward. "For so He giveth His beloved sleep." (Ps. cxxvii. 3.) The death of him who loves God is not called death, but sleep, so that he can truly say, "I will lay me down in peace and take my rest." (Ps. iv. 9.)

Father Saurez died in such peace that when dying he was able to say, "I did not think that it was so sweet to die." Cardinal Baronius having been advised by his physician not to think so much about death, replied, "And why? Is it perchance that I fear it? I do not fear, but I love it." Cardinal Fisher, as Saunders relates, when about to die for the faith, put on the best clothes he had, saying, that he was going to a wedding. When he came in sight of the scaffold he cast away his staff, saying, "Make haste my feet; make haste, for we are not far from Paradise." And before dying he sang Te Deum, in returning thanks to God, who had allowed him to die a martyr's death, for the holy faith, and thus being filled with joy, he placed his head under the axe. S. Francis of Assisi sang when dying, and invited the others to sing. One, brother Elias, made answer, saying, "We ought to weep, Father, and not to sing when we are dying." But the saint replied, "I cannot do less than sing, seeing that within so short a time I am going to enjoy God." A Teresian nun dying whilst she was young, and seeing the other nuns begin to weep, she said to them, "O God, wherefore do you weep, I am going to find my Jesus; if you love me rejoice with me." Father Granada relates that a certain huntsman found a solitary leper singing when dying: "Why is it," said the huntsman, "that thou canst sing when in this condition?" The hermit answered, saying, "Brother, between me and God there is only the wall of this my body; now I can see falling into pieces that which was my prison, and I am going to see God; and therefore it is that I comfort myself and sing." This longing to see God, made S. Ignatius the martyr say, that if the wild beasts did not come to take away his life, that he would irritate them, and thus provoke them to devour him. Catherine of Genoa would not allow any one to consider death a misfortune, for she said, "O beloved death, how ungraciously art thou welcomed! and why do you not come to me, when I call upon thee day and night?" S. Teresa desired death so much that she considered it death not to die, and accordingly she composed that celebrated hymn, "I die, because I do not die." Even such is death to the saints.

Affections and Prayers.

Ah my Sovereign Good, my God! if during the years that are past, I have not loved Thee, now will I be converted to Thee. I bid farewell to every creature, and I choose to love Thee alone, my sweetest Saviour. Tell me what Thou wishest me to do, that I may do it. I have already committed offences enough against Thee. The life that remains to me, I would wish to spend it all in pleasing Thee. Give me strength, in some way to atone with my love for the ingratitude, which, until now, I have shown towards Thee. I have deserved, all these years, to be cast into everlasting punishment. Thou hast sought me so many times, that at last Thou hast drawn me to Thee; let me now burn with the fire of Thy holy love. I love Thee, O Thou Infinite Good, Thou wishest me to love Thee only; and with reason, for Thou hast loved me more than all, and Thou alone art worthy to be loved, and I will love Thee only, for I would do all I can to please Thee. Do with me as Thou wilt. It is enough that I love Thee; and that Thou lovest me.

Third Point.

How is it then, that he can fear death, who hopes to be

crowned after death? S. Cyprian says, "We cannot fear to die, who await our crown when we are killed."

How can any one fear death, who knows that dying in grace, his body will become immortal: "This mortal must put on immortality." (1 Cor. xv. 53.) He who loves God and desires to see Him, regards life as a pain and death as a joy: "He lives patiently—he dies delightedly," says S. Augustine. S. Thomas of Villanova says, "that death, if it finds a man sleeping, comes as a thief, robs him, kills him, and casts him into the pit of hell;" but if death finds a man vigilant, it salutes him as the ambassador of God, and says, "The Lord expects thee at the nuptial feast; come, and I will lead thee to the blessed kingdom that thou hast desired."

Oh with what joy does he await death who is in the grace of God, hoping, as he does, soon to see Jesus Christ, and to hear Him say, "Well done, good and faithful servant; thou hast been faithful over a few things, I will make thee ruler over many things." (S. Matt. xxv. 21.) Oh how well then will he understand the force of the repentance, the prayers, the alienation from the things of this world, and all that he has done for God! "Say ye to the righteous, that it shall be well with him; for they shall eat the fruits of their doings." (Isa. iii. 10.) Then will he who has loved God enjoy the fruit of all his good works. Therefore did Father Hippolitus Durazzo, when a friend of his, a religious, was dying, with every sign of salvation, rejoice and not weep. For how absurd it would be, remarks S. John Chrysostom, to believe in an eternal heaven, and yet to pity any one who goes there. What joy it will bring to him, who has loved Jesus Christ, and who has often received Jesus Christ in the Holy Communion to see this same Jesus enter his room at the most solemn hour of death, to accompany him in his journey to the other life. Oh happy he who can then say with S. Philip Neri, "Behold my love, behold my love."

But some will say, "Who can tell what fate will be mine? Perhaps, after all, my end will be an unhappy one!" But to those who thus speak, I ask, "What is it that makes death dreadful?" Sin only; therefore it is sin that we ought to fear and not death. S. Ambrose observes, that "it is clear that the bitterness is not from death, but from sin; fear is not to be referred to death but to life." Therefore, if you desire not to fear death, live holily: "To him who fears the Lord it will be well in his last hour." Father Colombière considered it quite impossible, for him, who has been faithful to God all his life long, to die an unhappy death. And before him S. Augustine has remarked, "He cannot die badly who has lived well." He who is prepared for death, does not fear it, although it should be sudden. "But the just man, if he be prevented with death, shall be in rest." (Wisd. iv. 7.) And since we are unable to go to enjoy God, except we die, S. John Chrysostom exhorts us "to offer to God that which we are bound to render to Him." And let us understand, that he who offers his death to God, performs the most perfect act of love that can be done towards God; for by willingly embracing that death, which it pleases God to send us, and that time and manner of death which God wishes, he makes himself like unto the holy martyrs. He who loves God ought to long and sigh for death, because death unites us eternally with God, and frees us from the danger of ever losing Him again. It is a sign that we love God but little, if we have no desire soon to go to see Him, feeling certain that we shall never be able to love Him more. For the meantime, let us love God as much as we can in this life. For this alone should we live to increase in our love to Him; the measure of love to God in which death will find us, will be the measure of our love to God in a blessed eternity.

Affections and Prayers.

Bind me, my Jesus, to Thyself, so that I may never more be severed from Thee. Make me wholly Thine before I die, so that, when I behold Thee for the first time, I may behold Thee in peace. Thou hast sought me when I was fleeing from Thee; oh, do not drive me from Thee, now that I seek Thee. Pardon me whatever displeasure I may have caused Thee. From this day forward I wish to think of serving and loving Thee only. I am already too much indebted to Thee. Thou didst not refuse to shed Thy blood and give Thy life through love of me. I would wish to be entirely consumed for Thee as Thou wert for me.

O God of my soul, I would love Thee much in this life, so as to love Thee much in the life to come. Eternal Father, draw my whole heart to Thee, take from it all earthly affections, wound it, inflame it with Thy holy love. Hear me, through the merits of Jesus Christ. Give me holy perseverance, and give me the grace ever to ask it of Thee.

CONSIDERATION X

How we must Prepare for Death

"Prepare to meet thy God." Amos iv. 12.

First Point.

ALL confess that they must die, and die but once; and that there is nothing of greater consequence than this; for our eternal happiness or our eternal unhappiness depends upon the moment of death. We all know a happy or an unhappy death depends upon the life we have led. And yet, how is it that nearly all Christians live as if they would never have to die, and as if dying a happy or an unhappy death could be of little importance? Truly we lead a wicked life, because we think not upon death. "In all thy works remember thy last end, and thou shalt never sin." (Ecclus. vii. 40.) We must be persuaded that the hour of death is not the proper time to set our accounts in order, nor to make the great concern of our eternal salvation secure. The wise ones of this world, in worldly matters, take every precaution at the proper time towards obtaining that gain, that post, that matrimonial alliance; when the health of their body is concerned, they lose no time before applying the needful remedies. What would you say of any one who, having undertaken an academical contest, would defer preparing himself for it until the time was come? Would not that general be indeed mad, who should wait until besieged, to lay in stores of provisions and arms? Would not that pilot be mad, who should forget to provide himself with cable and anchors until the time of the tempest? That Christian is even in this state, to whom the hour of death arrives before his conscience is made clean in the sight of God. "When your fear cometh as desolation . . . . then shall they call upon me, but I will not answer, therefore shall they eat of the fruit of their own way." (Prov. i. 27, 28, 31.) The time of death is a time of tempest and confusion; then will sinners call upon God to help them, but only for fear of hell, to which they see themselves so near, and without a sincere conversion, and therefore God will not hear them. And therefore also very justly they shall then reap truly the fruits of their evil life. Alas for them, it will not be enough to take the Sacraments. It is necessary to die hating sin and loving God beyond all things; but how can he hate forbidden pleasures, who, until that time, has loved them so much? and how can he love God beyond all things, who, until that time, has loved the creature more than God?

The Lord called those virgins foolish—and, indeed, they were so—who wished to prepare their lamps when the bridegroom was nigh. A sudden death is dreaded by all, because there is then no time to settle our accounts. All confess that the saints were indeed wise, because they prepared for death before it came. And what are we doing? Do we wish to find ourselves in danger of being obliged to prepare for death when death is already near? therefore, now is the time in which we must do that, which we shall wish we had done when death is nigh. Oh, what anguish will the memory of the time we have lost, and even more, the time that has been badly spent, then cause us—a time given by God to make ourselves worthy, but a time that is past, and which will never return! What anguish will it then give us to hear, "Thou canst be no longer steward."

There will be no more time for repentance, to frequent the Sacrament, to hear sermons, and to pray. What will be done, will be done. We shall then require a sounder mind, a quieter time to make our confession as it should be made, in order to resolve many points of grave scruple, and thus to ease our conscience; but "time will be no longer."

Affections and Prayers.

Ah, my God, if I had died during one of those nights, of which Thou knowest, where now should I have been? I thank Thee for having waited for me, and I also thank Thee for all those moments which would have been spent in everlasting punishment from that time when I first offended Thee. Ah, give me light, and make me to understand the great wrong I have done Thee, by willingly losing Thy grace, which Thou hast merited for me in sacrificing Thyself upon the Cross for me. Ah, my Jesus, pardon me, for I repent with my whole heart, above every other evil, that of having despised Thy Infinite Goodness. I hope that Thou hast already pardoned me. Ah, help me, O my Saviour, so that I may never lose Thee more. Ah, my Lord, if again I should offend Thee as I used to do, after having received so many lights and graces from Thee, should I not deserve a special place of torment? Ah, through the merits of that Blood which Thou hast shed through love of me, never permit this. Give me holy perseverance; give me Thy love. I love Thee, O my Sovereign Good, and I wish never to cease to love Thee, even until my death. My God, have mercy upon me for the love of Jesus Christ.

Second Point.

Therefore, my brother, as it is certain that you will have to die, lose no time in casting yourself at the feet of your Crucified Lord; thank Him for the time that He in His mercy gives you to make your conscience clear in His sight; and then take all the wickedness of your past life in review, especially the wickedness committed in youth. Glance over the Divine commands; examine what you have done, the society you have been in the habit of visiting; make a note of all your failings, and make a general confession of your whole life, if you have not done so already. Oh, how much a good general confession assists a Christian in living a holy life! Consider that these are examinations for eternity, and therefore make them as if you were on the point of being examined by Jesus Christ, Who will be your Judge. Drive away from your heart every unholy affection, every spiteful feeling; remove now every scruple concerning the property of others, characters taken away, scandals noised abroad; and make up your mind to fly those occasions in which you may be in danger of losing God. Consider that what seems difficult to you now, at the moment of death will seem to be impossible.

It is of the greatest importance that you should make a resolution to practise every means to preserve yourself in the grace of God—namely, to attend daily Celebration, to meditate upon the eternal truths, to go to confession and to communicate at least every week, to examine your conscience every night, and, above all, to commend yourself very often to God, calling upon the most holy Name of Jesus, and this particularly at the time of temptation. By so doing we may at least hope to die a happy death, and to obtain our eternal salvation.

And as for the past, you must trust in the Blood of Jesus Christ, Who gives you these lights now, because He wishes you to be saved. By living thus, and trusting in Jesus, God gives us His help, and our souls gain strength! Therefore make haste, dear reader, and give yourself to God, Who thus calls you, and you will begin to taste that peace, of which your sin until now has deprived you. And what greater peace can any one feel than being able to say when lying down to rest at night, "If I should die this night, I hope to die in the grace of God?" If we are awaiting death with resignation when it is God's will, it is even consoling to hear the thunders roaring, and to feel the earth trembling.

Affections and Prayers.

Ah, my Lord, how I thank Thee for the light that Thou givest me. I have so often left Thee, and turned away from Thee; but Thou hast never left me. If Thou hadst, I should have remained blind, as I was willing to be during the years that are past; I should have remained obstinate in my sin; I should neither have felt the wish to leave it, nor the desire to love Thee. Now I feel very grieved for having offended Thee, and a great desire to remain in Thy grace. I feel a great aversion from those wretched pleasures which caused me to lose Thy friendship. All these feelings of sorrow for past sins, are graces which come from Thee, and make me hope that Thou art willing to pardon and to save me. Since, therefore, with all my sins, Thou hast not abandoned me, but hast wished to save me, behold, Lord, I give myself entirely to Thee; I repent beyond every other evil that of having offended Thee; and I would give my life many times over, if it were possible, rather than lose Thy grace. I love Thee, my Highest Good; I love Thee, my Jesus, Who once died for me, and I hope through Thy Blood that Thou wilt never more permit me to be separated from Thee. No, my Jesus, never more would I lose Thee. I would ever love Thee in life; I would love Thee in death; and I would love Thee for all eternity. Do Thou ever keep me, and do Thou increase my love towards Thee; and this I ask through Thy merits.

Third Point.

It is, moreover, necessary to endeavour each hour that we live to be in such a frame of mind as we should like to be when dying: "Blessed are the dead which die in the Lord." (Rev. xiv. 13.) S. Ambrose observes that those persons die a happy death who, when the hour of death arrives, are found already dead to the world, even to those things from which death will come to sever them by force. So that we must from this hour accept the spoiling of our inheritances, separations from our relatives, and from all the things of this world. If we do not do this willingly in life, we shall have to do it of necessity in death; but then with great grief and peril to our eternal salvation. And for this cause S. Augustine warns us that, in order to die in peace, it is necessary to settle our worldly interests during life, and now to dispose in a proper way of those earthly goods we shall have to leave, so that in death our time may be given up to the uniting of ourselves with God. At that time, our thoughts should be of God and Paradise only. Those last moments are too precious to be wasted upon the things of earth. The crown of the elect is perfected in death, for perchance it is then that we merit most the crown, by embracing those pains and that death with resignation and love.

But he will never have these holy feelings in death, who has not practised them in life. Some devout persons make a practice (and with great profit to themselves) of renewing every month a certain desire for death, imagining themselves to be on their death-bed, placing themselves as if in the presence of death.

That which is not done during life is very difficult to be done in death. Sister Catherine of S. Albert, who was a faithful servant of God, when dying, said, "I do not sigh because I fear death, because for twenty-five years I have been expecting it; but I sigh because I see many deceive themselves by leading a life of sin, and thus put off making their peace with God until the hour of death, when I feel as if I can hardly pronounce the name of Jesus."

Therefore examine yourself, my brother, and see whether your heart is fond of anything that is of the earth—that person, that honour, that house, that money, that conversation, those amusements; and reflect that you are not immortal. Some day you will have to leave all these things, and perhaps very soon. Why then are you so fond of them? and thus run the risk of dying a miserable death? From this hour offer everything to God, being ready to give up all when it shall please Him. If you wish to die submissive, you must resign yourself to all that may befall you, and divest yourself of every earthly affection. Reflect upon the moment of death, and as you would then despise all things do so now. S. Jerome observes, "He easily despises all things who ever regards himself as one about to die."

If you have not yet decided upon what life you shall lead, make choice of that which you will wish you had chosen at the moment of death, and that which will make you die a happy death. If you have already chosen it, do what you will wish to have done in that particular life. Act as if each day were the last of your life, each action were the last, each prayer the last, each confession the last, and each communion the last. Act as if each hour were your last, and stretched upon a bed you heard this intimated, "Depart out of this world."

This thought, Oh! how greatly will it help you to walk

through and to separate yourself from this world. "Blessed is that servant, whom when his Lord cometh He shall find so doing." (S. Matt. xxiv. 26.) He who expects death at every hour, even though he should die suddenly, will not fail to die well.

Affections and Prayers.

Every Christian ought to be prepared to say, when death shall be announced to him, Since therefore, my God, but so few hours remain to me, I would love Thee as much as it is possible for me to do during the short time I shall have in this life, so that I may love Thee more in the life to come. But little remains for me to offer Thee; therefore I will offer these my pains to Thee, and the sacrifice of my life, together with the sacrifice of Jesus Christ, made for me upon the Cross. O Lord, the pains which I am suffering are but few and very slight compared with what I deserve to suffer: such as they are I embrace in token of the love I have for Thee. I yield myself to every punishment that it may please Thee to send me. If only I may love Thee in eternity, punish me as Thou wilt, but do not deprive me of Thy love. I know that I do not deserve to love Thee any longer, because I have so often despised Thy love; but Thou wilt not spurn a repentant soul. I repent, O my Sovereign Good, for having offended Thee. I love Thee with all my heart, and trust everything to Thee. Thy death, O my Redeemer, is my hope. Into Thy wounded hands I commend my soul. "Into Thy hands I commend my spirit: for Thou hast redeemed me, O Lord, Thou God of truth." (Ps. xxxi. 6.) O my Jesus, Thou Who hast given Thy Blood to save me, do Thou never allow me to be separated from Thee. I love Thee, O Eternal God, and I hope to love Thee in eternity.

CONSIDERATION XI

The Value of Time

"Redeeming the time, because the days are evil." Eph. v. 16.

First Point.

WE are told in Holy Scripture to be careful of time, which is the most precious thing and the greatest gift that God bestows upon living man. The Pagans even understood the value of time. Seneca observed that "the value of time is priceless." But the saints have much better understood it. S. Bernardine of Sienna says, that one single moment of time is of very great importance, because at any one moment a man may, by one act of contrition or of love, gain the Divine grace and eternal glory.

Time is a treasure which can be found in this life alone; it is to be found neither in heaven nor in hell. This is the lamentation of the lost in hell, "Oh, that an hour were given." They would give anything for one hour in which they might be able to remedy their ruin, but this hour they will never have. In heaven there are no tears; but if the blessed could weep, this would be a cause for lamentation, that they had lost any time during this life in which they might have acquired greater glory—for such time they now can never have.

And you, my brother, how are you spending the time? And for what reason do you put off until to-morrow that which you can do to-day? Remember that the time which is already past away is no longer yours: the future is not in your power;

the present time alone you have for doing good. S. Bernard warns us, saying, "Wherefore do you presume upon the future, O miserable one, as if the Father had put the times in thy power." And S. Augustine asks, "Do you reckon upon a day, who canst not reckon upon an hour?" How canst thou promise thyself the day of to-morrow, if thou knowest not whether one more hour of life will be thine? S. Teresa thus concludes, and says, "If thou art not ready to die to-day, thou oughtest to fear lest thou shouldst die an unhappy death!

Affections and Prayers.

O my God, I thank Thee for the time Thou art giving me to atone, as far as I am able, for the sins of my past life. If at this moment Thou shouldst cause me to die, one of my greatest griefs would be to think of the time I have lost. Ah, my Lord, Thou didst give me the time to spend in loving Thee, and I have spent it in offending Thee. I deserved to be sent to hell from the first moment I turned away from Thee, but Thou hast called me to repentance, and Thou hast pardoned me. I promised never more to offend Thee, but since then, how many times have I not again offended Thee, and Thou hast again pardoned me? for ever blessed be Thy mercy. If it were not infinite, how could it thus have borne with me? Who else would have shown such patience towards me as Thou hast? How much I grieve for having offended a God so good! My dear Saviour, the patience alone Thou hast shown towards me ought to have inspired me with love for Thee. Ah, never more allow me to be ungrateful to the love Thou hast borne for me. Separate me from all things, and draw me wholly to Thy love. No, my God, I will no longer waste that time which Thou hast given me to atone for the evil I have done; I would spend it all in serving and loving Thee. Give me strength, give me holy perseverance. I love Thee, O Thou Infinite Goodness, and I hope to love Thee in eternity.

Second Point.

There is nothing that is more precious than time, but yet

there is nothing less valued, and more despised by men of the world. This is what S. Bernard deplores, when he says, "The days of salvation pass away, and no one reflects that the day which has passed away from him can never return." That gambler will be seen to waste both day and night in play; if he is asked what he is doing, he answers, "We are passing away the time." Another idler will be seen to loiter about the streets, for whole hours together, looking at those who pass by, either speaking of wicked, or else about useless things; if he is asked what he is doing, he answers, "I am passing away the time." Poor, blind ones! who are wasting so many days, but days that will never return.

O despised time, thou wilt be the thing most desired by the worldly at the time of death. They will desire one more year, one more month, one more day; but they will not have it, they will then hear it declared, that "time shall be no longer." What would not each one of those give for one more week, one more day, in order the better to clear his conscience. S. Laurence Justinian observes, that each one of these will then be willing to give up everything to obtain only one hour. But this hour will not be given to them; the priest who is with them will say, there is no more time for thee; "Depart, O Christian soul, from this world."

Nevertheless, the prophet bids us remember God, and obtain His grace before the light shall fail, "Remember now thy Creator . . . . while the sun or the light . . . . be not darkened. (Eccles. xii. 1, 2.) How it distresses a pilgrim when he finds out that he has wandered from the right way, and it is already night, and there is no longer time to get back to the right path. This will be the distress when death comes to him, of him who has lived for many years in the world, but who has not spent those years in loving God, "The night cometh, when no man can work." (S. John ix. 4.) Death will be to him the time of night, when he will be able to do nothing. "He hath called against me the time." (Lament. i. 15, Vulg.) His conscience will then remind him of the time he has had, and how he has spent it in the ruin of his soul; the many calls and graces that he has received from God to become holy, and yet was not willing to profit by all this, and then he will behold the way of doing any good closed against him. Then will he weep and say, "Oh, fool that I have been! Oh, time for ever lost! Oh, wasted life! Oh, years that are lost in which I could have become holy, but I did not do so, and now there is no longer time to become holy." But what will these lamentations and sighs avail, when his life's scene is for ever closing, the lamp is well nigh spent, and the dying man is drawing near to that last moment upon which his eternity depends?

Affections and Prayers.

Ah, my Jesus, Thou hast given away Thy whole life to save my soul, there has been no moment of it in which Thou hast not offered Thyself to the Eternal Father, in order to obtain pardon and eternal salvation for me; and I have lived so long in the world, and until now I have never spent any time in Thy service. Alas! for everything I remember to have done fills me with remorse of conscience. My sin has been very grievous. The good that I have done has been too little and too full of imperfection, of lukewarmness, of self-love, and of distraction. Ah, my Redeemer, it has all been thus, because I was forgetful of all that Thou hast done for me. I have been forgetful of Thee, but Thou hast never been forgetful of me. Thou hast sought me whilst I was flying from Thee, and hast so often called me to Thy love. Behold me, my Jesus, I will no longer resist Thee. Shall I, indeed, wait until Thou dost give me up? I repent, O my Sovereign Good, for having separated myself from Thee through my sin. I love Thee, O Thou Infinite Good, Thou Who art indeed worthy of infinite love. Ah, do not allow me ever to waste the time which Thou in Thy mercy dost grant me. Do Thou ever remember, my beloved Saviour, the love Thou hast borne for me, and the pains Thou hast suffered for me. Make me remember all this, so that, during the life that may remain to me, I may only think of loving Thee and pleasing Thee. I love Thee, my Jesus, my love, my all. I promise Thee ever to perform acts of love when I can remember to do so. Give me holy perseverance. I trust entirely in the merits of Thy Blood.

Third Point.

"Walk while ye have the light." (S. John xii. 35.) We must walk in the way of the Lord during life, even now that we have the light; for this light will be lost in death. The time of death is not the time to prepare, but to find ourselves prepared. "Be ye ready." When death comes, nothing can be done; what is then done is done. O God, if any one were to be told that before long a trial should take place upon which his life and all his property should depend, would he not hasten to obtain able counsel to plead his cause, and to find means to obtain favour! And what are we doing? We know for certain, that within a short time, and it may happen at any hour, the most important trial that we can undergo will take place, which will be the trial of our eternal salvation; and shall we lose time?

Some will say, but I am young, after some years I will give myself to God. But I answer, You know that the Lord cursed the fig-tree that He found without any fruit, although it was not the time for fruit, as is noticed in the Gospel. "For the time of figs was not yet." (S. Mark xi. 13.) By this Jesus Christ wished to show us, that man at every time—even at the time of youth, ought to yield the fruits of good works, otherwise he will be cursed, and for the future will yield no fruit. "No man eat fruit of thee hereafter for ever." Thus did the Redeemer speak to that tree; and even thus does He curse that one whom He calls, but who resists His call. The devil considers the time of our life to be but short, and for that reason he loses no time in tempting us. "The devil is come down unto you, having great wrath, because he knoweth he hath but a short time." (Rev. xii. 12.) The enemy loses no time in tempting us, so that we may be lost; and shall we lose any time in seeking to be saved?

Others will say, "But what harm can I be doing?" O God, is it not doing harm, to waste time in play, or in useless conversations, which can bring no profit to the soul? Perhaps God grants this time to you, so that you may waste it? Holy Scripture tells us no; for "defraud not thyself of the good day." (Ecclus. xiv. 14.) Those labourers, of whom S. Matthew writes, did not do evil, but they wasted their time; and for this they were reproved by the master of the vineyard. "Why stand ye here all the day idle?" (S. Matt. xx. 6.) At the day of judgment Jesus Christ will ask us for an account of every idle word spoken. Any time that is not employed for God is time that is wasted. Therefore does the Lord exhort us, saying, "Whatsoever thy hand findeth to do, do it with thy might; for there is no work, nor device, nor knowledge, nor wisdom in the grave whither thou goest." (Eccles. ix. 10.) A Teresian nun once observed that in the life of the saints there is no to-morrow; to-morrow is for sinners alone, who are ever saying, some day—some day—until death comes to overtake them. "Behold, now is the accepted time." (2 Cor. vi. 2.) "To-day, if ye will hear His voice, harden not your hearts." (Ps. xcv. 8.) God now calls upon thee to do good; do it at once; because, when to-morrow comes, either there may be no more time, or God may never call thee again.

And if during the time that is past you have unfortunately spent it in offending God, try to mourn over the sin during the life that remains to you. As King Hezekiah proposed to do, "I shall go softly all my years in the bitterness of my soul." (Isa. xxxviii. 15.) God gives you your life so that you may now in some measure redeem the time that is lost. "Redeeming the time because the days are evil." (Ephes. v. 16.) S. Austin comments upon this, and says, "Thou redeemest the time, if the things thou hast neglected to do, thou doest." S. Jerome observes of S. Paul, that although he was the last of the Apostles, yet he was the first in merits, because of all he did after he was called. Let us consider, that if there were nothing else, at each moment we could increase our store of eternal goods. If it were granted to you to gain as much land as you could walk round or as much money as you could count in one day, would you not make haste to walk round or to count it? And you can gain eternal treasures in one moment, and yet are you willing to waste the time? What you can do to-day, do not say you can do it to-morrow, because this day will be lost to you, and it will never return. S. Francis Borgia turned to God with such holy affection, when others spoke of the world, so that when his opinion was asked, he knew not what to answer. Being rebuked for this, he answered, "I would much rather be considered dull of understanding than waste my time."

Affections and Prayers.

No, my God, I will no longer waste that time which Thou in Thy mercy dost grant to me. I deserve now to be weeping fruitlessly in everlasting punishment. I thank Thee for having preserved me in life. Therefore, for the days which may remain to me, I will live only to Thee. If I were now in hell I should weep, but despairingly and without fruit. I wish to weep over the offences I have committed against Thee; and whilst weeping, I feel certain that Thou wilt pardon me; for the prophet assures me, that, "Thou shalt weep no more; He will be very gracious unto thee." (Isa. xxx. 19.) If I were now in hell I could never love Thee more; but now I love Thee, and hope ever to love Thee. If I were now in hell, I should never more be able to ask Thee for more grace; but now I can hear Thee saying, "Ask, and it shall be given you." Therefore, since I can still ask grace of Thee, these two gifts will I ask, O God of my soul; give me perseverance in Thy grace, and give me Thy love, and then do with me what Thou wilt. Grant that at every moment of life which may remain to me, I may ever commend myself to Thee, my Jesus, by saying, "Lord help me, Lord have mercy upon me; let me never more offend Thee; let me ever love Thee."

CONSIDERATION XII

The Importance of Salvation

"We beseech you, brethren, ... to do your own business." 1 Thess. iv. 10, 11.

First Point.

THE "business" of eternal salvation is assuredly an affair which is to us more important than any other, and yet it is the most neglected by Christians. They spare neither time nor diligence to attain that post, or to gain that lawsuit. To conclude that marriage, how many counsels, how many steps are taken? they neither eat nor sleep. And yet to secure eternal salvation, What do they do? how do they live? They do nothing, nay, they do all things to lose it; and the larger number of Christians so live, as if death, judgment, hell, heaven, and eternity could not be an article of faith, but fables invented by the poets. If they lose a lawsuit or a harvest, what grief do they not feel? What pains do they not take to repair the loss? If they lose a horse or a dog, what diligence do they not exercise to find it? They lose the grace of God; they sleep, they jest, and they laugh. Wonderful fact! All are ashamed to be called negligent in the affairs of the world, and yet how many are not ashamed to neglect the affairs of eternity, which is all-important! They deem the saints to be wise, since they have attended solely to their salvation; and then they attend to all other things of the world, and not at all to the soul! But, says S. Paul, do you, my brethren, do you, attend only to that great concern which you have, of your eternal salvation; for this is the affair which is important to you. "We beseech you, brethren, ... to do your own business." Let us then be persuaded that eternal salvation is for us the concern of the last *importance*—the *one* concern; and that it is an *irreparable* concern if ever we make a mistake.

It is the most *important* concern: yes, since it is an affair of the greatest consequence; it concerns the soul, which if lost all is lost. S. Chrysostom tells us that the soul ought to be more precious to us than all the goods of the world. It is sufficient to know, in order to understand this, that God Himself has given His Son to die to save our souls: "God so loved the world, that He gave His only-begotten Son." (S. John iii. 16.) And the Eternal Word did not refuse to purchase them with His own Blood. "Ye are bought with a price." (1 Cor. vi. 20.) So that, as a holy Father observes, "The redemption of man was effected at so precious a price, that man seemed to be of equal value with God." Hence our Blessed Lord said, "What shall a man give in exchange for his soul?" (S. Matt. xvi. 26.) If the soul, then, be of so great value, for what worldly goods truly, shall a man exchange and so lose it?

S. Philip Neri had reason to call him mad, who does not attend to the salvation of his soul. If on this earth there were men mortal as well as immortal, and the mortal men beheld those who were immortal wholly concerned with the things of this world—in the acquiring honours, possessions, and in worldly amusements—they would certainly exclaim, "Oh, madmen that ye are. You are able to gain eternal goods, and do you strive after these alone which are miserable and transitory? And is it for these that you condemn yourselves to eternal pains in the next life? Leave us, unhappy, who can only think of these earthly things, for whom all will end in death." But no—since we are all immortal, how is it that so many endanger the soul for the miserable pleasures of this world? How is it, says Salvian, that Christians believe that there is a judgment, a hell, an eternity, and yet live without fearing them.

Affections and Prayers.

Ah, my God, how have I spent the many years which Thou

hast given to me to the end that I might attain eternal salvation! Thou, my Redeemer, hast purchased my soul with Thy Blood, and Thou hast consigned it to me to the intent that I might attend to its salvation; and I have only attended to the losing of it, by offending Thee, Who has so greatly loved me. I thank Thee, that still to me Thou art giving time to repair this great loss which I have made. I have lost my soul and Thy bountiful favour. Lord, I repent, and grieve with my whole heart. Alas! pardon me, for I resolve from this day forth to sacrifice everything, even life, rather than Thy friendship. I love Thee above every good, and I resolve to love Thee ever, O Highest Good, worthy of infinite love. Help me, my Jesus, in order that this my resolution may not be like other past resolutions, which are all so many betrayals. Make me to die rather than to turn again and offend Thee, and cease to love Thee.

SECOND POINT.

The "business" of eternal salvation is not only the most important, but it is the *only* "business" that we have to do in this life. "But one thing is needful." S. Bernard weeps over the foolishness of Christians, saying that "the trifles of children are called trifles, but the trifles of grown-up people are called business." These trifles of adults are the greater trifles. Our Blessed Lord asks, "What is a man profited, if he shall gain the whole world, and lose his own soul?" (S. Matt. xvi. 26.) If you save this, my brother, it matters not if in this world you may be poor, afflicted, and despised; if you are saved, you will have no further woes, and you will be happy for all eternity. But if, on the other hand, you lose your soul, what will it serve you in hell, to have had all the pleasures of the world, and to have been rich and honoured? If the soul is lost, pleasures, honours, riches are lost—all is lost.

How will you answer Jesus Christ in the day of account? If a king had commanded his ambassador to transact some important business in a city, and he, instead of attending there to the business committed to him, attended solely to banquets, plays, and festivities; and by this means had badly executed his business, what account could he give to the king on his return? But, O God! what a much greater account will he have to render in that judgment, to the Lord, he who was placed on the earth—not to amuse himself, not to amass riches, not to acquire honours, but to save his soul—if he shall have attended to everything rather than to his soul? The worldly take thought of the present only; not of the future. S. Philip Neri once, in Rome, conversing with a young man of ability named Francis Zazzera, who was attached to the world, thus addressed him: "My son, you will make a large fortune; you will become a noted advocate; afterwards you will become a prelate, perhaps even at length a cardinal, and who knows, it may be a Pope; and then? and then?" "Go," he said in conclusion, "think upon these two last words." Francis retired home thinking upon these two words: *and then? and then?* He left his worldly studies, and entered into the same congregation of S. Philip, and began to attend to God alone.

The *one* "business," since we have but one soul. Benedict XII. was asked to grant a prince a favour which he could not concede without sin. The Pope answered the ambassador: "Tell your prince that, if I had two souls, I would lose one of them, and keep the other for myself; but as I have only one, I cannot, neither do I desire to betray it." S. Francis Xavier said, "that there is but one good and one evil in the world: the one good is to save, the one evil is to lose the soul." S. Teresa used to repeat to her nuns these words, "My sisters, one soul, one eternity;" wishing to say, "one soul—lose this and all is lost; one eternity—lose the soul once and it is lost for ever." Wherefore David prayed, "One thing have I desired of the Lord, which I will require, even that I may dwell in the house of the Lord all the days of my life." (Ps. xxvii. 4.) Lord, one thing I ask of Thee—save my soul, and I ask nothing more.

"Work out your own salvation with fear and trembling." (Phil. ii. 12.) He who does fear and tremble lest he be lost, will not save himself; therefore we must labour and do violence to ourselves to obtain salvation. "The kingdom of heaven suffereth violence, and the violent take it by force." (S. Matt. xi. 12.) To obtain salvation, it is needful that at our death, our life should be found like that of Jesus Christ—"conformed to the image of His Son." (Rom. viii. 29.) On the one hand, we must labour to avoid every occasion of sin; on the other, we must avail ourselves of the means necessary to obtain salvation. S. Bernard says, "The kingdom will not be given to the idle, but to those who are labouring willingly for the cause of God." Every one would wish to save himself without trouble. Great truth! S. Augustine says, that the devil so labours, and sleeps not, in the work of thy destruction, whilst thou art altogether careless in the matter of thy eternal weal or woe; "The enemy watches, and do you sleep?"

Affections and Prayers.

O my God, I thank Thee that at this time Thou allowest me to be at Thy feet and not in that hell which I have so often deserved. But what would avail me this life, which Thou art preserving to me, if I should continue to live deprived of Thy grace? Ah, may this never be my case! O my Chief Good, I have turned away from Thee. I have lost Thee—this now grieves me with all my heart: I would rather have died. I have lost Thee, but Thy Prophet makes me believe that Thou art all Goodness, and to be found of the soul that seeks Thee. "The Lord is good . . . . to the soul that seeketh Him." (Lam. iii. 25.) If, O King of my soul, if I have fled from Thee in the time past, now I seek Thee, and none beside Thee. With my every affection I love Thee. Accept me, do not disdain to make Thyself beloved by that heart that once despised Thee. "Teach me to do the thing that pleaseth Thee;" (Ps. cxliii. 10,) and that I may follow Thy entire will. Alas! my Jesus, save this soul, on behalf of which Thou hast poured out Thy Blood and Thy Life; and save me by giving me grace to love Thee, in this life and the next! I hope for this through Thy merits.

Third Point.

Salvation is the important, only, and *irreparable* "business." Eusebius says that "it is manifestly beyond every error to neglect the business of eternal salvation;" for there is no error like it in its consequences, for all errors but this, have their remedies. If a person lose his property, he may be able to recover it in some other way; if he lose a place, he may be able to regain it; even if he should lose this life and yet be saved, there is a remedy in all these cases. But for him who is lost, there is no further help. We die once; the soul lost once, it is lost for ever. Nothing now remains but to weep for ever in hell with those wretched ones, where the greatest punishment which torments them, will be the thought, that for them to remedy their misery, the time of all help has passed by. "The summer is ended, and we are not saved." (Jer. viii. 20.) Ask the wise ones of this world, who are in that pit of fire, what sentiments they now hold, whether they are contented to have made their future on earth, now that they are condemned to this eternal prison; hear how they weep and say, "On this account we erred." But what does it avail them to know the mistake they have committed, now that there is no escape from eternal condemnation? What grief would not any one feel in this world who had been able at a little cost to mend some defect in his palace, and yet one day afterwards, should find it fallen down: he would have good cause to reflect upon his own carelessness when he could no further remedy it.

This will be the greatest punishment of the lost; the thought that they have destroyed the soul, and that they are condemned for their own sin. "O Israel, thou hast destroyed thyself; but in Me is thine help." (Hos. xiii. 9.) S. Teresa says, that if any one lose, through their own fault, a coat, a ring, even the smallest trifle, he has no peace, he neither eats nor sleeps. O God! what grief will the condemned feel at that moment in which he enters hell, when he finds himself so shut up in that prison of torments and reflects upon his disgrace, and sees that through all eternity it can never be blotted out! Then he will say, I have lost my soul, lost heaven, lost God; I have lost all, and for ever, and for what? By my own fault.

But some will say, if I have committed this sin, wherefore am I condemned? "It may be, that still I may be saved." I answer, that it may be still—nay, I say it is much easier to be condemned; since Holy Scripture threatens with condemnation such obstinate transgressors as thou art now. "Woe to the rebellious children, saith the Lord." (Isa. xxx. 1.) "Woe unto them! for they have fled from me." (Hos. vii. 13.) Do you not by this sin, place your eternal salvation in great peril and doubt? And is this a matter to be placed in peril? It is not as if it concerned a house, a place; it concerns, says S. Chrysostom, the perishing in an eternity of torments, and the losing of an eternal heaven. And this matter, which signifies your all in all, you jeopardise by a "it is possible." You say, "Perchance, who knows I may not be condemned, I trust that afterwards God will pardon me." But in the meantime? In the meantime already you condemn yourself to hell. Tell me, would you throw yourself down a well, saying, "Who knows perhaps I may escape death?" No: how then dare you to make your salvation hang upon so feeble a hope, upon a "who knows?" Oh! how many have lost themselves by this most accursed hope. Do you not know, that the hope of the wilful sinner is not hope but delusion and presumption, which excites God not to pity, but to greater wrath. If you say that you cannot trust yourself now, to resist the temptation and the passion which governs you, how will you be able to resist afterwards, when by the habit of sin your strength of resistance will be diminished and not increased? Since, on the one hand, the soul will be more blinded and hardened in its wickedness; and, on the other, it will be wanting in the divine help. Do you hope, perchance, that God will increase this light and grace, after you have increased your sins?

Affections and Prayers.

O my Jesus, ever recall to me the death which Thou sufferedst for me, and give me confidence. I tremble, lest at my death the devil should make me despair, by showing me how great betrayals of Thee I have committed; how many promises have I not made not to offend Thee any more, by a sight of the light which Thou hast given me; and afterwards, have I not turned back and cast Thee behind me through the hope of pardon? And then because Thou hast not chastised me, have I not, even for this very reason, greatly injured Thee? Because Thou hast shown so great pity towards me, have I not the more outraged Thee?

My Redeemer, give me great grief on account of my sins ere I depart this life. I repent, O Highest Good, of having offended Thee. I promise Thee henceforth rather to die than to leave Thee. But meanwhile, grant me to feel that which Thou spakest to S. Mary Magdalene, "Thy sins are forgiven thee;" and before death comes to me, make me to feel very sorry for my sins; otherwise, I should fear that my death would prove to me unquiet and unhappy. In my last moments, O my Crucified Jesus, "be not a terror unto me, Thou art my hope in the day of evil." (Jer. xvii. 17.) Should I die ere I have wept over my sins, and have loved Thee, Thy wounds and Thy Blood would inspire me then with terror rather than with confidence. I do not ask Thee then for consolations and earthly possessions in this life; I ask of Thee sorrow and love. Hear me, my dear Saviour, for the sake of that love which led Thee for me to sacrifice Thy life on Mount Calvary.

CONSIDERATION XIII

The Vanity of the World

"What is a man profited, if he shall gain the whole world and lose his own soul?
S. Matt. xvi. 26.

First Point.

A CERTAIN ancient philosopher, named Aristippus, was shipwrecked on a voyage, and lost all his goods, but he reached the shore. Being much renowned for his knowledge, he was provided with all that he had lost by the inhabitants of the place; whence he wrote to his friends in his own country, that following his example they should care to provide themselves with those things only which could not perish in shipwreck. So precisely do our parents and friends who are in eternity speak to us, bidding us provide only in life such good things as death cannot destroy. The day of death is called "the day of destruction." (Deut. xxxii. 35.) For in that day all earthly goods, honours, riches, pleasures—all will be destroyed. Hence S. Ambrose says, "They are not our own possessions which we are not able to take away with us; our virtue alone accompanies us." What serves it then, says Jesus Christ, to gain the whole world, if losing the soul in death, we lose all. "What is a man profited, if he shall gain the whole world and lose his own soul?" Ah, this mighty truth! how many young men has it bidden to seek the cloister; how many hermits to live in deserts; how many martyrs to give their lives for Jesus Christ! S. Ignatius of Loyola by this truth, drew many souls to God, especially the beautiful soul of S. Francis Xavier who, living in Paris, gave himself up to the world. S. Ignatius said to him one day, "Remember, that the world is a traitor; that it promises, but it does not fulfil: if it should perform what it promises, it is not able to fill thy heart. But let us suppose that it could satisfy it, how long would this thy happiness endure? Can it last longer than thy life? and, in short, what canst thou carry into eternity? Is there perchance any rich man who has carried thither either a piece of money or a servant for his convenience? Is there any king who has carried a thread of the purple through his love of it?" On hearing these words, S. Francis left the world; he followed S. Ignatius, and he became a saint. "Vanity of vanities," so Solomon called all the goods of this world, although he had not denied himself one pleasure of all those that are in the world, as he himself acknowledges. "Whatsoever mine eyes desired I kept not from them; I withheld not my heart from any joy." (Eccles. ii. 10.) Sister Margaret of S. Anne, of the Barefooted-Carmelites, daughter of the Emperor Rudolph II., said, "Of what use are kingdoms at the hour of death." How wonderful! the saints tremble when they think upon their eternal salvation. Father Segneri trembled, in great terror, demanding of his confessor, "What say you, Father, shall I be saved?" S. Andrew Avellino trembled and wept, saying, "Who knows whether I shall be saved?" S. Louis Bertrand was so tormented by this thought even, that terrified in the night he sprang out of bed, saying, "And who knows but I shall be damned?" And sinners live condemned, and sleep, and jest, and laugh.

Affections and Prayers.

O Jesus, my Redeemer, I thank Thee that Thou hast made me to know my folly and the sin which I have committed in turning away from Thee, Who hast shed Thy Blood and Thy life for me. No, Thou hast not deserved to be treated by me as I have treated Thee. Behold, if death should come to me now, what should I find in myself, except sins and remorse of conscience, which would cause me to die in great disquiet? I confess, my Saviour, I have sinned, I have erred in leaving

Thee, my Highest Good, for the miserable pleasures of this world; I repent with my whole heart. Alas! by that grief which slew Thee on the Cross, give me such sorrow for my sins as may cause me to weep during all that remains of my life for the wrongs I have done Thee. My Jesus, my Jesus, pardon me, and I promise never more to offend Thee, and ever to love Thee. I am no longer worthy of Thy love since I have so despised it in the past time, but Thou hast said, "I love them that love Me." (Prov. viii. 17;) I love Thee, do Thou also love me; I will no longer live in Thy disgrace. If Thou wilt love me, I renounce all the pomps and pleasures of the world. Hear me, my Lord, for the love of Jesus Christ. I pray that Thou wouldst not banish me from Thy heart. I consecrate myself to Thee wholly; my life, my inclinations, my senses, my mind, my body, my will, and my liberty. Receive me; do not reject me as I deserve, for having so often rejected Thy friendship. "Cast me not away from Thy presence." (Ps. xxi. 11.)

SECOND POINT.

"The balances of deceit are in his hand." (Hos. xii. 17.) We ought to weigh all goods in the balances of God, not in the deceitful balances of this world. The goods of this world are miserable, they do not content the soul, and they quickly pass away, "My days are swifter than a post; . . . . they are passed away as the swift ships." (Job ix. 25, 26.) The days of our life pass and fly away; of the pleasures of this world, at the end, what remains? "They are passed away as the swift ships." Ships leave, indeed, no sign of where they have passed. "As a ship that passeth through the waves; whereof when it is gone by, the trace cannot be found, nor the path of its keel in the waters." (Wisd. v. 10.) Let us ask of so many wealthy, *literati*, princes, emperors, who are now in eternity, what find they now of the pomps, pleasures, and grand enjoyments of this earth? All answer, Nothing, nothing! "O man," says S. Augustine, "mark what he had here, and note what he takes away with him." Thou notest, says the saint, only the goods which the great have preserved; but observe what they take with them when they die — is it not a corrupt body and a few rags to decay with them? When the great ones of this world die, hardly, for a little time, are they spoken of, and then they are not even remembered, "Their memorial is perished with them." (Ps. ix. 6.) And if these miserable ones are afterwards in hell, what do they do, and what do they say there? They weep and say, "What hath pride profited us? or what advantage hath the boasting of riches brought us? All those things are passed away like a shadow." (Wisd. v. 8, 9.) In what have our pomp and our riches helped us, if the whole has now passed away as a shadow, and there remains nought save punishment, weeping, and eternal despair?

"The children of this world are in their generation wiser than the children of light." (S. Luke xvi. 8.) Great truth! that the children of this world are prudent in the things of the world! What fatigues do they not brave to obtain that post or this inheritance! What diligence do they not expend to preserve the health of the body! They choose the means, the most safe, the best medicines, the best physicians, the best air! And for the soul, then, they are so negligent! Yet it is certain that health, posts, possessions, will one day have an end; but the mind and eternity never end. S. Augustine says, "We observe how much men suffer for the things which they wrongly love." What does not the vindictive, the thief, the incontinent suffer, in order to obtain his depraved wish! And then for the soul, they are not willing to suffer anything! O God, at the hour of death, in that time of truth, worldlings both know and confess their madness. Then every one says, "Oh, that I had forsaken all, and that I had become a saint!"

Philip II., King of Spain, sent for his son when on his deathbed, and unfolding his royal robe, showed to him his breast eaten by worms, and then he said, "Prince, see how we die, and how the pomp of the world ends." And afterwards he exclaimed, "Oh, that I had been a lay brother in some monastery, and not a monarch!" At the same time, he caused them to fasten a wooden cross to his neck by a cord, and having prepared the things for his death, he said to his son, "I wished thee, my son, to be present at this act, that you may see how at the end, the world treats even monarchs, so that their death is the same as that of the poorest of the world; in short, he who lives best, has the best place with God." Afterwards this same son, who was Philip III., dying young, at the age of forty-three, said, "My subjects, preach nothing in my funeral sermon, but that sight which you now behold. Say that in death, it avails not to be a king, but that by this thought, greater torment is present to him." He then exclaimed, "Oh, that I had never been a king, and that I had lived in a desert to serve God; since now I should have dared with greater confidence to present myself before His tribunal, and I should not find myself in so great danger of being condemned!" But what do these desires avail, at the moment of death, save to bring greater pain and despair to him who has not loved God in life? Therefore, said S. Teresa, "We must make no account of that which ends with life; the true life is so to live as not to fear to die." If we wish to see the things of this world as they really are, let us behold them from the bed of death, and then say, "These honours, these amusements, these revenues, will one day end; we must then strive to become saints, rich in those goods above, which will go with us, and which will make us happy through all eternity."

Affections and Prayers.

Ah, my Redeemer, Thou hast suffered so many pains and ignominies for the love of me, whilst I have so greatly loved the pleasures and vanities of this world, that on their account I have often trampled Thy grace under foot. But if when I despised Thee Thou didst still follow me, I cannot fear, O my Jesus, that I shall be rejected, now that I follow Thee and love Thee with my whole heart; and I grieve more for having offended Thee than if I had suffered any other disgrace. O God of my soul, henceforth I will not willingly give Thee any displeasure, even in the smallest thing. Make me to know what is displeasing to Thee, and I will not willingly do it for any good in the world; and teach me to do what shall please Thee, for I am ready. I desire truly to love Thee. I embrace, O Lord, all the pains and crosses which Thou pleasest to send me. Give me that resignation which I ought to have. "Here burn—here cut;" chastise me in this life, that in the other life I may love Thee for all eternity.

Third Point.

"The time is short; . . . it remaineth that . . . they that use this world as not abusing it; for the fashion of this world passeth away." (1 Cor. vii. 29-31.) For what else is our life upon this earth, save a scene which passes and quickly ends? "The fashion of this world passeth away;" the fashion—that is, a scene, a play. Cornelius à Lapide says that "the world is like a stage, a generation passes away, a generation comes. He who plays the king does not take the people away with him. Tell me, O villa, O house, how many masters you have had?" When the play is finished, he who played the king is no longer a king; the master is no longer a master. Now thou possessest this villa or that palace, but death will come, and there will be other masters.

"The affliction of an hour maketh one forget great delights." (Ecclus. xi. 29.) The fatal hour of death makes all the pomps and the nobility, and the pageants of the world to be forgotten, and to be at an end. Cassimir, King of Poland, one day whilst sitting at table with the grandees of his kingdom, raising to his lips the cup to drink, died, and the scene closed for him. Celsus, the Emperor, at the commencement of the seventh day of his election, was slain, and the scene closed for him. Landislaus, King of Bohemia, a young man of eighteen years of age, whilst expecting his bride, the daughter of the King of France, and a splendid feast was being prepared, one morning was stricken with pain, and died; whereupon couriers were quickly despatched to the bride, to advise her to return to France, since the scene had closed for Landislaus. This thought of the vanity of the world made a saint of S. Francis Borgia who, (as already has been mentioned,) at the sight of the Empress Isabella, dead in the midst of her splendour, and in the flower of her youth, resolved to give himself wholly to God, saying, "What! do the greatnesses and the crowns of this world end thus? I desire, then, henceforth to serve a Master Who cannot die."

Let us endeavour so to live, that it may not be said to us in death, as it was said to the fool in the gospel, "Thou fool, this night thy soul shall be required of thee." (S. Luke xii. 19.) Whence S. Luke concludes, "So is he who layeth up treasure for himself, and is not rich towards God." Afterwards, he says, Seek to become rich, not indeed in the possessions of this world, but towards God—in virtue, in merit, which things are really good—which will be eternal with you in the heavens. "Provide yourselves a treasure in the heavens; where no thief approacheth, neither moth corrupteth." (S. Luke xii. 33.) Therefore let us strive to acquire the great treasure of Divine love. S. Augustine asks, "What has the rich man if he has not love? If the poor man has love, what has he not?" If he has all riches, and has not God, he is the poorest man in the world; whilst the poor man who has God, possesses all things. And who has God? He who loves Him. "He that dwelleth in love, dwelleth in God, and God in him." (1 S. John iv. 16.)

Affections and Prayers.

Ah, my God, I will not, that the devil should have further power over my soul. I desire that Thou alone shouldst be my Master, and rule over it. I desire to forsake all to obtain Thy favour; and I value this more than crowns or kingdoms. Who ought I to love, if not Thee, Who art infinite sweetness, infinite good, beauty, bounty and love? In the past time I have left Thee for creatures; this is to me now, and ever will be, a grief which will pierce my heart, to have offended Thee, Who had so much love for me. But after Thou hast bound me, my God, by so great favours, I will not trust myself any longer to see myself deprived of Thy love. Take to Thyself, my love, my whole will, and all that is mine, and do with me according to Thy pleasure. If formerly I allowed myself to be permitted by contrary events, I ask Thy pardon. I will no longer repine, my Lord, at Thy dispensations; I know that they are all, holy, and all, for my good. O my God, do what Thou wilt, and I promise to be always contented, and ever to thank Thee. Grant that I may love Thee, and I ask Thee for nothing more. I desire only God.

CONSIDERATION XIV

Life is a Journey to Eternity

"Man goeth to his long home." Eccles. xii. 5.

First Point.

FROM the beholding, that in this world so many evil-livers live in prosperity, and that so many righteous men, on the contrary, live in adversity, even the Gentiles recognised by the light of nature alone, this truth—that, as there is a God, and as this God is just, so there must be another life in which the wicked will be punished and the good rewarded. What these Gentiles saw by the light of reason alone, that we, Christians, confess by faith: "Here we have no abiding city, but we seek one to come." (Heb. xiii. 14.) This world is not truly our country, but for us it is a place of passage, through which we must pass quickly to our "long home." "Man goeth to his long home." Therefore, my reader, the house in which you dwell is not your house; it is an hostel from which, quickly and when you least expect it, you will have to depart. Know that when the time of your death has arrived, those most dear, will be the first to thrust you out. And what will be your real home? A grave will be the home of your body until the day of judgment; and your soul will have to go to its long home, either to paradise or to hell. Wherefore S. Augustine addresses you: "Thou art a guest; thou beholdest; and thou passest onwards." That traveller would be insane who, passing through a country, would wish to lay out there all his patrimony in the purchase of a villa or a house in that place which in a few days he must leave. Reflect, yet, says the saint, that in this world thou art a passenger; do not place thy affections on what thou seest; behold and pass on, and procure a good home where you will have to dwell for ever.

If thou art saved, happy art thou. Oh, what a beautiful home is heaven! All the palaces, so exceedingly rich, of monarchs are hovels when compared with the city of heaven, which can alone be called "the perfection of beauty." (Lam. ii. 15.) In that place, you will not have anything left to desire; remaining in the company of the saints and of Jesus Christ, without further fear of harm. In short, you will live in an ocean of delights, and in perpetual joy which will never end: "Everlasting joy upon their heads." (Isa. xxxv. 10.) This joy will be so great, that through all eternity, at every moment, it will appear to be ever new. But if thou art lost;—unhappy thou. Thou wilt be confined in a lake of fire, abandoned by all, and without God. And for what time? Perchance, when a hundred thousand years shall have passed by, your punishment will be ended? What end! A hundred thousand million years, and ages will pass by, and your hell will be ever at its beginning. For what are a thousand years in comparison with eternity? Less than a day that has passed, "A thousand years in Thy sight are but as yesterday, seeing that it is past as a watch in the night." (Ps. xc. 4.) Do you wish to know what will be your home, which will receive you in eternity? It will be exactly that which you deserved, and which you chose by your own actions.

Affections and Prayers.

Behold, then, O Lord, the home which I have deserved by my life; alas, hell! where, from the first sin which I committed, I ought to remain, abandoned by Thee, deprived of the hope of being able to love Thee more. Let Thy mercy for ever be blessed, which, having waited for me, also gives me time to atone for my sin. Let the Blood of Jesus Christ be blessed, which has obtained this mercy for me. No, my God, I do not desire further to abuse Thy patience. I repent, above every other sin, having grieved Thee, not so much on account of having deserved hell, as that I have abused Thy infinite goodness. Never more, my God, never more; let me die rather than offend Thee more. If I were now in hell, O my Sovereign Good, I could not love Thee any more, neither couldst Thou further love me. I love Thee, and I desire to be loved by Thee. I do not deserve this; but Jesus Christ merits it, Who so sacrificed Himself upon the Cross that Thou mightst be able to pardon and love me. Eternal Father, for the love, then, of Thy Son, give me grace to love Thee ever, and to love Thee much. I love Thee, O my Father, for having given Thy Son to me. I love Thee, O Son of God, for Thou hast died for me.

SECOND POINT.

"If the tree fall toward the south, or toward the north, in the place where the tree falleth, there it shall be." (Eccles. xi. 3.). Wheresoever the tree of thy soul shall fall in death, there it will have to abide for ever. There is no middle way: either a king for ever in heaven, or a slave for ever in hell; either for ever blessed in a sea of joy, or despairing for ever in a pit of torments. S. Chrysostom, considering the feaster who was counted happy in this world because he was rich, but who was afterwards confined in hell; and considering Lazarus, on the other hand, who was reckoned miserable because he was poor, but who was afterwards happy in paradise, says, "O unhappy happiness which drew the rich man into eternal unhappiness! O happy unhappiness which led the poor man into the happiness of eternity!"

What does it serve to trouble yourself, as some do, by saying, "Am I among the number of the reprobate or the predestined?" When the tree is cut down, where does it fall? It falls as it inclines. To which side do you incline, my brother? What life are you leading? Study ever to incline towards the south; preserve yourself in the grace of God; fly from sin; and by so doing you will save yourself and will be numbered with the elect. To avoid sin, have ever before your eyes the great thought of eternity, called by S. Augustine "the great thought." This thought has caused so many youths to fly from the world and to live in deserts, so as to attend to their souls alone; and they have saved them. Now that they are saved, they find a happiness which will be theirs for ever.

A lady who was living far from God was converted by a certain Father M. Avila merely saying, "Lady, meditate upon these two words, *always* and *ever*." Paul Segneri, by a thought which he once had of eternity, was unable to sleep for many nights, and from that time he dedicated himself to a more ascetic life. Drexelius narrates, that this thought of eternity caused a bishop to lead a holy life, ever repeating to himself, "I stand at the gate of eternity every moment." A monk shut himself up in a cave, and there did nothing but exclaim, "O eternity! O eternity!" Avila says, that he who believes in eternity, if he does not become a saint, ought to be shut up in a madhouse.

Affections and Prayers.

O my God, have pity upon me! I truly know that I condemned myself to an eternity of pain in sinning; and I was content to oppose Thy will, and to have all this punishment; and for what? For a miserable gratification. Ah, my Lord, pardon me, for I repent with all my heart. I do not wish any more to oppose myself to Thy holy will. Wretched me! hadst Thou caused me to die in the time of my evil life, I should now have had to remain for ever in hell to hate Thy will; but now I love Thee, and I desire to love Thee ever. "Teach me to do Thy will." Teach me, and give me strength to perform to-day and henceforth Thy good pleasure. I desire not to thwart Thee further, O Infinite Goodness, and I ask Thee for this grace alone. "Thy will be done on earth as it is in heaven." Grant me to fulfil Thy will perfectly, and I ask nothing else. And what more dost Thou desire, O my God, but my good and my salvation? Ah! Eternal Father, hear me for the love of Jesus Christ, Who has taught me ever to pray to Thee, and in His Name I beg Thee, "Thy will be done." O blessed me, if during the remainder of my life, and to its end, I may perform Thy will.

THIRD POINT.

"Man goeth to his long home," says the Prophet. "Goeth" signifying that each one "goeth" to that home which he chooses; he will not be carried there, but he will go there of his own accord. It is certain that God wills all, but He will not force all, to be saved. "Before man is life and death." He has placed before each of us life and death; and "that which he shall choose shall be given him." (Ecclus. xv. 18.) Similarly, Jeremiah says, that the Lord has given to us two ways in which to walk; the one of heaven, the other of hell. "I set before you the way of life, and the way of death." (Jer. xxi. 8.) It remains with us to choose. But how can he who chooses to walk in the way of hell, ever hope to find himself in heaven? It is a great truth that all sinners desire to be saved, and meanwhile they condemn themselves to hell, by saying, "I hope to save myself." But who ever, says S. Augustine, is so mad as to take poison with the hope of being cured? And yet so many Christians, so many who are mad, condemn themselves to death by sinning, with the saying, "Afterwards, I will think of the remedy." O deceit, which has ordered so many to hell!

Let us not be so mad as these; let us remember that it concerns eternity. How great pains do men take, to build themselves a house, convenient, airy, and healthy, considering that they will have to dwell in it all their lives! And why then are they so careless about that home in which they will have to dwell for eternity? "Eternity is the object for which we contend," says S. Eucher; not to treat of a home more or less convenient, more or less airy, but of a resting, either in a place full of all delights amongst the friends of God; or in a pit, full of every torment amongst an infamous crew of so many wicked heretics and idolaters. And for how long a time? Not for twenty, nor for forty years, but for all eternity. It is an all important point; it is not an affair of small moment, but one of vast moment. When Sir Thomas Moore was condemned to death by Henry VIII., his wife, Louisa, tried to persuade him to submit himself to the will of Henry; but he said to her, "Tell me, Louisa—

for you see how old I am now—how many years do you think I may be able to live?" She answered, "You might live for twenty years." "O foolish tradeswoman!" he lovingly said; "for another twenty years of life on this earth, you would have me forfeit a happy eternity, and condemn myself to an eternity of pain."

O God, give us light! If this question of eternity were doubtful, or a probable opinion only, even then we ought to make it our whole study to live well, so as not to expose ourselves to the danger of being eternally unhappy, if ever this opinion should prove true. But not so. This point is not doubtful, but certain; it is not an opinion, but an article of faith, "Man goeth to his long home." Alas! says S. Teresa, that the want of faith should be such, as to cause so great sins, and the condemnation of so many Christians. Let us then ever rekindle faith by saying, I believe "in the life everlasting." I believe that after this life, there is another life which shall never end, and with this thought always before the eyes, let us seize the means to secure our eternal salvation. Let us frequent the Holy Sacrament; let us every day meditate, and reflect upon eternal life; let us flee from opportunities which are dangerous; and, if necessary, let us leave the world, since no security can be enough to make sure of this great point of eternal salvation. S. Bernard says, "That no security is excessive, where eternity is in danger."

Affections and Prayers.

Therefore, my God, there is not a middle way; either I must be happy for ever, or for ever unhappy; either in a sea of delights, or in a sea of torments; either ever with Thee in paradise, or for ever afar off and separated from Thee in hell. I know for certain that I have often merited this hell; but I also know that Thou dost pardon him who repents, and that Thou deliverest from hell him who hopes in Thee. Thou assurest me of it, "He shall call upon me, and I will hear him . . . . I will deliver him, and bring him to honour." (Ps. xcv. 15.) Make haste, then, my Lord, make haste to pardon me and to deliver me from hell. I repent, O Highest Good, above every other evil, the having offended Thee; make haste to restore me to Thy favour, and give to me Thy holy love. If I were now in hell I could no longer love Thee, I should be compelled to hate Thee for ever. O my God, what evil hast Thou done to me that I should hate Thee? Thou hast loved me even unto death. Thou art worthy of infinite love. O Lord, do not allow me again ever to be separated from Thee. I love Thee, and I will ever love Thee, "Who shall separate us from the love of Christ?" (Rom. viii. 35.) O my Jesus, sin alone can separate me from Thee. Permit it not, I pray Thee, by that Blood which Thou hast shed for me. Suffer me sooner to die.

CONSIDERATION XV

Of the Evil of Deadly Sin

"I have nourished and brought up children, and they have rebelled against me."
Isa. i. 2.

First Point.

WHAT does he do who commits a deadly sin? He insults God, he dishonours God, he embitters God. In the first place, by the deadly sin that he commits, he *insults* God. As S. Thomas observes, the malice of an injury is measured according to the person that does it and the person who receives it. It is very wicked to insult a peasant, but it is worse to insult a nobleman, and still much worse is it, to insult a monarch. Who is God? He is the King of kings: "Lord of lords and King of kings." (Rev. xvii. 14.) God is of infinite majesty, with respect to Whom all the princes of the earth, the saints, and the angels in heaven, are less than a grain of dust, "As a drop of a bucket . . . . and as the small dust of the balance." (Isa. xl. 15.) Nay, says Isaiah, compared with the greatness of God all creatures are as the smallest things, even as though they had never been: "All nations before him are as nothing." (Isa. xl. 17.) Even such is God; and who is man? S. Bernard answers, even a sack of worms, and food for worms, who, in a short time, will be devoured by worms, "Miserable, and poor, and blind, and naked." (Rev. iii. 17.) Man is a miserable worm that can do nothing; he is blind, and can see nothing; and poor and naked, and has nothing. And this miserable worm dares to insult God!

S. Bernard exclaims, "What terrible majesty for vile dust to dare to irritate! The Angelic Doctor is right when he says, "that the sin of man contains a malice almost infinite. Sin has a certain infinity of malice from the infinity of the Divine Majesty." Nay, S. Augustine calls sin absolutely an "infinite evil!" Therefore it is, that if all men, and all angels, were to offer themselves to die, and to annihilation, they would not be able to make satisfaction for one single sin. God punishes deadly sin with the great punishment of hell; but however much God punishes the sinner for it, all theologians agree in saying that God punishes it "*Citra condignum*,"—that is to say, with less punishment than deadly sin deserves. And what punishment can be great enough for a worm that tries to set itself up against its Lord? God is Lord of all, because He has created all things. "All things are in Thy power. . . . . Thou hast made all things." (Esther xiii. 9, 10, Vulg.) And in fact all creatures obey God: "The winds and the sea obey Him;" (S. Matt. viii. 27.) "Fire and hail, snow and vapours; wind and storm, fulfilling His word." (Ps. cxlviii. 8.) But what does man do when he sins? He says to God, Lord, I do not wish to serve Thee! "I have broken Thy yoke, and burst Thy bands." (Jer. ii. 20.) The Lord says to him, "Revenge not thyself;" and he answers, "I will revenge myself!" "Take not the property of thy neighbour." He replies, "But I wish to take it." "Give up this wicked pleasure." He returns, "I will not give it up!" The sinner says to God, even what Pharaoh said to Moses when he brought him the command from God that he should let the people go. The rash one answered: "Who is the Lord that I should obey His voice. . . . . I know not the Lord." (Exod. v. 2.) Even thus does the sinner say, "Lord, I know Thee not; I wish to do what pleases me." In short, he despises God, and turns away from Him; and it is indeed committing a deadly sin to turn away from God—"A turning away from the unchangeable good," as S. Thomas observes.

Of this does the Lord complain. "Thou hast forsaken me," saith the Lord; "thou art gone backward." (Jer. xv. 6.) Thou hast been ungrateful, says God, thou hast left Me, since I would never have left thee; thou hast turned away from Me. God has declared that He hates sin, therefore He cannot do otherwise than hate him who sins, "For the ungodly and his ungodliness are both alike hateful unto God." (Wisd. xiv. 9.) When man sins, he is bold enough to declare himself the enemy of God. "He stretcheth out his hand against God, and strengtheneth himself against the Almighty." (Job xv. 25.) God is that powerful One Who, from nothing, but as it were with a "beck," has created the heaven and the earth: "God made them of things that were not." (2 Macc. vii. 28.) And if He wishes, He can with another "beck" destroy them all. "Who at a beck can cast down . . . . all the world." (2 Macc. viii. 18.) And when the sinner consents to sin, he stretches out his hand against God. He stretches out his neck —that is to say, pride, and flies in the face of God; he arms himself with a thick shield, that is to say, with ignorance—thickness being a symbol of ignorance—and says: "What have I done? what harm is there in the sin I have committed? God is merciful; He pardons sinners." O my God, keep me from such boldness and blindness.

Affections and Prayers.

Behold, O my God, at Thy feet the rebellious one; the bold one, who has had the boldness to insult Thee so many times, and to turn away from Thee; but now I seek for mercy from Thee. Thou hast said, "Call unto Me, and I will answer thee." (Jer. xxxiii. 3.) I know that hell is a fitting punishment for me; but Thou knowest that I feel very sorry for having offended Thee, O Thou Infinite Goodness; more sorry than if I had lost everything I possess, and my life even. Ah, my Lord, pardon me, and never let me offend Thee more. Thou hast waited for me, so that I may for ever bless Thy mercy, and love Thee. Yes, I do bless and love Thee, and hope because of the merits of Jesus Christ, never more to be separated from Thy love. Thy love has freed me from hell; and for the future, it must free me from sin. I thank Thee, my Lord, for this light, and for the desire ever to love Thee, which Thou dost give me. Ah, take me entirely into Thy possession, my soul, my body, my powers, my senses, my will, and my liberty, "I am Thine,

O save me." Thou Who art my only good, my only adorable one, be also my only love. Give me zeal in loving Thee. I have offended Thee often enough, therefore it will not suffice to love Thee; I must love Thee very much, so that I may in some measure atone for the wrongs I have committed against Thee. I hope for it from Thee, O Thou Who art Omnipotent.

Second Point.

Not only does the sinner insult God, but he *dishonours* Him. "Through breaking the law dishonourest thou God." (Rom. ii. 23.) Yes, it is because He renounces His grace, and for a miserable pleasure treads under foot the friendship of God. If a man loses the Divine friendship to gain a kingdom for himself, and even the whole world, he would nevertheless commit a great evil, because is not the friendship of God worth far more than the world, or a thousand worlds? "Wherefore should the wicked blaspheme God?" (Ps. x. 14.)

For a little earth, for a fit of anger, for an impure pleasure, for a vapour, for a caprice: "Will ye pollute me . . . . for handfuls of barley, and for pieces of bread?" (Ezek. xiii. 19.) When the sinner begins to deliberate, whether or not he shall consent to sin, then, so to speak, he takes the scales in his hand, and ascertains which weighs the most, the grace of God, or that fit of temper, that vanity, and that pleasure; and when he consents to sin, he declares, as far as he is concerned, all these things are of far more importance than the Divine friendship. Behold God insulted by the sinner! When David was contemplating the grandeur and the majesty of God, he exclaimed, "Lord, who is like unto Thee?" (Ps. xxxv. 10.) But, on the contrary, when God sees a miserable pleasure compared to, and preferred rather than Himself, He says, "To whom then will ye liken Me, or shall I be equal?" (Isa. xl. 25.) Therefore the Lord says, "Is that vile pleasure worth more than My grace?" "Thou hast . . . . cast Me behind thy back." (Ezek. xxiii. 35.) You would not have committed that sin, if by committing it, you would lose your hand, or any sum of money, however small. Therefore God alone, as Salvian observes, is so contemptible in your sight that He deserves to be neglected for some worldly passion, or for a miserable pleasure. "In comparison with other things, God only was esteemed vile by thee."

Besides, when the sinner, because of some pleasure, offends God, that pleasure becomes his god, because he makes it his ultimate aim. S. Jerome observes: "That which any one desires, if he venerates it, becomes his god; a vice in the heart is an idol upon the altar." And S. Thomas says, "If you love pleasures, they are called thy god." And S. Cyprian, "Whatever man places before God, he makes a god to himself." When Jeroboam rebelled against God, he tried to draw the people with him into idolatry, and therefore he presented his gods unto them, and cried, "Behold thy gods, O Israel." (1 Kings xii. 28.) Even so, does the devil present some gratification to the sinner, and say, "What hast thou to do with God? this pleasure is thy god, this passion; take it, and leave God." And when the sinner consents, he in his heart adores that pleasure as a God.

When the sinner dishonours God, he not only dishonours Him in His presence, but He dishonours Him to His face, because God is everywhere present. "I fill heaven and earth." (Jer. xxiii. 24.) And the sinner knows this, and for all that ceases not to provoke God, even in His presence. "A people that provoketh Me to anger continually to My face." (Isa. lxv. 3.)

Affections and Prayers.

Therefore, my God, Thou art an infinite good, and yet I have many times exchanged Thee for a miserable pleasure which was hardly obtained, before it vanished away. But Thou, although Thou hast been despised by me, dost now offer me pardon, if I desire it; and Thou dost promise to receive me into Thy grace, if only I repent for having offended Thee. Yes, my Lord, I repent with all my heart for having thus provoked Thee; I hate my sin more than any other evil. Behold, now that I return to Thee, Thou dost receive me and embrace me as a son. I thank Thee, O Infinite Goodness.

But now do Thou help me, and never more let me drive Thee from me. Hell will never cease to tempt me, but Thou art more powerful than hell. I know that if I always commend myself to Thee, I shall never more be separated from Thee. Therefore this is the grace that Thou must grant me, that I may always commend myself to Thee, and pray to Thee even as I now say to Thee, "Lord, assist me—give me light, give me strength, give me perseverance, give me Paradise, but above all, give me Thy holy love, which is the true Paradise of the soul. I love Thee, O Thou Infinite Good, and I would ever love Thee. Hear me, for the love of Jesus Christ."

THIRD POINT.

The sinner insults and dishonours God, and, by doing so, grieves Him very much. There is no bitterness more acute, than to be repaid with ingratitude by a person who has been loved and benefited. Who is it, then, that the sinner grieves? Even the God Who has created Him, and Who has loved him so much as to give His Blood and His life for the sinner's love. And the sinner, by committing a deadly sin, drives God away from his heart. God comes and dwells in a soul that He loves. "If a man love Me . . . . My Father will love him, and We will come unto him, and make Our abode with him." (S. John xiv. 23.) Take notice, "We will make Our abode." God enters the soul, ever to stay there, so that He never leaves it unless the soul drives Him away; and He does not leave it unless He is driven from it. But, Lord, Thou knowest that within a short time that ungrateful one will drive Thee away; why, therefore, dost Thou not now leave him? Why wait until he drives Thee away? Leave him before he shall offer Thee this great insult. But God says, "No, I will not leave him, until by his own free will he doth send Me away."

Therefore, when the soul consents to sin, it says, Lord, depart from me: "They say unto God, Depart from us." (Job xxi. 14.) It says so, not in words, but in actions, as S. Gregory observes, "Depart, not in words, but in deeds." The sinner knows full well that God cannot stay in the same place with sin; he knows that when he commits sin, God is forced to depart; therefore he exclaims, "Since Thou canst not remain when I commit sin, farewell, go." And, driving God away from his soul, he allows the devil to enter in immediately, to take possession of it. By the same door through which God departs, the enemy enters; "Then goeth he and taketh with himself seven other spirits more wicked than himself, and they enter in and dwell there." (S. Matt. xii. 45.) When a child is baptized, the devil is commanded to depart from it with the words: "Depart, thou unclean spirit, and make room for the Holy Ghost." Yes, because that soul, by receiving grace, becomes the temple of God. "Know ye not that ye are the temple of God?" (1 Cor. iii. 16.) But when a man consents to sin, he does the contrary, for he says to God, Who is dwelling in his soul, "Depart from me, O Lord, give place to the devil."

Would it not grieve you very much if you were to receive a great injury from some one to whom you had been very kind? This is the grief you have caused your God, Who gave His life even to save you.

The Lord calls upon heaven and earth, as it were, to pity Him because of the ingratitude which sinners show to Him. "Hear, O heavens, and give ear, O earth: for the Lord hath spoken, 'I have nourished and brought up children, and they have rebelled against Me.'" (Isa. i. 2.) In fact, sinners with their sins give sorrow to God. "They rebelled and vexed His Holy Spirit." (Isa. lxiii. 10.) God is not able to feel grieved, but if He were, one deadly sin alone would be sufficient to cause Him great sorrow. As S. Bernard observes, "Sin, so far as it is possible, would destroy God Himself." Therefore, the sinner, when he commits a deadly sin, gives, as it were, a poison to God. "The ungodly is so proud, that he careth not for God." (Ps. x. 4.) And, as S. Paul declares, he "hath trodden under foot the Son of God," (Heb. x. 29,) for he despises all things that Jesus Christ hath done and suffered, to take away the sin of the world.

Affections and Prayers.

Therefore, my Redeemer, whenever I have committed sin, I have sent Thee away from my soul. Now I can hear Thee ask me, "Tell Me what I have done to Thee—what have I done to offend Thee, that thou shouldst cause Me to feel so displeased?" Lord, dost Thou ask me what evil Thou hast done to me? This is the evil that Thou hast done me—Thou hast given me my being, and Thou hast died for me. What answer, then, can I make? I can only say I deserve hell many times over, and that Thou hast just cause to send me there. But call to mind that love which made Thee die for me, upon the Cross: call to mind that Blood which Thou didst shed for me, and have mercy upon me. But I feel that Thou dost not wish me to despair; nay, Thou makest me to feel that Thou art standing at the door of my heart, from which I had driven Thee away, and that Thou art knocking with Thy inspirations, at this door to enter therein. "Behold, I stand at the door, and knock." (Rev. iii. 20.) Thou dost tell me to open to Thee, "Open to Me, My sister." (Sol. Song v. 2.) Yes, Lord Jesus, I drive away every sin from my heart, I grieve with all my heart because of my sin, and I love Thee above all things. Enter, my love, the door is open—enter, and do Thou never more go away. Bind me to Thee with Thy love, and never allow me to be separated from Thee. No, my God, never more will I willingly be separated from Thee. I embrace Thee and I bind Thee to my heart, but do Thou give me holy perseverance. Grant that I may never be separated from Thee.

CONSIDERATION XVI

Of the Mercy of God

"Mercy rejoiceth against judgment." S. James ii. 13.

FIRST POINT.

GOODNESS is diffusive in its nature, that is to say, it inclines ever to communicate its goods to others. Now, God—Who by nature is infinite goodness—has a sovereign desire to communicate His happiness to us; and therefore it is not His nature to punish, but to show mercy to all. As Isaiah says, punishment is opposite to the inclination of Almighty God. "He shall be wroth . . . . that He may do His work, His strange work." (Isa. xxviii. 21.) And when the Lord chastises in this life, He chastises so that He may show mercy in the next. "Thou hast also been displeased; O turn Thee unto us again." (Ps. lx. 1.) He appears to be angry, so that we may repent and detest our sins. "Thou hast showed Thy people heavy things: Thou hast given us a drink of deadly wine." (Ps. lx. 3.) And if He sends us any punishment, He sends it because He loves us, and that we may be delivered from eternal punishment. "Thou hast given a token for such as fear Thee: that they may triumph because of the truth. Therefore were Thy beloved delivered." (Ps. lx. 4, 5.)

And how can the mercy be ever admired and praised enough which God shows towards sinners in waiting for them, in calling them, and in receiving them when they return? And, in the first place, Oh, how great is the patience which God exercises towards us in waiting for our repentance! My brother, when thou wast offending God, He could have caused thee to die, but He waited for thee, and instead of chastising thee, He conferred His benefits upon thee. He preserved thy life and provided for thee. He feigned not to see thy sins, so that thou mightest repent. "Thou overlookest the sins of men for the sake of repentance." (Wisd. xi. 24.) But how is it, Lord, that Thou Who canst not endure the sight of a single sin, yet remainest quiet when Thou beholdest so many?"

Thou beholdest that dishonest one, that revengeful one, that blasphemer, whose offences increase daily; but yet Thou punishest them not, and why so much patience? "Therefore will the Lord wait, that He may be gracious unto you." (Isa. xxx. 18.) God waits for the sinner, so that he may amend his ways, and thus He may pardon and save him.

S. Thomas observes, That all creatures—fire, earth, air, water—would punish the sinner by instinct, to avenge the wrongs done to the Creator, for "all creation, in its service to Thee, the Creator, turns against the impious." Yet God in His mercy withholds them. But, Lord, Thou dost wait for these wicked ones that they may repent, yet dost Thou not see that they are making use of Thy mercy to offend Thee more? "Thou hast increased the nation, O Lord, Thou hast increased the nation: Thou art glorified." (Isa. xxvi. 15.) And wherefore then so much patience? Because God willeth not the death of the sinner, but that he should be converted and live. "As I live, saith the Lord God, I have no pleasure in the death of the wicked; but that the wicked turn from his way and live." (Ezek. xxxiii. 11.) S. Augustine goes so far as to say, that if God were not God, "He would be unjust on account of the long-suffering that He shows towards sinners." To wait for that one who makes use of God's patience only to become more sinful, would appear unjust to the Divine honour. "We sin," the Saint goes on to say, "We sin, and are attached to it, and some make their peace with sin; they sleep in sin for months and for years; "We rejoice in sin," some even boast of their wickedness, "and art Thou appeased?"

It would seem as if we were striving with God—we were provoking Him to punish us—and He inviting us to pardon.

Affections and Prayers.

Ah, my Lord, full well do I know, that at this very hour my place ought to be in hell, "Hell is my home." But because of Thy mercy I am not there, but in this place, even at Thy feet, and I can hear Thee telling me, that Thou dost wish to be loved by me. "Thou shalt love the Lord thy God." And Thou dost assure me of Thy pardon if only I repent of the offences which I have committed against Thee. Yes, my God, since Thou desirest to be loved even by me, who am a miserable rebel against Thy Majesty, I will love Thee with all my heart, and I will repent for having offended Thee, more than any other sin into which I may have fallen. Ah, enlighten me, O Infinite Goodness, and make me to know the wrong I have done Thee. No, I will no longer resist Thy calls. I will no more displease the God Who has loved me so much, and Who has pardoned me so many times, and with so much love. Ah, would that I had never offended Thee, O my Jesus! Pardon me, and grant, that from this day forward, I may love none other than Thee; that I may live for Thee alone, Thou who didst die for me. Grant that I may suffer for Thy love, since Thou hast suffered so much for mine. Thou hast loved me from eternity; grant that I may burn with Thy love in eternity. I hope for all things because of Thy merits.

Second Point.

Consider, moreover, the mercy which God uses in calling the sinner to repentance. When Adam rebelled against the Lord, and afterwards hid himself from His face, behold God, Who having lost Adam, goes to seek him, and calls him, saying, "Where art thou?" Father Pereira observes, "They are the words of a father who is seeking his lost son." Very often, my brother, has God done the same with you. You were flying from God, and God has sought you, calling you, sometimes by inspirations, sometimes by a remorseful conscience, sometimes by a sermon, sometimes by trouble, and sometimes by the death of your friends. Jesus Christ comes to you, saying, "I am weary of crying; My throat is dry." (Ps. lxix. 3.) My son, I have almost lost My voice in calling thee. "Be warned, O sinners," observes S. Teresa, "for that same Lord Who is now calling you, will one day be your Judge." My Christian brother, how many times have you not turned a deaf ear to God when He has called you? You deserve that He should never call you again. But no, your God will never cease to call you, because He wishes to be at peace with you and to save you. And Who was He that called you? Even a God of Infinite Majesty. And what are you but a miserable worm? And wherefore does He call you? For nothing else than to give you back the life of grace which you have lost. "Wherefore turn yourselves, and live ye." (Ezek. xviii. 32.) It would be doing but little to live in a desert for a whole life, if by so doing we could gain Divine grace; but God offered His grace to you in one moment, if you chose to accept it, by doing one act of repentance; and you have refused it. And yet God has not abandoned you; but He has sought you, saying, Why wilt thou condemn thyself, my son? "For why will ye die, O house of Israel?"

When a man commits a deadly sin, he drives God away from his soul. "Therefore they say unto God, Depart from us; for we desire not the knowledge of Thy ways." (Job. xxi. 14.) But what does God do? He stands at the door of that ungrateful heart. "Behold, I stand at the door, and knock." (Rev. iii. 20.) And He entreats, as it were, the soul to admit Him: "Open to Me, My sister." (Song of Sol. v. 2.) And He wearies Himself with entreating. "Yes," observes S. Dionysius the Areopagite, "God follows the sinner about like a discarded lover, entreating him not to be lost."

And S. Paul signifies the same when he writes to his disciples, "We pray you in Christ's stead, be ye reconciled to God." (2 Cor. v. 20.) And the reflection is indeed beautiful that S. Chrysostom makes, commenting upon this, "Christ Himself beseeches you. What does He beseech? That ye may be reconciled to God; for it is not He that is your enemy, but yourselves." And the saint wishes to say that there is indeed no need for the sinner to strive to make his peace with God, for he only has to form the wish to make it, since it is he himself, and not God, that flies away from peace.

This good Lord is ever seeking sinners, and saying to them : "Ungrateful ones, do not flee away from Me; tell Me why you flee? I love your good, and I have no other desire than to make you happy. Why therefore do you wish to be lost?" But, Lord, wherefore do all this? Why dost Thou exercise so much patience, and feel so much love for these rebellious ones? What good dost Thou hope from them? Does it not lessen Thy honour to show Thyself so compassionate towards these miserable sinners who fly from Thee? "What is man that Thou shouldst magnify him? and that Thou shouldst set Thine heart upon him?" (Job vii. 17.)

Affections and Prayers.

Behold, Lord, at Thy feet the ungrateful one who implores Thy mercy. I call Thee Father, because Thou wished that I should so call Thee. My Father, pardon me. I do not deserve compassion, because, since Thou hast been so good to me, I have been more ungrateful to Thee. Ah, because of Thy goodness, which has kept Thee from abandoning me when I fled from Thee—because of that, receive me now that I come to Thee. Give me, my Jesus, a great grief for the offences I have committed against Thee, and give me Thy kiss of peace. I repent more because of the evil I have committed against Thee, than because of any other evil. I detest and abhor it, and I join this my hatred to it with that which Thou, my Redeemer, didst feel for it in the Garden of Gethsemane. Ah, pardon me through the merits of that Blood which Thou didst shed for me in that garden. I promise Thee to strive never more to depart from Thee, and to drive away from my heart every affection that is not Thine. My Jesus, my Love, I love Thee beyond everything, and I wish ever to love Thee, and Thee only; but give me strength to do so, and make me wholly Thine.

THIRD POINT.

The princes of the earth disdain even to look upon rebellious subjects who come to seek their pardon; but God does not so with us. "For the Lord your God is gracious and merciful, and will not turn away His face from you, if ye return to Him." (2 Chron. xxx. 9.) God will never turn away His face from him who returns to His feet; no, because He Himself invites him, and promises to receive him directly he returns. "Yet return again to me, saith the Lord." (Jer. iii. 1.) "Turn ye unto me, saith the Lord of Hosts, and I will turn unto you." (Zech. i. 3.) Oh, the love and tenderness with which God embraces the sinner who returns to Him! Jesus Christ wished us to understand this, when He gave us the parable of the lost sheep, which when the shepherd had found he laid on his shoulders, saying, "Rejoice with me; for I have found my sheep which was lost." (S. Luke xv. 6.) And afterwards Jesus adds, "There is joy in the presence of the angels of God over one sinner that repenteth." (Ibid. 10.) And much more did the Redeemer wish us to understand this, by the parable of the prodigal son, signifying that He is that Father, Who, seeing His lost son return, runs to meet him, and before he can speak embraces him, and kisses him, "And ran and fell on his neck, and kissed him." (S. Luke xv. 20.)

The Lord goes on to say, that if the sinner repents, his sins will be forgotten, as if they had never been committed. "But if the wicked will turn from all his sins that he hath committed, ... he shall surely live, he shall not die." (Ezek. xviii. 21.) Then He adds, "Come now, let us reason together, saith the Lord; though your sins be as scarlet, they shall be as white as snow." (Isa. i. 18.) As if He had said, Come, sinners, "let us reason together;" if I do not pardon you, reprove Me, and treat Me as an unfaithful one. But no; for God will never cast a heart from Him that humbles itself and repents. "A broken and contrite heart, O God, shalt Thou not despise." (Ps. li. 17.)

The Lord glories in showing mercy and in pardoning sinners: "And therefore will He be exalted, that He may have mercy upon you." (Isa. xxx. 18.) And how long dost thou wait to be pardoned? Not one moment: "Thou shalt weep no more; He will be very gracious unto thee." (Isa. xxx. 19.) Sinner, says the prophet, thou hast not long to weep; for at the first tear the Lord will be moved to pity thee: "He will be very gracious unto thee at the voice of thy cry; when He shall hear it, He will answer thee." (Isa. xxx. 19.) God does not act with us as we do with Him. God calls us, and we turn a deaf ear to His call; but God, "when He shall hear, will answer thee;" directly thou repentest, and seekest pardon from Him, God will answer and pardon thee.

Affections and Prayers.

O my God, with Whom have I been contending? Even with Thee, Who art so good, Who hast created me, and Who hast died for me. And why hast Thou borne with me after having betrayed Thee so often? Ah, the sight alone of the patience which Thou hast had with me, ought to make me live for ever glowing with Thy love. And who is there who would have borne all the offences which I have committed against Thee, except Thou? Ah, wretched me, if again I should offend Thee, and become condemned! These mercies Thou hast shown me would be more painful to me than hell itself. No, my Redeemer, never allow me again to turn from Thee. Better to let me die. I know that Thy mercy will not bear with me much longer. I repent, O Thou Highest Good, for having offended Thee. I love Thee with all my heart, and am resolved to give the life that remains to me, to Thee only. Hear me, Eternal Father, through the merits of Jesus Christ; give me holy perseverance, and Thy holy love. Hear me, my Jesus, through the Blood Thou hast shed for me. "We therefore pray Thee help Thy servants whom Thou hast redeemed with Thy precious Blood."

CONSIDERATION XVII

Of the Abuse of Divine Mercy

"Not knowing that the goodness of God leadeth thee to repentance?" Rom. ii. 4.

First Point.

WE read in the parable in S. Matthew xiii. that the tares, having grown in a field together with the corn, the servants wished to go and pluck them up. "Wilt Thou then that we go and gather them up?" But the Master answered, "Nay; . . . . Let them both grow together until the harvest: and in the time of harvest I will say to the reapers, Gather ye together first the tares, and bind them in bundles to burn them." From this parable we learn the patience which the Lord shows to sinners, and also the severity which He shows to those who are obstinate. S. Augustine observes, that the devil deceives men in two ways, "By despair and by hope." After the sinner has committed the sin, he tempts him to despair, through fear of the Divine Justice; but before the sin is committed, he tempts the sinner to commit it, by telling him of the Divine Mercy. Therefore the saint warns every one, by saying, "After sin, hope for mercy; before sin, fear justice." Yes, because he who makes use of mercy to offend God, does not deserve mercy. Mercy is shown to him who fears God, not to him who makes use of it so as not to fear God. He who offends justice, observes Abulensis, can fly to mercy; but he that offends the same mercy, to whom can he fly?

It is but seldom a sinner is found so hopeless, as to wish to be condemned. Sinners are willing to sin, but they are not willing to give up the hope of being saved. They commit sin, and say to themselves, God is merciful; I will commit this sin, and afterwards confess it. Behold, says S. Augustine, this is how sinners talk: "God is good, I will do what it pleaseth me;" but O God, how many, who are now in hell, have said the same!

The Lord tells us not to say that the mercies of God are great, and that although we may commit many sins, by one act of sorrow they will be pardoned. "Say not the mercy of the Lord is great, He will have mercy on the multitude of my sins." (Ecclus. v. 6.) God tells us not to say this, and wherefore? "For mercy and wrath quickly come from Him, and His wrath worketh upon sinners." (Ecclus. v. 7.) The mercy of God is infinite, but the acts of this mercy, are finite. God is merciful, but He is also just. S. Basil observes that sinners will only consider God in one aspect. "The Lord is good, but also just; we are unwilling to think of God in His half-nature." To bear with him who makes use of the mercy of God, only to do Him more offence, observes Father Avila, would not be mercy, for justice would be lacking. Mercy is promised to him who fears God, not, indeed, to him who abuses it, as the holy Virgin sang, "His mercy is on them that fear Him." To the obstinate, justice is threatened, and, as S. Augustine observes, God never fails in His promises, neither does He fail in His threats.

Take care, says S. Chrysostom, when the devil, but not God, promises thee Divine Mercy, that thou mayest commit sin.

Woe, adds S. Augustine, to him who hopes, so that he may sin, "Woe to that perverse hope." Oh! exclaims the saint, how many there are, whom this vain hope has deceived and caused to be lost!

Unhappy, indeed, is he who abuses the mercy of God by offending him more! S. Bernard observes that it was for this reason that Lucifer was so soon punished by God, because he rebelled, in the hope that he should not be punished for rebelling. King Manasseh was a sinner, but he became afterwards converted, and God pardoned him. Amon, his son, seeing his father was so easily pardoned, gave himself up to an evil life, at the same time hoping to be pardoned; but for Amon there was no pardon. S. Chrysostom observes that it was even for this reason that Judas was lost, because he committed the sin, trusting in the mercy of Jesus Christ, "in the meekness of his Master." In short, although God endures for some time, yet He will not endure for ever. If God were to suffer sin for ever, no one would be lost; but it is the general opinion, that the greater part even of Christians, and those adults, are lost. "For wide is the gate, and broad is the way, that leadeth to destruction, and many there be which go in thereat." (S. Matt. vii. 13.)

He who offends God, hoping to be pardoned, "is a derider, and not a penitent," observes S. Augustine. But on the contrary, S. Paul says, that "God is not mocked." (Gal. vi. 7.) It would be mocking God to continue to offend, and afterwards to go to heaven, "For whatsoever a man soweth, that shall he also reap." (Gal. vi. 7.) He that sows in sin, has no right to hope for anything but punishment and hell. The snare into which the devil draws almost all those Christians and the deceit is, by telling them to sin freely, because, notwithstanding all their sins, they will be saved. But God curses him who sins in the hope of pardon. "Cursed is the man who sins in hope." The sinner's hope, when he is repentant, even after he has committed the sin, is indeed dear to God; but the hope of those who are obstinate, is an abomination to God. "Their hope shall be as the giving up of the ghost." (Job xi. 20.) Such a hope as this only provokes God to punish them, even as a master would be provoked by that servant who should offend him, even though the master be good.

Affections and Prayers.

Ah, my God, I have been one of those who offended Thee notwithstanding Thou wast good to me. Lord, wait for me, do not abandon me; because I hope, Thy grace helping me, never more to provoke Thee to abandon me. I repent, O Thou Infinite Goodness, for having offended Thee, and for having thus abused Thy patience. I thank Thee that Thou hast waited for me until now. From this day forward, I will never more abuse Thee as I have done in the time that is past. Thou hast borne with me so long, that Thou mightest one day see me made a lover of Thy goodness. That that day be already come, is my hope. I love Thee more than anything, and I prize Thy grace more than all the kingdoms of the world; rather than lose it, I would lose my life, if it were possible to do so, many times over. My God, for the love of Jesus Christ, give me holy perseverance until death, with Thy most holy love. Never allow me to betray Thee any more, neither to cease to love Thee.

SECOND POINT.

Some will say, God has shown me so many mercies during the time that is past, that I hope He will continue to do so for the future. But I answer, for what reason has He shown you so many mercies? Is it because He wishes you to return and offend Him? Therefore, as S. Paul says, "Despisest thou the riches of His goodness, and forbearance, and long-suffering, not knowing that the goodness of God leadeth thee to repentance?" (Rom. ii. 4.) When thou art trusting in Divine mercy, if thou art not willing to put an end to thy sin, God will put an end to it for thee. "If a man will not turn, He will whet His sword." (Ps. vii. 13.) "To me belongeth vengeance and recompence." (Deut. xxxii. 35.) God waits, but when the time of revenge arrives, He will wait no longer; but He will then punish.

"And therefore will the Lord wait, that He may be gracious unto you." (Isa. xxx. 18.) God waits for the sinner that he may repent, but when He sees that he, to whom time is given to weep over his sins, only employs the time in increasing his sin, then He calls upon that same time to judge him. S. Gregory observes, "The time itself, comes to be judged." So that the very time that is given, the same mercies which have been shown, will only serve to make his punishment more severe, and his abandonment more quick. "We would have healed Babylon, but she is not healed: forsake her." (Jer. li. 9.) And how does God forsake the sinner? He sends death to him, or allows him to die in sin, or else deprives him of His abundant grace, and leaves him with that grace only which is sufficient for the sinner to be saved, but which the sinner will not make use of. The mind darkened, the heart hardened, the evil habit which is done, will render his salvation morally impossible, and thus will he remain if not absolutely, at least, morally abandoned.

"I will take away the hedge thereof, and it shall be eaten up." (Isa. v. 5.) Oh, what a punishment! When the master of the vineyard breaks down the hedge, and allows any one who may wish to enter the vineyard, both man and beast, it is a sign that he has abandoned it. When God abandons a soul, He does even this—He takes away the hedge of fear, remorse of conscience, and leaves the soul in darkness, and then all the monsters of vice enter into the soul. "Thou makest darkness that it may be night: wherein all the beasts of the forest do move." (Ps. civ. 20.) And when the sinner is thus left in darkness, he will despise every thing, the grace of God, Paradise warnings; he will even laugh at his own damnation. "When the wicked cometh, then cometh also contempt." (Prov. xviii. 3.)

God very often leaves the sinner without punishment in this life; but the sinner's greatest punishment often is, that he is not punished. "Let favour be showed to the wicked, yet will he not learn righteousness." (Isa. xxvi. 10.) S. Bernard observes upon this text, "I do not desire this compassion, it is worse than any anger."

Oh, what a punishment is it, when God leaves the sinner to his sin, and when He appears to ask for no account of his sin, nor to be angry with him. "So will I make My fury toward thee to rest, and My jealousy shall depart from thee." (Ezek. xvi. 42.) And when He seems to leave him to follow all that he desires in this world; "So I gave them up unto their own heart's lusts, and let them follow their own imaginations." (Ps. lxxxi. 13.) Alas, for those miserable sinners who prosper in this life! It is a sign that God is waiting to make them the victims of His justice in the life to come. Jeremiah inquires, "Wherefore doth the way of the wicked prosper?" (Jer. xii. 1.) And then he answers, "Pull them out like sheep for the slaughter." (Jer. xii. 3.) There is no greater punishment, than when God permits a sinner to add sin to sin, according to what David says, "Let them fall from one wickedness to another; .... let them be wiped out of the book of the living." (Ps.

lxix. 28, 29.) Concerning which Bellarmine observes, "There is no punishment greater, than when sin becomes the punishment of sin." Far better would it have been for any one of these unhappy ones, had the Lord allowed him to die after having committed the first sin; for dying after so many sins, he will suffer even as he has sinned.

Affections and Prayers.

My God, in this miserable state I know full well that I deserve to be deprived of Thy grace and of Thy light, but seeing that Thou dost still grant me light, and feeling that Thou dost still call me to repentance, it is a sign that Thou hast not yet forsaken me. And since Thou hast not left me, arise, O Lord, increase Thy mercy towards me; increase my light; increase my desire to serve and to love Thee. Change me, O my God, and from a traitor and rebel, which I have been, make me a lover indeed of Thy goodness, so that one day I may come to heaven, there to praise Thy mercy for ever. Thou art therefore willing to pardon me, and I desire nothing else than Thy pardon and Thy love. I repent, O Infinite Goodness, for having given Thee so much displeasure. I love Thee, O my Sovereign Good, because Thou commandest me to love Thee. I love Thee because Thou art worthy of being loved. Ah, my Redeemer, through the merits of Thy Blood, make Thyself to be loved by a sinner whom Thou hast loved so much, and whom Thou hast borne with for so many years. My hopes are all in Thy mercy. I hope to love Thee, from this day forward, even until death, and afterwards in eternity. I will praise Thy mercy, my Jesus, for ever.

THIRD POINT.

My brother, when the devil tempts you to sin again, if you wish to condemn yourself, it is in your power to sin; but do not in that case say that you wish to be saved. As long as you choose to sin, look upon yourself as condemned, and picture to yourself that God thus writes your condemnation, "What should have been done more in My vineyard that I have not done in it?" (Isa. v. 4.) Ungrateful one, what more is there that I ought to do for you that I have not done? So, then, since you choose to be condemned, it is your own fault.

But you will say, "Where then is the mercy of God?" Ah, unhappy one! does not the mercy of God appear in having borne for so many years with so many sins? You ought ever to remain with averted face, thanking Him, and saying, "It is of the Lord's mercies that we are not consumed." (Lam. iii. 22.) In committing a mortal sin, you have been guilty of a greater fault than if you trod under foot the loftiest monarch of a world. You have committed so many sins, that if the injuries which you have done to God, you had done to your fleshly brother, he would not have endured the sight of you; whilst God not only has waited for you, but He has also so often called you, and invited you to pardon. "What could have been done more?" if God stood in need of you, or if you had done him some great favour, could He use greater compassion towards you? This being so, if you turn again to offend Him, His pity will be turned to anger and punishment.

If that fig-tree, which the Master found without fruit after the year which was granted for its cultivation, should still have produced no fruit, who could have expected that the Lord should have given to it a longer time, and spared the cutting of it down? Attend, therefore, to that which S. Augustine warns you of: "Oh, fruitless tree, the axe was only deferred; be not secure, thou shalt be cut down." The Saint says that the punishment has been delayed, but not done away with; if you further abuse the Divine compassion, "you shall be cut down;" finally, vengeance will overtake you. Do you wish to wait, that God Himself may send you to hell? But if He should send you there, truly you know, that there is no further help for you; the Lord is silent, but not for ever: when the time of vengeance is come, He is silent no longer. "These things hast thou done, and I held My tongue, and thou thoughtest wickedly that I am even such an one as thyself; but I will reprove thee, and set before thee the things that thou hast done." (Ps. l. 21.) The mercies which He has shown to you God will set before you, and He will cause these very mercies both to judge and to condemn you.

Affections and Prayers.

Ah, my God, unhappy me, if from this day henceforth I am not faithful to Thee, and if I should turn again to betray Thee after the lights which now Thou givest to me, this light is a sign that Thou wilt pardon me. I repent, O Highest Good, of all the injuries that I have done in giving offence unto Thy Infinite Goodness. I hope for pardon through Thy Blood; and I hope with certainty; but I feel, that if I were to turn away again from Thee, I should deserve a hell formed for me. And this is what made me tremble, O God of my soul; that I can turn away and lose Thy grace. I remember how many times I have promised to be faithful to Thee, and how afterwards again I have revolted from Thee. O Lord, do not permit it; do not abandon me to the great disgrace of becoming again Thine enemy; send me any punishment, but not this. "Do not suffer me to be separated from Thee." Grant me rather to die if Thou seest that I shall again offend Thee. I am content to die any death, however painful, rather than have to weep over the wretchedness of being deprived of Thy grace. "Do not permit me to be separated from Thee;" and thus I repeat again and again; grant me ever so to do. I love Thee, my dear Redeemer; by the merits of Thy death give me a stronger love that shall bind me to Thee, so that I shall never be able to sever myself from Thee any more.

CONSIDERATION XVIII

Of the Number of Sins

"Because sentence against an evil work is not executed speedily, therefore the heart of the sons of men is fully set in them to do evil." Eccles. viii. 11.

First Point.

IF God were at once to chastise offences, He would not be insulted as He is now; but because the Lord delays His punishment, and waits, sinners take courage to further offend Him. We must understand, that though God waits and endures, He will not wait and suffer for ever. It is the opinion of many of the holy Fathers, that like as God has determined for each man the days of his life, the state of his health, the talents He wills to bestow upon him—"Thou hast ordered all things in measure, number, and weight" (Wisd. xi. 21)—so has He determined for each one, the number of sins which He will pardon, which, being fulfilled, He pardons no more. S. Augustine says, "We should remember that for a certain time the long-suffering of God bears with each one of us, but when this time is completed, no pardon is reserved for him." Eusebius of Cæsarea also says that "God waits up to a certain number, and afterwards leaves the sinner."

This opinion of the Fathers is supported by Holy Scripture. In one place it says that the Lord delayed the ruin of the Amorites. "For the iniquity of the Amorites is not yet full." (Gen. xv. 16.) In another, "I will no more have mercy upon the house of Israel." (Hos. i. 6.) Again, "Because all those men . . . . have tempted Me now these ten times. . . . . Surely they shall not see the land which I sware unto their fathers." (Num. xiv. 22, 23.) In another place Job says, "My transgression is sealed up in a bag." (Job xiv. 17.) Sinners keep no account of their sins, but God does, strictly, that He may punish when the harvest is ripe; that is, when the number is completed. "Put ye in the sickle, for the harvest is ripe." (Joel iii. 13.) Again, "Be not without fear about sin forgiven, and add not sin upon sin." (Ecclus. v. 5.) Which is as much as saying, Sinner, you should fear for the sins which have been forgiven you, for if you add another sin, it may be, that the new sin with those pardoned will complete the number, and then there will remain no more mercy for you; and this Holy Scripture plainly declares, "The Lord patiently expecteth, that when the day of judgment shall arrive, He may punish them in the fulness of their sins." (2 Macc. vi. 14.) So that God waits until the day in which the measure of sins is filled up, and then He punishes.

Of this delayed punishment, there are many examples in Holy Scripture, and especially in the case of Saul, who was forsaken by God for his last disobedience, and who prayed that Samuel would intercede for him, saying, "I prav thee, pardon my sin, and turn again with me, that I may worship the Lord." (1 Sam. xv. 25.) But Samuel answered, "I will not return with thee: for thou hast rejected the word of the Lord, and the Lord hath rejected thee." (Ib. xv. 26.)

There is also the example of Belshazzar, who, when he was feasting, prepared the vessels of the temple, and there saw a hand which wrote on the wall, "Mene, Mene, Tekel, Upharsin." Daniel coming and explaining these words, said, amongst other things, "Thou art weighed in the balances, and art found wanting." (Dan. v. 25-27.) He gave him to understand, that the weight of his sins had already weighed down the scale of Divine justice; in fact, that same night he was slain.

Oh, to how many miserable sinners does it not happen, that they live for many years in their sins, but when their number is filled up, they are seized by death and are sent to hell. "They spend their days in wealth, and in a moment go down to the grave." (Job xxi. 13.) Some apply themselves to searching out the number of the stars, the number of the angels, or the length of life which some have, but who can apply himself to searching out the number of sins which God will pardon in each of us? Therefore we should tremble. Who knows, my brother, that after that first unworthy gratification, that first allowed thought, that first sin which you may commit, God will ever pardon you?

Affections and Prayers.

Oh, my God, I thank Thee; how many, for less sins than mine are now in hell, and for them there is no more pardon or hope! Whilst I am still living, I am out of hell, and I have, if I desire it, the hope of pardon and of heaven. Yes, my God, I desire pardon. I repent, above every other sin, the having offended Thee, because I have offended Thy infinite Goodness. Eternal Father, "Look upon the face of Thine Anointed." (Ps. lxxxiv. 9.) Look upon that Son Who died upon that Cross for me; by His merits, have pity upon me. I promise to choose death rather than to offend Thee more. I may justly fear, thinking upon the sins that I have committed, and the graces which Thou hast bestowed upon me, that should I add another sin, my measure would be filled up, and I should be condemned. Oh, help me by Thy grace: from Thee I look for light and strength to be faithful to Thee, and if ever Thou seest that I should again offend Thee, let me die in this moment, in which I trust that I am in Thy grace. I love Thee, my God, above all things, and I fear more than death itself, to find myself again out of Thy grace; in mercy grant that this may never be.

Second Point.

The sinner says, "But God is merciful;" I answer, "Who denies it? The compassion of God is infinite, but in spite of all this mercy, how many are daily lost?" "He hath sent Me to bind up the broken-hearted." (Isa. lxi. 1.) He heals those who have a right disposition. He pardons sin, but He cannot pardon the desire to sin. The sinner will answer, "I am young." You are young, but God counts sins and not years. And this assessment of sins is not the same for all: to some God pardons a hundred, to others a thousand sins; He casts another into hell after the second sin. How many has the Lord sent there after the first sin? When our Blessed Lord in the gospel had cursed the barren fig-tree, we are told that "presently the fig-tree withered away." (S. Matt. xxi. 19.) The Prophet tells us that the Lord said, "For three transgressions of Damascus, and for four, I will not turn away the punishment thereof." (Amos i. 3.) Perhaps some presumptuous man may demand of God, why He wills to pardon three sins and not four? In this matter we must adore the Divine judgments, and say with the Apostle, "O the depth of the riches both of the wisdom and knowledge of God! how unsearchable are His judgments, and His ways past finding out." (Rom. xi. 33.)

S. Augustine says that "God knows well whom He may spare, and whom not. To whom mercy is given, it is granted as a favour; to whom it is not given, it is denied of justice."

The obstinate sinner will plead, "But I have so often offended God, and He has pardoned me, and therefore I trust that He will pardon this other sin." But I reply, And because God has not punished you as yet, will He ever thus spare you? No; He will fill up the measure, and He will punish you. Samson, continuing to wanton with Delilah, hoped nevertheless to liberate himself from the hands of the Philistines as he had done before. "I will go out, as at other times before, and shake myself." (Judg. xvi. 20.) But this last time he was taken, and lost his life. "Say not, I have sinned, and what harm hath befallen me? for the Most High is a patient rewarder." (Ecclus. v. 4.) That is to say, the time will come when He will repay all; and by how much greater has been this mercy, by so much greater will be this punishment. S. Chrysostom holds that God "is more to be feared when He bears with sin, than when He quickly punishes it;" "because," as S. Gregory says, "those whom He waits for a long time, He condemns the more heavily; and often those who have been borne with for a long time are suddenly snatched away by death, so that there was no time even to be converted before death." Especially since the greater has been the light which God has given, the greater will be the blindness and obstinacy in sin. S. Peter says, "For it were better for them not to have known the way of righteousness, than, after they have known it, to turn from the holy commandment." (2 S. Pet. ii. 21.) And S. Paul adds, "It is impossible (speaking morally) for those who were once enlightened, and have tasted of the heavenly gift, ... if they shall fall away, to renew them again unto repentance." (Heb. vi. 4-6.)

Terrible, indeed, is it, what the Lord says against those who are deaf to His calls. "Because I have called, and ye refused; . . . . I also will laugh at your calamity; I will mock when your fear cometh." (Prov. i. 24-26.) Mark carefully these two words, "I also;" they signify that as the sinner has mocked God, confessing Him, promising, and afterwards ever betraying Him; so the Lord will mock at the hour of his death. Moreover, the Wise Man says: "As a dog returneth to his vomit, so a fool returneth to his folly." (Prov. xxvi. 11.) Denis explains this passage: "That as it is most abominable and disgusting to take again that which has been vomited, so is it to repeat sins which have been blotted out."

Affections and Prayers.

Behold me, O my God, at Thy feet; I am that unclean being who has so often returned to feed upon that forbidden fruit which I at first hated. I do not deserve mercy, O my Redeemer; but the Blood which Thou hast shed for me, encourages me and allows me to hope for it. How often have I offended Thee, and Thou hast pardoned me! I have promised never to offend Thee again, and then I returned to the vomit, and Thou hast again pardoned me. Do I wait for Thee to send me direct to hell, or to give me over into the hand of my sin, which would be a heavier punishment than hell? No, my God, I will amend; and that I may be faithful to Thee, I put all my confidence in Thee; and when I am tempted, I will fly to Thee instantly and ever. In times past I have trusted in my promises and resolutions, and I have neglected to commend myself to Thee in temptation, and this has caused my ruin. Lord, from this day henceforth Thou shalt be my hope and my strength, and then shall I be able to do all things. "I can do all things through Christ, Who strengtheneth me." (Phil. iv. 13.) Give me, then, grace through Thy merits, O my Jesus, to commend myself ever to Thee, and to implore Thy help in my needs. I love Thee, O Highest Good, amiable above every good, and Thee only will I love; but give Thou help to me.

Third Point.

"My son, hast thou sinned? do so no more; but, for thy former sins, also pray that they may be forgiven Thee." (Ecclus. xxi. 1.) Behold, O Christian, how that good Saviour advises you, since He desires your salvation, "My son, do not return to offend Me, but from this day henceforth be mindful to ask pardon for your sins." My brother, the more you have offended God, so much the more you ought to fear to offend Him further, since the other sin which you commit will sink the scale of Divine justice, and you will be condemned. I do not say positively, that after another sin there will be no more pardon for you, since I know not this; but I say that this can be so. Therefore, when you are tempted, say, "Who knows whether God will not further pardon me, and I shall be condemned?" Of your favour, tell me, if there were a likelihood that poison were in some food, would you take it? If with probability you believed that your enemies lay in wait in a certain road, would you go along that road, having another way more secure? And thus, what security, what probability even, have you, that if you again sin, you will afterwards have a true sorrow, and not return again to sin; or that in the act of sinning, God will not strike you dead, and that He will not abandon you after it?

O God, if you buy a house even, you take every care to obtain the legal securities, and not to waste your money; if you take medicine, you seek to be well assured that it cannot harm you; if you pass a stream, to seek to secure yourself from falling into it—and yet for a wretched gratification, for an animal pleasure, you are willing to risk your eternal salvation; and you say, "I will repent of it to-morrow." And who promises you this to-morrow? S. Augustine says: "Do you hold fast to a day, who canst not hold an hour?" He who has promised pardon to the penitent, has not promised to-morrow to the sinner; He may give it, or He may not. If you sin now, perhaps God may give you a time for repentance, and perhaps He may not; and if He should not, what will become of you for all eternity? Meanwhile, for a wretched pleasure, truly you lose your soul, and run the risk of losing it for ever? Would you for a brief pleasure cast away all, money, houses, estates, liberty, and life? No. And how then, for that wretched pleasure, are you willing in a moment to lose all truly—the soul, heaven, and God? Tell me, are these things true which faith teaches, or are they fables? Is there such a thing, as heaven, hell, eternity? Do you believe that if death should overtake you in a state of sin, you would be lost for ever? And what temerity, what madness is it, to condemn oneself to an eternity of pain, saying, "I trust to remedy it afterwards." S. Augustine says that "no one under the hope of being cured, desires to fall ill." No one is so mad as to take poison, and then to say, I am able afterwards to be cured by remedies; and do you choose to condemn yourself to an eternal death, saying, "Perhaps I may afterwards deliver myself from it?" O folly, which has cast, does still cast, so many souls into hell. According to the threat of the Lord, "Thou hast trusted in thy wickedness, ... therefore shall evil come upon thee; thou shalt not know whence it riseth." (Isa. xlvii. 10, 11.) Thou hast sinned, rashly confiding in the Divine mercy; the punishment will fall suddenly upon you, without your knowing whence it comes.

Affections and Prayers.

Behold, O Lord, one of those foolish ones, who in the hope of recovering it, has so often lost his soul and Thy grace. If Thou hadst caused me to die in that moment, or in that night, when I was in sin, what should have become of me? I thank Thy mercy which has waited for me, and which now makes me to know my folly. I see that Thou desirest my salvation, and I desire to be saved. I repent, O Infinite Goodness, of having so often turned away from Thee. I love Thee with my whole heart. I trust, O my Jesus, through the merits of Thy Passion, to be no longer so foolish. Pardon me quickly, and receive me into Thy grace, for I wish never more to leave Thee. "In Thee, O Lord, have I trusted; let me never be confounded." Oh no; I hope, O my Redeemer, never again to endure the disgrace and the confusion of finding myself deprived of Thy grace and of Thy love. Give me holy perseverance; and grant, that I may always ask it of Thee, and especially when tempted, calling for the aid of Thy holy name, saying, "My Jesus! help me;" for as long as I turn to Thee, I shall never be more overcome. If the temptation continues, grant to me that I may not forsake the perpetual calling upon Thee.

CONSIDERATION XIX

The Gift of Grace is a great Good, and the Loss of Grace is a great Evil

"Man knoweth not the price thereof." Job xxviii. 13.

First Point.

THE Lord says, "If thou take forth the precious from the vile, thou shalt be as My mouth." (Jer. xv. 19.) He who knows how to separate things precious from things vile, becomes like God; he rejects the evil and he chooses the good. Let us mark how blessed is the gift of the grace of God, and how sad is the loss of it. Men do not consider the value of Divine grace, they know not "the price thereof," and therefore they barter it away for nothing—for a passing vapour, for a little land, for an animal pleasure; yet it is an infinite treasure, one which renders us worthy of the friendship of God. "He is an infinite treasure to me, which they that use, become the friends of God." (Wisd. vii. 14.) So that a soul in grace, is a friend of God. The heathen who were deprived of the light of faith deemed it impossible that the creature should have any friendship with God; and speaking according to natural light, they said justly, since friendship can only exist amongst equals; or, as S. Jerome says, "Friendship either finds or makes equals." But God has in many places of Holy Scripture declared, that by means of His grace we may become His friends if we observe His laws, "Ye are my friends if ye do whatsoever I command you: henceforth I call you not servants, but I have called you friends." (S.

John xv. 14, 15.) Whence S. Gregory exclaims, "Oh, marvellous condescension of Divine goodness, we are not worthy to be called slaves, and we are called friends."

How fortunate would he reckon himself to be, who had a king for his friend! But it would be temerity in a subject to claim to have a friendship with his prince; but yet it is not temerity for a soul to claim to be the friend of its God. S. Augustine relates, that two courtiers were once in a monastery of hermits, and that one of them took up the life of S. Anthony the Abbot to read; "He read, and his heart was drawn out from the world." Then turning to his companion he spake thus, "What do we seek? Have we any greater hope than that of being friends of the emperor? And through how many dangers is this the greater danger arrived at? And how long will this friendship last?" "Friend," he said, "fools, that we are; what do we seek? can we hope by serving the emperor for more than his friendship? If we obtain it, we expose ourselves to the greater danger of losing our eternal salvation. But no, we shall not succeed in this, so difficult will it be to obtain Cæsar for a friend. But if I will it, even now, I can become the friend of God."

Whoever, then, is in the grace of God, becomes His friend, nay, rather, he becomes the child of God. "Ye are gods, ye are all the children of the Most Highest." (Ps. lxxxii. 6.) This is the "high calling" that the Divine love has obtained for us through the mediation of Jesus Christ. "Behold what manner of love the Father hath bestowed upon us, that we should be called the Sons of God. (1 S. John iii. 1.) Moreover, the soul that is in grace becomes the spouse of God. "I will even betroth thee unto Me in faithfulness." (Hos. ii. 20.) Therefore, the father of the prodigal son, when he restored him to his favour, ordered, in token of his espousal, to "put a ring on his hand." (S. Luke xv. 22.) The soul becomes also the temple of the Holy Ghost. "Ye are the temple of God, and the Spirit of God dwelleth in you." (1 Cor. iii. 16.)

Affections and Prayers.

Therefore, O my God, my soul, whilst it remained in Thy grace, was Thy friend, Thy child, Thy spouse, Thy temple;

but then in sinning it lost all, and became Thy enemy and the slave of hell. But I thank Thee, O my God, that Thou hast even given me time to recover Thy grace. I grieve that I have offended Thee, more than for every other evil, O Infinite Goodness, and I love Thee above all things. Ah, receive me again into Thy friendship, and in Thy pity do not reject me. I know well, that I have deserved banishment from Thee; but Jesus Christ merits that, being penitent, Thou shouldst receive me again, for the sake of the sacrifice of Himself which He made to Thee on Calvary. "Thy Kingdom come." My Father—for so has Thy Son taught me to call Thee—"come" by Thy grace to reign in my heart. Grant that it may serve Thee only, live for Thee only, love Thee only. "And lead us not into temptation." Ah! do not suffer the enemies that I have, so to tempt me that they may conquer me. "But deliver us from evil;" from hell; but first from that sin which alone can bring me to hell; from the great evil of falling into sin, and so of being deprived of the grace of God.

Second Point.

S. Thomas Aquinas says that the gift of grace exceeds every other gift that the creature can receive, "since it is a participation of the Divine nature." Before him, S. Peter had said, "That by these ye might become partakers of the divine nature." (2 S. Peter i. 4.) So great things has Jesus Christ merited for us by His Passion: He has communicated to us the same glory that He had received from God. "The glory which Thou gavest me I have given them." (S. John xvii. 22.) In brief, he who is in the grace of God is one with God. "He that is joined to the Lord is one spirit." (1 Cor. vi. 17.) And the Redeemer said that in the mind that loves God the entire Holy Trinity comes to dwell. "If a man love Me, ... My Father will love him, and We will come unto him, and make Our abode with him." (S. John xiv. 23.) The soul in grace is so beautiful in the eyes of God that He Himself praises it. "Behold, thou art fair, My love; behold, thou art fair." (Cant. iv. 1.) The Lord seems not to know how to take His eyes away from a soul that He loves; neither to close His ears from anything that it may ask. "The eyes of the Lord are over the righteous, and His ears are open unto their prayers." (Ps. xxxiv. 16.)

How many acquisitions of merit can a soul in grace obtain? Each moment it may be made worthy of eternal glory. Why then do we envy the great ones of the world? If we are in the grace of God, we can continually obtain far more greatness in heaven. Moreover, only he who experiences it, can realise the peace that is enjoyed even in this world by a soul in the grace of God. "O taste and see how gracious the Lord is." (Ps. xxxiv. 8.) The words of the Lord cannot fail. "Great is the peace that they have who love Thy law." (Ps. cxix. 165.) The peace of him who is united with God exceeds all the pleasures that the world and the senses can give: it is "the peace of God, which passeth all understanding." (Phil. iv. 7.)

Affections and Prayers.

O, my Jesus, Thou art that Good Shepherd Who sufferedst Thyself to be slain that Thou mightest give life to Thy sheep. When I fled from Thee Thou didst not cease to follow me, and seek for me. Receive me now that I seek Thee, and, penitent, return to Thy feet. Give me Thy grace again, which I have miserably lost by my sin. I repent with my whole heart. I could die of very grief when I think, how often I have rejected Thee. Pardon me by the merits of that bitter death which Thou sufferedst for me on the Cross. Bind me with the sweet chains of Thy love, and suffer me no further to fly from Thee. Give me strength to bear with patience every cross which Thou imposest upon me, since I have merited the eternal pains of hell. Grant that I may embrace with love the insults which I may receive from men, since I have deserved to be trampled under the feet of devils eternally. Grant, in short, that in all things I may obey Thy inspirations, and subdue all human regards for Thy sake. I am resolved from this day forward to serve Thee only. Others may say what they will, I desire to love Thee alone, O my sweetest Lord. Thee alone do I desire to please. But Thou must give me Thy help, without which I can do nothing. I love Thee, O my Jesus, with all my heart, and I confide in Thy Blood.

THIRD POINT.

Let us now consider the misery of a soul that is not in the grace of God; it is separated from its highest good, which is God. "Your iniquities have separated between you and your God." (Isa. lix. 2.) So that no longer it belongs to God, nor God to it. "Ye are not My people, and I will not be your God." (Hos. i. 9.) God not only does not belong to the soul, but He loathes it, and condemns it to hell. The Lord does not hate any of His creatures. "Thou lovest all things that are, and hatest none of the things which Thou hast made." (Wisd. xi. 25.) But God cannot avoid hating sinners. "Thou hatest all them that work vanity." (Ps. v. 3.) Yes, because God cannot help hating sin, which is an enemy wholly contrary to His will; and therefore in hating sin He necessarily hates the sinner also who is united to sin. "But to God the wicked and his wickedness are hateful alike." (Wisd. xiv. 9.)

O God, if any one has for an enemy an earthly prince, he can never enjoy a quiet sleep, justly fearing death in any moment; and he who has God for an enemy, how can he have peace? One can fly from the anger of an earthly prince by hiding oneself in a wood, or by going afar off into another country; but who can escape from the hands of God? "Lord," said David, "If I climb up into heaven, Thou art there; if I go down to hell, Thou art there also; . . . . even there also shall Thy hand lead me." (Ps. cxxxix. 8, 9.)

Poor sinners, they are cursed by God, by the angels, by the saints, even in this world every day by all the priests, the religious who proclaim their curse in reciting the Divine office: "Cursed are they that do err from Thy commandments." (Ps. cxviii. 21.) Moreover, the loss of God's grace, implies the loss of all merit; for if the greatest saint or missionary commits but one act of sin, he loses all. "All his righteousness that he had done shall not be mentioned." (Ezek. xviii. 24.) Mark the ruin which the loss of God's grace brings with it—the child of

God, becomes the slave of Lucifer—the beloved friend, becomes an enemy greatly hated—the heir of heaven, is condemned to hell. S. Francis of Sales said, that if the angels could weep, when they beheld a soul that had committed deadly sin, and had lost divine grace, they would be ready to weep through compassion. But the greater misfortune is, that whilst the angels would be ready to weep, were they capable of doing so, the sinner weeps not. S. Augustine says, that when a man has lost a small sheep, one of the flock, he neither eats nor sleeps, but weeps; yet if he have lost the grace of God, he both eats, and sleeps, and weeps not.

Affections and Prayers.

Behold, O my Redeemer, the miserable state into which I have reduced myself. To make me worthy of Thy grace, Thou didst spend thirty-three years of toil and of pain, and I, for one moment of poisoned pleasure, for a mere nothing, have despised it and lost it. I thank Thy compassion for still giving me time in which I can recover it at my will. Yes, I wish, as far as I can, to recover it. Tell me what I must do to receive Thy pardon. Dost Thou wish me to repent? Yes, my Jesus, I repent with all my soul for having offended Thy Infinite Goodness. Dost Thou wish me to love? I love Thee above all things. I have hitherto most unworthily employed my heart in loving the creature, and upon vanity; from this day forth I will live for Thee alone, I will love Thee only, my Lord, my treasure, my hope, my strength. "I will love Thee, O Lord, my strength." (Ps. xviii. 1.) O my Jesus, Thy wounds and Thy merits shall be my hope and my strength. From Thee I hope for strength to be faithful. Receive me, then, with Thy grace, O my Saviour, and do not let me leave Thee any more. Separate me from worldly affections, and inflame my heart with Thy holy love.

CONSIDERATION XX

The Folly of the Sinner

"The wisdom of this world is foolishness with God." 1 Cor. iii. 19.

FIRST POINT.

THE Venerable John Avila would divide the world into two prisons, one for those who do not believe, the other for those who believe and yet live in sin far from God, to whom belonged the prison of fools. But the great misery and disgrace of those unhappy ones is, that they deem themselves to be wise and prudent, whilst they are the most stupid and foolish people in the world; and what is worst of all is, that the number of these is innumerable. Some are mad for the honours, others for the pleasures and the defilements of this world. And these, then, dare to call the saints fools, who despise the goods of this world, that they may gain eternal salvation, and the True Good, which is God. They call it foolishness to accept insults and to pardon injuries; foolishness to deprive themselves of the pleasures of the senses, and to embrace the mortifications; to renounce honours and riches, and to love solitude, and a life both humble and hidden. But they do not observe, that their wisdom is called foolishness by the Apostle, "The wisdom of this world is foolishness with God." (1 Cor. iii. 19.) Ah, one day they will truly confess their folly; but when? When there will be no further remedy, and they will say in despair, "We fools esteemed their life madness, and their end without honour." (Wisd. v. 4.) Ah, wretched that we have been, we counted folly, the life of the saints, but now we know that we have been the fools. "Behold, how they are numbered among the children of God, and their lot is among the saints." (Wisd. v. 5.) Behold, they are now collected into the happy number of the children of God, and they have made their lot with the saints, which will be an eternal one, which will make them blessed for ever, and we shall be placed amongst the slaves of the devil, condemned to burn in a pit of torment for all eternity. The lost will continue their lamentation, "We have erred from the way of truth, and the light of justice hath not shined unto us." (Wisd. v. 6.) Therefore, we have been deceived by having chosen to close our eyes to the Divine light; and that which will make us the more unhappy is, that for our error there is not, and there will not be, any remedy while God shall be God.

What folly, then, for a worthless gain, for a little vapour, for a brief delight, to lose the favour of God! What does not a subject do, to obtain the favour of his prince? O God, for one miserable gratification to lose the Highest Good, which is God! to lose heaven, to lose even peace in this life by granting an entrance of sin into the soul, by which its remorse will ever torment it, and condemn it voluntarily to eternal misery.

Would you catch at that forbidden pleasure if, by touching it, you were afterwards to have your hand burnt, or to be enclosed within a sepulchre for a year? Would you commit that sin if it cost you the loss of a large sum of money? And after you know and believe, that by sinning you forfeit heaven and God, and will be for ever condemned to the fire—will you still sin?

Affections and Prayers.

O God of my soul, what should I have been at this moment if Thou had not shown to me so many mercies? I should have been in hell, in the place of fools; as I have been. I thank Thee, O Lord, and I pray Thee, not to abandon me in my blindness; I deserve to be deprived of Thy light, but I see that Thy favour has not forsaken me. I feel that it calls me with tenderness, wishing me to ask for pardon of Thee, and to hope for great things from Thee, notwithstanding the great offences that I have committed against Thee. Yes, my Saviour, I hope to be accepted of Thee as a son. I am, indeed, not worthy thus to be called, because so often I have insulted Thee to Thy face. "Father, I have sinned against heaven and before Thee, and am not worthy to be called Thy son." But I know that Thou searchest out the lost sheep, and that Thy consolation is to embrace Thy lost children. My dear Father, I repent that I have offended Thee, I cast myself at and I embrace Thy feet, and I will not go if Thou dost not pardon and bless me. "I will not let Thee go except Thou bless me." Bless me, O my Father, and may Thy blessing give me great grief for my sins, and great love towards Thee. I love Thee, O my Father, I love Thee with all my heart. Do not allow me to be separated from Thee again; deprive me of all things, save of Thy love.

Second Point.

Poor sinners! They toil, they weary themselves to acquire earthly knowledge or the art of gaining the good things of this life which have to end in a short time; whilst they neglect the good things of that life which shall never end. They lose their reason in such wise that they become not fools only, but brute beasts; and so living, they do not consider what is good and what is evil, but they follow the brutish instincts of sense, alone embracing that which of the present is pleasing to the flesh, without thinking of what they lose, and of that eternal ruin which they have drawn down upon themselves—this is to act like brutes, not like men. S. Chrysostom says, "We call him a man who preserves intact the image of man. But what is the image of man? To be rational." To be a man is to be rational, that is, to act according to reason and not according to sensual appetite. If God were to give a beast the use of reason, and it were to act according to reason, we should say it acted like a man; so, on the other hand, when man acts according to sense, contrary to reason, we say, that man acts like a beast.

"Oh that they were wise, that they understood this, that they would consider their latter end!" (Deut. xxxii. 29.) He who acts with prudence, according to reason, foresees the future, which is what must follow at the end of life, death, judgment, and after that, heaven or hell. Oh how much wiser is the peasant who saves his soul, than the king who loses it! "Better is a poor and wise child than an old and foolish king, who will no more be admonished." (Eccles. iv. 13.) O God! would he not be accounted mad by all, who, to gain more present pleasures, risks the loss of all his goods? And he, who for one brief satisfaction, loses his soul and risks its loss for ever—shall we not hold him to be foolish? This causes the ruin of so many souls which are lost—the care for present goods and ills alone, and the carelessness for those which are eternal.

God has certainly not placed us in the world to grow rich, to gain honours, or to gratify our senses, but to obtain eternal life; "And the end everlasting life." (Rom. vi. 22.) To follow this ought to be our aim; "One thing is needful." (S. Luke x. 42.) But this end is that which sinners most despise; they think only of the present, they walk down to death, they approach the threshold of eternity, and they know not where they go. S. Augustine asks, "What would you say to a pilot, who, being asked where he was going, said that he did not know?" would not every one exclaim—"This fellow steers the ship to destruction!" "Such an one," he concluded, "is he who runs out of the way." Such are these wise ones of the world, who know how to amass wealth, to follow pleasures, to obtain places; but who do not know, how to save the soul. The glutton was wise in making riches, but "he died, and was buried, and in hell he lifted up his eyes." (S. Luke xvi. 22, 23.) Alexander the Great was wise in acquiring so many kingdoms, but after a few years he died and was lost for ever. How many miserable ones now weep and cry in hell, "What hath pride profited us? and what advantage hath the hoarding of riches brought us? All those things are passed away like a shadow." (Wisd. v. 8, 9.) As a shadow they are gone, and nought remains of them now, but weeping and eternal suffering.

"Before man is life and death, and good and evil, that which he shall choose shall be given him." (Ecclus. xv. 18.) My fellow Christian, in this life are placed before you life and death, that is, either to deprive yourself of the pleasures of this life to gain life eternal, or to accept them with death eternal. What do you say? Which will you choose? Choose as a man, and not as a beast; choose as a Christian who has faith, and says, "What is a man profited if he should gain the whole world and lose his own soul?" (S. Matt. xvi. 26.)

Affections and Prayers.

Ah, my God, Thou hast endowed me with reason; Thou hast given me the light of faith, whilst in time past I have acted like a brute beast, losing Thy grace for the sake of the miserable pleasures of my senses, which are passed away as a wind, leaving nothing save remorse of conscience, and an account with Thy Divine justice. "Enter not into judgment with thy servant." O Lord, do not judge me after my merits, but deal with me according to Thy mercy. Give me light; give me sorrow for my sins; give me pardon. "I have gone astray like a sheep that is lost; O seek Thy servant:" for if Thou seekest me not, I shall remain lost. Have pity upon me, by that Blood which Thou hast shed for my sake. I repent, O my Chief Good, of having left Thee, and of having willingly renounced Thy grace. I would that I could die of grief; but do Thou give me greater sorrow. Grant that I may attain heaven to sing of Thy compassion.

THIRD POINT.

We understand that the really wise are they, who know how to obtain the Divine favour and heaven. Let us ever pray, then, to the Lord, that He may give to us the science of the saints, which the Lord gives to those who seek for it. Oh, how sweet a science is it to know how to love God, and to save the soul, which knowledge consists in knowing how to choose the way of eternal salvation, and to follow the means which lead to this end. The matter of saving the soul is of all matters most necessary; if we know everything, and do not know how to save ourselves, it would serve us nothing, and we should be for ever miserable; but on the contrary, we should be for ever blessed if we knew how to love God, although we may be ignorant of all else. S. Augustine says, "Blessed is he who knows Thee, although he knows not anything besides Thee."

"The unlearned arise and seize heaven," says the same saint. How many ignorant peasants there are who, knowing not how to read, yet know how to love God, and to save themselves. How many learned of the world who lose themselves! But the former, not the latter, are truly wise. How truly wise have those been who, leaving the world, have embraced the cloistered life. How truly wise the many martyrs and virgins who renounced the nuptials of the great to go and die for Jesus Christ. And this truth even the worldly recognise; and they do not fail to say of any one who has given himself to God, "Blessed is he who understands, and who saves his soul." In short, they who leave the things of the world to give themselves to God are called "the undeceived." What, then, should those be called who leave God for the things of this world? Deceived men.

My brother, to which of these classes do you wish to belong? S. Chrysostom advises you to go to the graveyards to learn to choose well; they are a good school in which to learn the vanity of worldly goods, and the science of the saints. S. Chrysostom says, "Tell me if you can distinguish there who has been a prince, a noble, a man of letters? For my part, I see nothing, save rottenness, bones, worms. Everything is a fable, a dream, a shadow." All the things of the world in a short time will end and vanish away like a play, a dream, a shadow. But my fellow Christian, if you wish to become wise, it is not sufficient to know the importance of your end; you must seize the means of obtaining salvation. All wish to be saved, and to become saints; but since they do not adopt the means, they not only do not become saints, but they are lost. We must avoid the occasions of sin, frequent the Sacrament, pray, and, before all, ground the heart in the precepts of the Gospel. "What is a man profited, if he shall gain the whole world and lose his own soul?" (S. Matt. xvi. 26.) "He that loveth his life shall lose it." (S. John xii. 25.) That is to say, we must even sacrifice the life, to save the soul. "If any man will come after Me, let him deny himself." (S. Matt. xvi. 24.) That is, to follow Him we must deny our self-love the gratification which it seeks. "In His pleasure is life." (Ps. xxx. 5.) Our salvation consists in fulfilling the Divine will, in these and in many like precepts.

Affections and Prayers.

O Father of mercies, look upon my miseries, and have pity upon me; grant me light, and make me to know my past folly, that I may weep, and Thy Infinite Goodness, that I may love it. My Jesus, "Shut not up my soul with the sinners." (Ps. xxvi. 9.) Thou hast shed Thy Blood for my salvation. Grant that I may never again become the slave of Satan as I was in time past. I repent, O Highest Good, the having left Thee. I detest all those moments in which I willingly consented to sin; and I embrace Thy holy will, which alone desires my good. Eternal Father, through the merits of Jesus Christ, give me strength to follow all things that may please Thee. Let me rather die than any more oppose Thy will. Help me, by Thy grace, to repose in Thee alone all my love, and to banish all affections which do not tend to Thee. I love Thee, O God of my soul, I love Thee above all things; and from Thee I hope for all my good; for pardon, for perseverance in Thy love, and for heaven, where I may love Thee for ever.

CONSIDERATION XXI

The Unhappy Life of the Sinner, and the Happy Life of the Saint

"There is no peace, saith the Lord, unto the wicked." Isa. xlviii. 22. "Great is the peace that they have who love Thy law." Ps. cxix. 165.

FIRST POINT.

ALL men in this life weary themselves to find peace—the merchant, the soldier, and he who has a lawsuit—they all try to find peace, thinking that by winning that gain, obtaining that post, gaining that lawsuit, to make a fortune, and thus to find peace. Poor worldly ones, who seek peace in this world, which cannot give it to them! God alone can give us peace, as the Church prays, "Give unto Thy servants that peace which the world cannot give." No; the world with all its riches cannot satisfy the heart of man, because man was not created for these riches, but for God alone; therefore it is God alone that can satisfy him. Animals are created for the delights of sense only; these find their happiness in earthly things. Give a horse a bundle of grass; give a dog a piece of flesh; they are both content—they desire nothing more. But the soul which is created to love and to be united to God alone, will never be able to find peace in all the pleasures that sense can give. God alone can render it truly happy.

That rich man whom S. Luke records, whose ground brought forth plentifully, said within himself, "Soul, thou hast much goods laid up for many years; take thine ease, eat, drink, and be merry." (S. Luke xii. 19.) But this unhappy one was called a fool; and with reason, as S. Bernard observes. "Hast thou the soul of a hog?" "Ah, wretched one," exclaims the saint, "perhaps thou art like a beast, so that thou canst be satisfied with eating, with drinking, with sensual pleasures?" S. Bernard observes, that a man may be filled with the good things of this world, but not satisfied. The goods of the world are apparent goods, and therefore cannot satisfy the heart of man. "Ye eat, but ye have not enough." (Hag. i. 6.) And for this reason, the more the avaricious man acquires, the more does he seek to acquire. S. Augustine observes, that increased riches do not close, but rather extend, the jaws of avarice! When Alexander the Great had acquired many kingdoms, he wept, because he could conquer no more.

If the riches of this world could satisfy a man, the rich and those who govern, would be fully happy; but experience teaches us the contrary. Solomon observes the same thing, even he who asserts that he never denied his senses one thing. "And whatsoever mine eyes desired I kept not from them." (Eccles. ii. 10.) But notwithstanding, what does he say? "Vanity of vanities; .... all is vanity." (Eccles. i. 2.) As if he had said, all that is in the world is mere vanity, deceit, and folly.

Affections and Prayers.

Ah, my God! what is there remaining to me of all the offences I have committed against Thee, but trouble, bitterness, and the feeling that I deserve hell? The bitterness which I feel does not displease me; nay, it rather consoles me, for it is the gift of Thy grace, and causes me to hope, since Thou dost give it to me, that Thou art willing to pardon me. That which does displease me, is the bitterness I have caused Thee, my Redeemer, Thou who hast loved me so much. My Lord, I deserved to be left by Thee then; but, instead of leaving me, Thou dost offer me pardon; nay, Thou art the first to ask for peace. Yes, my Jesus, I would be at peace with Thee, and I desire Thy grace more than any other good. I repent, O Thou Infinite Goodness, for having offended Thee. I would die of grief. Ah, through that love which Thou didst bear for me when dying on the Cross, pardon me, and take me to Thy heart, and change my heart in such a way that I may please Thee in the time to come, as much as I have displeased Thee in the time that is past. For Thy love I now renounce all the pleasures the world can give me, and resolve rather to lose my life than Thy grace. Tell me what I can do to please Thee, for I wish to do it. I care not for pleasures, honours, riches; I only wish for Thee, my God, my Joy, my Glory, my Treasure, my Life, my Love, my All. Give me, Lord, Thy help, in order to be faithful to Thee. Grant that I may love Thee, and then do with me what Thou wilt.

SECOND POINT.

Not only does Solomon exclaim that the riches of this world are vanity which cannot satisfy, but he says that they are pains which torment the mind. "Behold, all is vanity and vexation of spirit." (Eccles. i. 14.) Poor sinners! they think to be happy in sin; but they only find bitterness and remorse. "Destruction and unhappiness is in their ways, and the way of peace have they not known." (Ps. xiv. 7.) What peace! what peace! No, saith God, "There is no peace, ... unto the wicked." (Isa. xlviii. 22.) In the first place, sin bears about with it the fear of Divine Justice. If any one has a powerful enemy, he can neither eat nor sleep in peace; and he who has God for an enemy, how can he rest in peace? "but destruction shall be to the workers of iniquity." (Prov. x. 29.) When he who is living in sin feels the earth quake, and hears the thunders roar, Oh! how he trembles? Every leaf that moves affrights him. "A dreadful sound is in his ears." (Job xv. 21.) He is ever flying away without seeing who follows him. "The wicked flee when no man pursueth." (Prov. xxviii. 1.) And who pursues him? Even his own sin. After Cain had killed his brother Abel, he said "that every one that findeth me shall slay me." (Gen. iv. 14.) And although the Lord assured him that no one should hurt him: "Therefore, whosoever slayeth Cain, vengeance shall be taken on him sevenfold;" nevertheless, Holy Scripture tells us, that Cain ever went from one place to another. Who was the persecutor of Cain but his own sin?

Besides this, sin bears about with it the remorse of conscience, which, like a cruel worm, is ever gnawing. The wretched sinner may seek amusement in various ways—at the play, in the dance, at the banquet; but his conscience is ever whispering to him, "Thou art at enmity with God; if thou shouldst die, whither wilt thou go?" The remorse of conscience is, even in this life, a torment so great that some, to free themselves from it, have deliberately deprived themselves of life. Such an one was Judas, who, as we all know, went and hanged himself. It is related of another that, having murdered a child, to flee from the anguish of remorse he took monastic vows; but finding no peace, he confessed his crime to the judge, and was condemned to die.

What is a soul that lives without God? Holy Scripture tells us that it is like a stormy sea. "But the wicked are like the troubled sea, when it cannot rest." (Isa. lvii. 20.) I ask, if some one were taken to a musical festival, or to a ball, or to a feast, and there had to be suspended by the feet, with his head downwards, would he enjoy this amusement? Even such is that man who lives with his soul turned upside down, living in the midst of the riches of this world, but without God. He may eat, he may drink, he may dance, he may wear that rich dress, he may receive those honours, he may obtain this post, that possession; but he will never find peace. "There is no peace unto the wicked." Peace can be obtained alone from God, and God grants this peace to His friends, but not to His enemies.

S. Vincent Ferrer observes, that the riches of this world are external—they enter not into the heart. "They are waters which do not enter space, where there is thirst." The sinner may wear a beautiful embroidered robe, he may have a costly diamond on his finger, he may feast according to his desire, but his poor heart will remain filled with bitterness; and therefore he will be, notwithstanding all his riches, pleasures, and amusements, ever restless; and when anything opposes his will, he will become furious and angry like a dog that is mad. When things go wrong with him who loves God, he resigns himself to the will of God, and therefore there is no need for him to quiet himself. The unhappy sinner serves the devil—serves a tyrant who repays him with sorrow and bitterness. Ah, the word of God can never come to fail, which says, "Because thou servedst not the Lord thy God with joyfulness . . . . thou shalt serve thy enemy which the Lord thy God shall send against thee, in hunger, and in thirst, and in nakedness, and in want of all things." (Deut. xxviii. 47, 48.) What does not that revengeful man suffer, after he is revenged? that dishonest one, after he has fulfilled his design? that ambitious one? that avaricious one? Oh how many there are, who, if they suffered for God that which they suffered to bring themselves to condemnation, would become great saints.

Affections and Prayers.

Oh my lost life! O my God, that I had but suffered the pains in serving Thee which I have suffered in offending Thee. I should, with Thy help, have become in part, worthy of heaven! Ah, my Lord, and wherefore did I leave Thee, and lose Thy grace? for pleasures that are brief and empoisoned, which vanished away ere I possessed them, and left my heart full of woe and bitterness. Ah! my sins, I detest you, and curse you a thousand times; but I bless Thy mercy, my God, which with so much patience has endured with me. I love Thee, O my Creator and Redeemer, Who hast given Thy life for me; and because I love Thee, I repent with all my heart for having offended Thee. My God, my God, wherefore have I lost Thee? and for what have I exchanged Thee? Now I know the evil that I have done, and I resolve to lose everything, even life itself, rather than Thy love. Grant me light, Eternal Father, for the love of Jesus Christ; make me feel how very good Thou art, and make me understand how base are the pleasures which the devil presents to me, to make me lose Thy grace. I love Thee, but I desire to love Thee more. Grant that Thou mayest be my only thought, my only desire, my only love. I trust in Thy goodness through the merits of Thy Son.

Third Point.

Therefore, since all riches and pleasures of the world are not able to satisfy the heart of man, who is there that can do so? Even God alone. "Delight thou in the Lord, and He shall give thee thy heart's desire." (Ps. xxxvii. 4.) The heart of man is ever seeking some good that may satisfy it. It obtains riches, pleasures, honours, but it is not content, because these things are finite, and it is created for things which are infinite; but if it finds God, and is united to Him, behold it is quite content—nothing more is desired. "Delight thou in the Lord, and He shall give thee thy heart's desire." S. Augustine found no peace when he was leading a life of sensual pleasure, but afterwards, when he gave himself to God, then he confessed to the Lord and said: "Unquiet is our heart, until it rests in Thee." My God, now do I understand that everything is vanity and trouble, and that Thou alone art the true peace of the soul. All things are toilsome, and Thou alone art not. And afterwards he wrote, "What seekest thou, O manikin—seeking good things? Seek thou the one good in which are all good things?"

When King David was living in sin, he partook of all worldly amusements, but these amusements whispered to him and said: "David, thou oughtest not to be contented with us—no, we are not able to satisfy thee." "Where is now thy God?" Go and find thy God—for He alone can satisfy thee; and, therefore, in the midst of all his pleasures, David did nothing but weep. "My tears have been my meat day and night, while they daily say unto me, Where is now thy God?" (Ps. xlii. 3.)

But, on the contrary, how well does God know how to satisfy the faithful souls of those who love Him! S. Francis of Assisi, having left all for God, although he was barefooted and almost dead with cold and hunger, having only a tattered garment to cover him, nevertheless said, "My God, and my all;" thus did he experience, in some degree, the joys of Paradise. S. Francis Borgia, after he became a religious, and was obliged during his travels to sleep upon straw, felt such great joy that he could scarcely sleep. God will never fail in His promise when He says that He will give him who leaves the riches of this world for the love of Him, even in this life, an hundredfold of peace and contentment. "And every one that hath forsaken houses, or brethren, or sisters, or father, or mother, or wife, or children, or lands, for my name's sake, shall receive an hundredfold, and shall inherit eternal life." (S. Matt. xix. 29.)

Whom, therefore, are we seeking? Let us seek Jesus Christ Who calls us, and Who says, "Come unto Me, all ye that labour and are heavy laden, and I will give you rest. (S. Matt. xi. 28.) Ah, the soul that loves God, finds that peace which surpasses all the pleasures and satisfactions which the senses and the world can give. "The peace of God that passeth all understanding." (Phil. iv. 7.) It is true that in this life even the saints suffer, for this earth is a place of suffering, and we cannot be saved without it; but S. Bonaventure observes, that Divine love is like unto honey, which makes the bitterest things sweet and lovely. He who loves God, loves the will of God, and therefore rejoices in spirit although in affliction, for, by embracing it, he knows he is pleasing God. O God, sinners are willing to despise the spiritual life, but without trying it! S. Bernard says, "They see the cross, but they do not see the unction;" they only regard the mortifications which those who love God endure, and the pleasures of which they are deprived, but they see not the spiritual joys with which the Lord caresses them. Oh, if sinners would but taste the peace which that soul enjoys who desires nothing but God! David exclaims, "Oh, taste and see how gracious the Lord is." (Ps. xxxiv. 8.) My brother, begin to make daily meditations. Very often receive the most Holy Communion. Endeavour to leave the world and to be reconciled to God, and you will see that the Lord will comfort you more in that short time which you spend with Him, than the world has ever comforted you with all its amusements. "Oh, taste and see." He who does not taste can never understand how fully God satisfies the soul that loves Him.

Affections and Prayers.

My dear Redeemer, how is it that I have been so blind during the time that is past as to leave Thee, Thou Infinite Good, Thou Fountain of Consolation, for the short and miserable satisfactions of sense! I marvel at my blindness, but much more do I marvel because of Thy mercy which has borne with me for so long with so much goodness. I thank Thee, that Thou makest me now to understand my folly and my great duty to love Thee. I love Thee, my Jesus, with all my soul, and I desire to love Thee more. Increase this desire and this love. Inspire me with love for Thee, Thou Who art infinitely lovely, Who hast done everything to make me love Thee, and Who desirest my love so much. "If Thou wilt, Thou canst make me clean." (S. Matt. viii. 2.) Ah, my dear Redeemer, purge my heart from every impure affection which may prevent me from loving Thee as I ought. I have not the power to make my heart burn with love towards Thee, and to love no other than Thee; it must be through the strength of Thy grace which can do all that it wishes to do. Separate me from all things, drive away from my soul every affection that is not Thine, and make me wholly Thine. I grieve beyond every evil, because of having so often offended Thee as I have done. I resolve to consecrate the life that remains to me entirely to Thy holy love; but it is Thou Who must enable me to do it. Enable me through that Blood which Thou didst shed for me with so much grief and so much love. Let it be to the glory of Thy power to make my heart, which was once filled with earthly affections, now to be consumed with love towards Thee, O Thou Infinite Good.

CONSIDERATION XXII

The Habit of Sin

"When the wicked cometh, then cometh also contempt." Prov. xviii. 3.

FIRST POINT.

ONE of the greatest evils which the sin of Adam caused us, is the wicked inclination to sin. This made the Apostle weep when he found himself impelled by concupiscence towards those same sins which he detested. "But I see another law in my members . . . . bringing me into captivity to the law of sin." (Rom. vii. 23.) And therefore it happens with us, that being infected by this concupiscence, and with so many enemies who urge us on to do evil, that we find it so difficult to reach the blessed country without sin. Now, such being our frailty, I ask, What would you say of a traveller who would have to cross the sea in a storm in a shattered bark, and yet should wish to load it with a weight which, even were the bark a strong one, and there were no storm, would be enough to send it to the bottom? What would you predict concerning the life of such an one? Now, we say the same of the habitual sinner, who, having to pass over the sea of this life—a sea which is very tempestuous and where many are lost—in a weak and shattered bark, which is our flesh, and to which we are united, is willing to weigh it down with habitual sins. For in this one it is very difficult to be saved, because the evil habit darkens the mind, and hardens the heart, and by doing so, easily renders him obstinate, even to death.

In the first place, the evil habit produces blindness. And why is it that the saints ever beg God to give them light, and why do they fear lest they should become the greatest sinners in the world? It is because they know that if for one moment they were to lose the light, they might commit any wickedness. How is it that so many Christians have been willing to live in sin, until they have at last condemned themselves? "Their own malice blinded them." (Wisd. ii. 21.) Sin has deprived them of sight, and so they have become lost. Each sin produces blindness, so that when the sin increases, so does the blindness increase. God is our light; the more, therefore, the soul withdraws itself from God, the more does its darkness increase: "His bones are full of the sin of his youth." (Job xx. 11.) As the light of the sun cannot enter in a vessel filled with earth, so the Divine light cannot enter a heart that is filled with vices. And therefore it is that we see many relaxed sinners lose this light, and go on from sin to sin, and never again think of amending their ways. "The ungodly walk on every side." (Ps. xi. 9.) These miserable sinners have fallen into that dark pit, where they can do nothing but sin, speak only of sin, think only of sin, and, at last, they scarcely recognise that there is any evil in sin. S. Augustine observes, that "the habit itself of evil does not suffer sinners to see the evil which they do." So that they live as if they no longer believed in a God, a paradise, a hell, or an eternity.

And, behold, for that sin which, at one time, caused them to feel great horror, through the evil habit, no longer causes them to feel it. "Make them like unto a wheel; and as the stubble before the wind." (Ps. lxxxiii. 13.) "Observe," says S. Gregory, "with what ease a bit of straw is moved by the slightest puff of wind;" even thus do we often see some, who, before they fell, once resisted, at least, for some time, and strove against the temptation, but after the sin became habitual, they yielded to every temptation, and every occasion to sin that was presented to them. And wherefore? Because the evil habit has deprived them of light. S. Anselm tells us that the devil acts with many sinners, like any one who holds a bird tied by a string, who allows it to fly, but directly it flies he pulls it back again to earth. Even so, as the saint observes, does it happen with habitual sinners, "Entangled by a bad habit, they are holden by the enemy; flying, they are cast down into the same vice." S. Bernardine of Sienna adds, that some continue to sin even without the occasion. The saint remarks, that habitual sinners are like unto windmills which turn round at every breath of wind; and turn round more when there is no corn to grind, and although the miller does not wish them to turn. An habitual sinner will be seen, who, without occasion, will indulge in bad thoughts; who without desire, and who almost without wishing it, will be drawn by force to do evil. As S. Chrysostom observes, "Habit is a hard thing, which sometimes compels those who are unwilling to do what is wrong." Yes, because, according to S. Augustine, the bad habit at last becomes a sure necessity. And S. Bernardine also adds, "Habit is changed into nature;" for, as it is necessary for man to breathe, even so to habitual sinners who are made the slaves of sin, it seems necessary to sin. I say slaves of sin; there are servants who serve and are paid, but slaves serve because they are obliged to do so, and without any pay. Even to this do some miserable ones come—even to sin without feeling any pleasure in doing so. "When the wicked cometh, then cometh also contempt." (Prov. xviii. 3.) S. Chrysostom well applies this to the habitual sinner, who being placed in that pit of darkness, despises corrections, sermons, censures, hell, and even God; who despises every thing, and becomes like the vulture, which rather than leave the dead body is willing to be killed upon it. S. Bernard tells us even that for habitual sinners it is no use to pray—we must weep for them as for those who are lost. But how can they avoid the precipice if they can no longer see? They need a miracle of grace. These wretched ones will open their eyes in hell, when there will be no longer any good in opening them, except to weep more bitterly over their folly.

Affections and Prayers.

My God, Thou hast indeed favoured me with Thy blessings in blessing me more than others; and I have clearly, by my offences, displeased Thee more than any other that I know.

O sorrowful heart of my Redeemer, Who upon the Cross wast afflicted and tormented when beholding my sins, give me, through Thy merits, a living knowledge and grief for my sins. Ah, my Jesus, I am full of wickedness; but Thou art Omnipotent; truly canst Thou fill me with Thy holy love. Therefore in Thee do I trust—Thou Who art good and of infinite mercy. I repent, O Sovereign Good, for having offended Thee. Oh, would that I had died, rather than have given Thee this offence. I have been forgetful of Thee, but Thou hast never been forgetful of me. I can see it through that light which Thou dost now grant me. Since, therefore, Thou dost grant me that light, grant me also the strength to be faithful to Thee. I promise Thee that I would rather die a thousand times, if it were possible so to do, than ever again to turn away from Thee; but I hope alone in Thy help. O Lord, in Thee have I trusted, let me never be confounded. In Thee, O my Jesus, do I hope never more to be confounded in sin, and deprived of Thy grace.

Second Point.

Again, the habit of sin hardens the heart. And God allows it to do so, as a punishment for the resistance made against His calls. The Apostle observes, that "therefore hath He mercy on whom He will have mercy, and whom He will He hardeneth." (Rom. ix. 18.) S. Augustine explains this passage thus—"It is not indeed that God hardens the habitual sinner; He withdraws His grace from him as a punishment for the ingratitude shown towards His graces; and thus does the heart of the sinner remain hard, and like unto stone." "His heart is as firm as a stone; yea, as hard as a piece of the nether millstone." (Job xli. 24.) Hence it is that when others become affected, and weep when they are told of the rigour of Divine judgment, of the pains of those who are condemned, of the Passion of Jesus Christ, the habitual sinner is quite unmoved. He will speak, and will hear all these things spoken of with indifference, as if they were things in which he had no part; and he will become more hardened in sin, even "as hard as a piece of the nether millstone."

Even sudden deaths, earthquakes, thunders, and lightnings, will not affright him; instead of awaking him, and making him repent, they produce that sleep of death in him in which he is sleeping hopelessly. Sinful habits by little and little destroy even remorse of conscience. To habitual sinners, even the most enormous sins seem as nothing. S. Augustine observes that "sins, however horrible, when they become habitual, seem to be small, or no sins at all." Doing evil, naturally brings with it a certain sense of shame; but S. Jerome tells us, that habitual sinners lose even the feeling of shame when they sin. S. Peter compares such an one to the swine that wallows in the mire. (2 S. Pet. ii. 22.) As the swine turning again to the mire does not observe the smell, even thus does it happen with the habitual sinner; that corruption which is noticed by all others, is not noticed by him. And supposing the mire has deprived him of sight, what need is there to marvel, as S. Bernardine observes, if he does not amend even when God is chastising him? Therefore it happens that instead of being sorry for their sins, they rejoice in sin, they laugh at it, and they make a boast of it, "Who rejoice to do evil." (Prov. ii. 14.) "It is as sport to a fool to do mischief." (Prov. x. 23.) S. Thomas of Villanova inquires, What signs are these of such diabolical hardness? They are all signs of damnation. "Hardening is an indication of condemnation." My brother, fear lest the same should happen to thee. If thou hast any bad habit, endeavour quickly to leave it, now that God calls thee; and as long as thy conscience smites thee, be joyful, because it is a sign that God has not yet abandoned Thee. But repent, and leave the evil habit soon; because if not, the wound will mortify, and thou wilt be lost.

Affections and Prayers.

O Lord, how can I thank Thee as I ought for the many favours Thou hast shown me? How many times Thou hast called, and I have resisted! Instead of being grateful to Thee, and loving Thee for having delivered me from hell, and for having so lovingly called me, I have continued to provoke Thy wrath, answering Thee with insults. No, my God, no longer do I wish to offend Thy patience; I have already offended

Thee too much. Thou alone, Who art of Infinite Goodness, couldst have put up with me until now. But already do I see that Thou canst not endure me much longer, and Thou art right. Pardon me, therefore, my Lord and my Highest Good, all the injuries I have committed against Thee, for which I repent with my whole heart; and I purpose for the future never more to offend Thee. And wherefore? Perhaps I shall ever continue to provoke Thee! Ah! be at peace with me, O God of my soul, not through my merits, to which nothing but punishment and hell belong, but through the merits of Thy Son and my Redeemer, in Whose merits I place my hope. For the love, therefore, of Jesus Christ, receive me into Thy grace, and give me perseverance in Thy love. Take from me every impure affection, and draw me all to Thyself. I love Thee, O Highest God, O Sovereign lover of my soul, Who art worthy of infinite love. Oh, that I had ever loved Thee!

Third Point.

When the light shall be lost, and the heart shall be hardened, it will generally happen that the sinner's end will be a bad one, and that he will die obstinate in his sins. "A hard heart shall fear evil at the last." (Ecclus. iii. 27.) The just continue to walk in the right way. "The way of the just is uprightness." (Isa. xxvi. 7.) Habitual sinners, on the contrary, ever walk round about. "The ungodly walk on every side." (Ps. xii. 9.) They leave sin for a time, and then return to it. S. Bernard announces condemnation to such as these, "Woe to the man who follows this course." But some will say, I am willing to repent before I die; but the difficulty is for an habitual sinner to amend even should he come to be old. Holy Scripture tells us to "train up a child in the way he should go: and when he is old, he will not depart from it." (Prov. xxii. 6.) The reason truly is, as S. Thomas of Villanova observes, because our strength is very weak: for "the strong shall be as tow." (Isa. i. 31.) Therefore it happens, as the saint continues, that the soul, being deprived of grace, cannot remain without committing more sins.

Moreover, would not any one be very foolish, who should wish to play, and who should willingly lose all his money, hoping to win it back at the last stake? This is even the madness of that one who continues to live in sin, but who hopes to make amends for all his sin at the last moment of his life. Can the Ethiopian or the leopard change the colour of his skin? And how can any one lead a good life who for a long time has contracted a habit of sin? "Can the Ethiopian change his skin, or the leopard his spots? then may ye also do good, that are accustomed to do evil." (Jer. xiii. 23.) Hence it is, that the habitual sinner is at last given up to despair, and thus finishes his life.

Upon this passage in Job, "He breaketh me with breach upon breach, He runneth upon me like a giant," (Job xvi. 14), S. Gregory remarks, "When a person is attacked by an enemy, at the first wound which he receives he may still be able to defend himself; but the more wounds that he receives so much more strength does he lose, until in the end, he is slain." Even in this way does sin act. After the first and second sin, the sinner still has strength to withstand—be it ever understood that he has this strength by means of the Divine grace which assists him; but if afterwards he continues to sin, the sin becomes like a giant, it "runneth upon him like a giant." On the other hand, the sinner, finding himself much weaker, and having so many wounds, how can he avoid death? Sin, according to Jeremiah, is like unto a heavy stone which oppresses the soul. "They have . . . . cast a stone upon me." (Lam. iii. 53.) Now, S. Bernard observes, it is as difficult for a sinner to arise from an evil habit, as it is difficult for one who has fallen under a heavy stone, and who has not sufficient strength to remove it, to free himself from it. "He arises with difficulty whom the weight of evil habit presses."

Therefore will the habitual sinner exclaim, Then I am despaired of? No; thou art not despaired of, if thou art willing to amend. But justly does an author observe, that for very great sins very great remedies are required.

If a man who was sick, in danger of death, were unwilling to apply the proper remedies, because he was not aware of the danger of his disease, the doctor would say, "Friend, thou wilt die if thou dost not take the medicine." The sick man would answer, "Behold, I am ready to take anything if my life is in danger."

My Christian brother, I will say the same to you if you have contracted the habit of some sin, You are unwell, and are one of those infirm ones who are "seldom cured." As S. Thomas of Villanova remarks, you are ready to be condemned. If, therefore, you are willing to be cured, there is the remedy; but you must not expect a miracle of grace; you must, on your part, exert all your strength, to deliver yourself from the occasion to sin; you must avoid evil companions; resist when you are tempted, by commending yourself to God. You must use every means, frequently confessing, and reading a spiritual book daily. You must exert all your strength, otherwise the threat of the Lord against the obstinate will be fulfilled in you, "Ye . . . . shall die in your sins." (S. John viii. 21.) And if, now that God grants you light, you do not amend, you will afterwards amend with great difficulty. Listen to God, who calls you, "Lazarus, come forth." Poor sinner, already dead, come forth from this dark tomb of your evil life. Answer quickly, and give yourself to God, and fear lest this should be the last call for you.

Affections and Prayers.

Ah, my God, and for what shall I wait—until Thou dost abandon me, and send me to hell? Ah, Lord, wait for me, for I wish to change my life, and give myself to Thee. Tell me what I am to do, that I may do it. O Blood of Jesus, do Thou help me. And Thou, O Eternal Father, through the merits of Jesus, have mercy upon me. I repent, O God of infinite goodness, for having offended Thee, and I love Thee beyond all things. Pardon me, through the love of Jesus Christ, and give me Thy love. Give me also a great fear for my eternal ruin, should I offend Thee again. Light, my God; light and strength. I hope for everything because of Thy mercy. Thou didst grant me many graces when I wandered far from Thee; much more do I hope for, now that I return to Thee, being resolved to love none other than Thee. I love Thee, my God, my Life, my All.

CONSIDERATION XXIII

The Delusions which the Devil puts in the Mind of Sinners

"That they may recover themselves out of the snare of the devil." 2 S. Tim. ii. 26.

First Point.*

LET us picture to ourselves some young person once fallen into grievous sin, but who now has confessed it, and has regained the Divine grace. The devil again tempts such an one to fall, but he resists still; but already he wavers, because of the delusions which the enemy puts into his mind. I say to such an one, "Young man, tell me what thou dost wish to do? Art thou willing to lose the grace of God, which thou hast regained, and which is worth more than all the world, in order to obtain that miserable satisfaction? Dost thou wish to write the sentence of thy eternal death—to condemn thyself to burn for ever in hell?" Thou sayest, No, I do not wish to condemn myself, I wish to be saved; if I commit this sin—I will confess it afterwards. This is the *first delusion* which the devil presents to you. Thou sayest that afterwards thou wilt confess it? But in the meanwhile thou art losing thy soul. Tell me, whether, if thou hadst a jewel in thy hand, which was worth a very large sum of money, wouldst thou throw it into the river saying, "Presently I will search carefully, and then I shall hope to find it again?" but thou hast in thy hand that most beautiful jewel—

* Author's Note.—Many of the sentiments in this Consideration have been expressed before; they are collected for their especial application to the wiles of the devil.

thy soul, which Jesus Christ has bought with His Blood; and thou art willingly throwing it into hell—for by sinning thou art already condemned according to the present justice—and thus casting it away, thou art saying, I hope to regain it by confessing. But if thou shouldst not regain it? For in order to regain it, a true repentance is necessary, which is the gift of God. And if God should not grant this repentance? And if death should come and deprive you of the time for confession?

Thou sayest that thou wilt not allow a week to pass without confession. But who promises thee this week? Thou sayest that thou wilt confess to-morrow. But who promises thee to-morrow? S. Augustine writes thus—God has not promised to give thee to-morrow, perhaps He will give it to thee, and perhaps He will refuse to give it to thee; even as He has denied it to so many, who at night have gone to bed alive, and in the morning have been found dead. How many, indeed, in the act itself of sin, has the Lord struck dead, and sent to everlasting punishment? And if He should do the same with thee, how couldst thou amend thy eternal ruin? Know, that because of this mistake, in saying, "Afterwards I will confess," the devil has borne many thousands of Christian souls to hell; for it is very seldom that a sinner is found in such a desperate state, as to wish of his own free will to be condemned. All, when they sin, sin in the hope of confessing their sin, and thus have so many miserable ones been condemned, and now they can no longer remedy their condemnation.

But thou sayest, "I am not strong enough to resist that temptation;" this is the *second delusion* of the devil who tries to make thee feel that thou hast not strength to resist the present passion.

Firstly, we must understand that God, as the Apostle tells us, is faithful, and will not suffer us to be tempted above that we are able. (1 Cor. x. 13.) Moreover, I ask thee, if now thou art not strong enough to resist, how canst thou gain strength afterwards? Afterwards, the enemy will not cease to tempt thee to commit other sins; and then he will be much stronger against thee, and thou wilt be much weaker. If therefore, now thou art not strong enough to extinguish that flame, how wilt thou be able to do so, when the flame is much greater? Thou sayest that God will give thee His help. But God already gives His help to thee; why, therefore, with His help canst thou not resist? Perhaps thou art hoping that God will increase His help and His graces, after that thou hast increased thy sins? But if now thou requirest greater help and strength, why not ask God to grant them to thee? Perhaps thou art doubting God's faithfulness, when He promised to give thee all that thou seekest from Him? "Ask, and it shall be given you." (S. Matt. vii. 7.) God cannot fail; fly to Him; He will give thee that strength which is necessary for thee to resist. Ancient Fathers have declared that "God does not command things impossible to be performed; but by commanding, bids you both do what you can, and to pray for what you cannot do, and He helps you to do it." God does not command us to do impossible things; but He gives us His precepts, and admonishes us to do all that we can, with the actual aid that He bestows upon us; and when that aid is not sufficient to enable us to resist, then He exhorts us to seek for greater help, and if we ask for it, then truly will He give it to us.

Affections and Prayers.

Therefore, my God, is it because Thou hast been so good towards me that I have been so ungrateful towards Thee? We have, as it were, been striving together; I, in flying from Thee, and Thou in seeking me; Thou in doing me good, and I in doing evil against Thee. Ah, my Lord, if there were no other reason, the goodness alone which Thou hast shown me, ought to have inspired me with love towards Thee; for after I have increased my sins, Thou hast increased Thy graces. And whenever have I deserved the light which Thou art giving to me? My Lord, I thank Thee with all my heart, and I hope to come to heaven, there to thank Thee for that light through all eternity. I hope, through Thy Blood, to be saved, and I hope it with certainty, because Thou hast shown so many mercies to me. In the meantime I hope that Thou wilt grant me strength never more to betray Thee. I would rather, with thy grace helping me, die many times over, if it were possible, than again offend Thee. I have offended Thee often enough. In the life that remains to me I wish to love Thee. And how can I help loving a God, Who, after having died for me, has borne with me with so much patience, notwithstanding the many insults I have offered to Him? O God of my soul, I repent with all my heart; would that I could die of grief. But if during the past, I have turned from Thee, now do I love Thee beyond every thing, much more than I love myself. Eternal Father, through the merits of Jesus Christ, succour a miserable sinner who wishes to love Thee.

SECOND POINT.

The sinner exclaims, "But God is merciful!" This is the *third delusion* which is common to sinners, and through which so many are lost. A learned author observes, that the mercy of God sends more souls to hell than the justice of God; because these miserable ones, boldly trusting in His mercy, never cease to sin, and thus are they lost. God is very merciful. Who is there that can say He is not? But notwithstanding this, how many are there who are daily sent to hell? God is merciful—but He is also just, and for that reason He is obliged to punish those who offend Him. He uses mercy, but to whom? Even to those who fear Him. "So great is His mercy also toward them that fear Him. . . . . So is the Lord merciful unto them that fear Him." (Ps. ciii. 11–13.) But to those who despise Him, and abuse His mercy in order the more to despise Him, He executes His justice upon them. And very rightly. God pardons sin; but He cannot pardon the wish to sin. S. Augustine declares, that he who sins, thinking to repent after he has committed the sin, is not a penitent, but a mocker of God. And, on the other hand, the Apostle tells us, that God will not be mocked, "Be not deceived; God is not mocked." (Gal. vi. 7.) It would be mocking God to offend Him as we please, and how we please, and afterwards to expect to reach heaven.

But, as during my past life God has shown so many mercies towards me, and has not punished me, therefore do I hope He will show mercy for the future. This is the *fourth delusion.* Therefore, because God has had compassion upon thee, for this reason, He must ever show mercy to thee, and must never chastise thee? No, indeed, for the greater have been His mercies to thee, the more oughtest thou to tremble lest He should never pardon thee again, but should chastise thee if again thou dost offend Him. We are told not to say, "I have sinned, and what harm hath befallen me? for the Most High is a patient rewarder," (Ecclus. v. 4,) for God endures, but will not do so for ever; when the mercies which He is willing to show towards a sinner come to an end, then does He punish the sinner for his sins altogether. And the longer He has waited for the sinner to repent, so much the more severe will be the sinner's punishment; as S. Gregory observes, "Those whom He waits for the longer, He punishes the more severely." If, therefore, my brother, thou feelest that thou hast offended God many times, and that God has not sent thee to hell, thou oughtest to say, "It is of the Lord's mercies that we are not consumed." (Lam. iii. 22.) Lord, I thank Thee that Thou hast not sent me to hell as I deserved. Think of the number who have been condemned for less sins than thine. And with this thought thou oughtest to seek as far as thou canst to atone for the offences thou hast committed against God, by repentance, prayer, and good works. The patience that God has shown towards thee ought to animate thee, not, indeed, to displease Him more, but to serve Him better and to love Him more; seeing that He has shown so many mercies to thee, which He has not shown to others.

Affections and Prayers.

My crucified Jesus, my Redeemer, and my God, behold the traitor at Thy feet. I blush to appear before Thee. How many times have I not mocked Thee; how many times have I not promised never more to offend Thee, but my promises have all proved treacherous; for when the occasion to sin presented itself, was I not forgetful of Thee, and did I not again turn away from Thee? I thank Thee that I am not in hell, but that Thou art keeping me at Thy feet, and that Thou art enlightening me and calling me to Thy love. Yes, for I wish to love Thee, my Saviour and my God, and I wish never more to despise Thee. Thou hast already borne with me long enough. I feel that Thou wilt not bear with me any longer. Ah, wretched me, if after so many graces I should again offend Thee! O Lord, I do sincerely wish to change my life, and as much as I have hitherto offended Thee, so much do I wish to love Thee. I am consoled, for I have to do with Infinite Goodness, Which, indeed, Thou art. I repent beyond every other evil for having so despised Thee, and I promise to give Thee all my love for the future. Pardon me through the merits of Thy passion; remember no more the sins I have committed against Thee; and give me strength to be faithful to Thee in the life that remains to me. I love Thee, O my Sovereign Good, and I hope ever to love Thee. My beloved Lord, never more will I leave Thee.

THIRD POINT.

"But I am young; God takes compassion upon youth; when I am old, I will give myself to God." This is the *fifth delusion.* Art thou young? But dost Thou not know, that God takes not account of the years, but the sins of each one? Art thou young? But how many sins hast thou committed? There may be many old men, who perhaps have not committed one-tenth part of the sins which have been committed by thee. And knowest thou not, that the Lord has fixed the number and the measure of the sins which He will pardon to each one? "The Lord patiently expecteth, that when the day of judgment shall come, He may punish them in the fulness of their sins." (2 Macc. vi. 14.) That is to say, God has patience, and waits until a certain time; but when the measure of the sins which He has determined upon pardoning is full, He no longer pardons, but He chastises the sinner; either by sending him a sudden death in the same state of condemnation in which he has been living, or else by leaving him to his sin, which punishment is worse than death. "I will take away the hedge thereof, and it shall be eaten up." (Isa. v. 5.) If thou hadst a garden, around which thou shouldst have planted a hedge, and shouldst have cultivated it for many years, and spent much labour upon it; and notwithstanding all this, thou shouldst see that it brought forth no fruit; what wouldst thou do? Thou wouldst take away the hedge, and leave it to itself. Therefore fear lest God should do the same with thee. If thou continuest to sin, thou wilt lose remorse of conscience; thou wilt think upon eternity no longer, nor of thy soul; thou wilt lose all light; thou will lose fear; behold the hedge is taken away; and thus wilt thou be abandoned by God.

But thou wilt say, "It is true, that by this sin I lose the grace of God, and I shall be condemned to hell, and perhaps through this sin I may be already condemned; but it may also happen that I shall confess and be saved." Behold the *last delusion*, Yes, I grant that thou mayest still be saved; for I am not a prophet, and therefore I cannot say for certain, whether, after having committed this sin, God will no longer show mercy to thee. But thou canst not deny, that after the many graces the Lord has shown thee, if thou shouldst again offend against Him, thou wilt be very likely to be lost. Even thus does Holy Scripture assure us, "A hard heart shall fear evil at the last." (Ecclus. iii. 27.) "Wicked doers shall be rooted out." (Ps. xxxvii. 9.) The wicked shall at last be cut off by Divine justice: "for whatsoever a man soweth, that shall he also reap." (Gal. vi. 7.) He that sows in sin at length shall reap only punishment and torment. "Because I have called, and ye refused; .... I also will laugh at your calamity; I will mock when your fear cometh." (Prov. i. 24, 26.) I have called thee, says God, and ye have mocked me; but I will mock thee when death cometh upon thee. "To Me belongeth vengeance and recompense." (Deut. xxxii. 35.) To Me belongeth vengeance, and I will repay when the time shall arrive. Even thus does Holy Scripture speak of those sinners who are obstinate, for justice and right require it.

Thou sayest, "But for all that I may be saved." And I answer, Yes, perhaps thou canst be; but is it not great madness to allow the salvation of thy immortal soul to depend upon a "perhaps," and upon a "perhaps" which is so uncertain? Is this a case to be placed in such great peril?

Affections and Prayers.

My dear Redeemer, I cast myself at Thy feet, and I thank Thee that, after so many sins, Thou hast not abandoned me. How many who have offended Thee much less than I have, will never have the light which Thou art now giving to me? I see that Thou dost indeed wish me to be saved; and I wish to be saved chiefly that I may give Thee pleasure. I wish to praise these Thy many mercies to me, which Thou dost show me for ever in heaven. I trust that Thou hast already pardoned me; but if I should still be in disgrace with Thee, and that because I have not known how to repent as I ought for the many sins committed against Thee, now indeed do I repent with my whole heart, and I grieve for them beyond all evils. Pardon me, through Thy mercy, and do Thou ever increase in me a sorrow for having offended Thee, my God, Who art so good. Give me sorrow and give me love. I love Thee beyond all things; but still I love Thee too little. I would love Thee much, and I ask and hope for this love from Thee. Do Thou hear me, my Jesus, for Thou hast promised to hear those who pray to Thee.

CONSIDERATION XXIV

The Particular Judgment

"For we must all appear before the judgment-seat of Christ." 2 Cor. v. 10.

FIRST POINT.

LET us now consider the soul's appearance before God; the accusation, the examination, and the sentence. And, in the first place, speaking of the appearance of the soul before the Judge, it is the general opinion of theologians, that the particular judgment takes place at the very moment when man expires, and that, at the same place in which the soul is separated from the body, it is judged by Jesus Christ, Who will not send, but will come Himself to judge its cause, "for the Son of Man cometh at an hour when ye think not." (S. Luke xii. 40.) S. Augustine observes, "He will come with love for us; with terror for the ungodly." Oh, what fear will that one feel, when he beholds the Redeemer for the first time, and beholds Him in wrath! "Who can stand before His indignation?" (Nah. i. 6.) To see the wrath of the Judge will be the forerunner of condemnation. "The wrath of a king is as messengers of death." (Prov. xvi. 14.) S. Bernard remarks, that the soul will suffer more in seeing Jesus wrathful, than in being even in hell itself. Very often criminals are seen to perspire with a cold perspiration upon being brought before some earthly judge. When Piso appeared before the Senate in a criminal's dress, he was so troubled that he committed suicide. What grief is it to a son to see his father really offended; or to a subject to see his prince deeply annoyed! But what greater punishment can a soul experience than to see Jesus Christ, Whom all his life long has been despised? "they shall look upon Me Whom they have pierced." (Zech. xii. 10.) That Lamb, Who during life has shown so much patience, the souls will afterwards behold very wrathful, without the hope of ever again being able to appease Him; so that they will feel obliged to call upon the mountains to fall upon them, and thus to hide them from the anger of the Lamb. "Fall on us, and hide us from the . . . . wrath of the Lamb." (Rev. vi. 16.) S. Luke, speaking of the judgment, says, "And then shall they see the Son of Man." (S. Luke xxi. 27.) Oh, what anguish will it bring to the sinner, when he beholds the Judge in the form of a man! Because the sight of Him, Who as Man once died for his salvation, will reproach him very deeply for his ingratitude. When the Saviour ascended into heaven, the angels said to His disciples, "This same Jesus, Which is taken up from you into heaven, shall so come in like manner as ye have seen Him go into heaven." (Acts i. 11.) Therefore the Judge will come to judge, with those same wounds with which He departed into heaven. Those wounds will console the just, but they will affright the sinners. When Joseph said unto his brethren, "I am Joseph your brother, whom ye sold," (Gen. xlv. 4), Holy Scripture tells us that they "could not answer him; for they were troubled at his presence." (Gen. xlv. 3.) But what will the sinner answer Jesus Christ? Perhaps he will take courage to entreat His mercy, at that time when he will first of all have to render to Him an account of the contempt which he has shown for the mercies granted to him? S. Augustine inquires, What will the sinner do, whither will he fly, when he beholds the Judge, Who will be very wrathful, sitting above him; underneath him, hell already open; on the one side the sins which will accuse him; on the other, the devils ready to execute the sentence; and within, the conscience which will sting him?

Affections and Prayers.

O my Jesus, I wish ever to call Thee my Jesus; Thy Name consoles me, and gives me courage, reminding me that Thou art my Saviour, Who didst die to save me. Behold me at Thy feet; I confess that I have been guilty of hell each time that I have offended Thee by committing deadly sin. I do not deserve pardon, but Thou hast died to pardon me. Therefore, my Jesus, do Thou quickly pardon me before Thou dost come to judge me. For then I could no longer beg for mercy; but now I can beg for it, and hope to receive it. Then will Thy wounds affright me; but now they give me confidence. My dear Redeemer, I repent more than for any other evil, that of having offended Thy infinite Goodness. I would wish to accept every chastisement, every loss, rather than lose Thy grace. I love Thee with all my heart. Have mercy upon me. "Have mercy upon me, O God, after Thy great goodness."

Second Point.

We will consider the accusation and the examination. "The judgment was set, and the books were opened." (Dan. vii. 10.) Those books will be two—the Gospel, and the conscience. In the Gospel, it will be read what the guilty ought to have done; in the conscience, what he has done. In the scales of Divine justice, riches will not weigh, nor dignity, nor nobility, but works alone. "Thou art weighed in the balances, and found wanting," (Dan. v. 27,) said Daniel to King Belshazzar. On which F. Alvarez comments thus, "Neither God nor riches were put in the balance; the king alone, was weighed."

Then will come the accusers. The first of these will be the devil. S. Augustine here observes, "The devil will stand before the tribunal of Christ, and he will recite the words of our profession. He will cast in our teeth all things that we have done, in what day, and at what hour, we have sinned." "He will recite the words of our profession." That is to say, he will bring forward all our vows which we have failed in performing; and he will charge us with all our sins, telling us of the day and the hour in which we committed them. Then he will say to the Judge, as S. Cyprian tells us, "I, for these things, have endured neither blows nor scourgings; I, for this guilty one, have suffered nothing; but he left Thee, Who once died to save him, to become my slave, therefore he is mine." Even the guardian angels will become accusers, as Origen observes, "Each one of the angels will give evidence as to how many years he has laboured on his behalf, and how he spurned the warnings."

Therefore at that time "all her friends have dealt treacherously with her." (Lam. i. 2.) Even those walls, within which the guilty one shall have sinned, will become accusers. "The stone shall cry out of the wall." (Hab. ii. 11.) His own conscience will be an accuser. "Their conscience also bearing witness . . . . in the day when God shall judge." (Rom. ii. 15.) Their own sins then will speak, as S. Bernard says, and cry out, "Thou hast made us, we are thy work; we will not desert thee."

Finally, as S. Chrysostom observes, the wounds of Jesus Christ will become accusers: "the nails will complain of thee; the scars will speak against thee; the Cross of Christ will proclaim against thee."

And then will the examination commence. The Lord declares that "at that time I will search Jerusalem with candles." (Zeph. i. 12.) Mendozza observes that the lamp will penetrate into every corner of the house. Cornelius à Lapide, explaining these words, "with lamps," teaches us, that God will then place before the guilty the example of the saints, and will remind them of all the lights and the inspirations which He has given to them during life, and also of all the years which He has granted them, during which they ought to have done good. "He hath called an assembly against me." (Lam. i. 15.) So that he will then, according to S. Anselm, have to render an account of every glance. "He shall purify the sons of Levi." (Mal. iii. 3.) As gold is purified by being separated from the dross, even so will our good works be examined—our confessions, and our communions. "When I receive the congregation, I shall judge according unto right." (Ps. lxxv. 3.) Indeed, as S. Peter tells us, the righteous will scarcely be saved in the judgment. "And if the righteous scarcely be saved, where shall the ungodly and the sinner appear?" (1 S. Peter iv. 18.) If he shall have to render an account of every idle word, what account will he be able to render of so many evil thoughts which have been yielded to—

of so many idle words? S. Gregory asks: "If account is to be taken of the idle, what about the impure words?" And particularly does the Lord forewarn those infamous sinners who have robbed Him of souls, "I will meet them as a bear that is bereaved of her whelps." (Hos. xiii. 8.) And then, speaking of works, the Judge will say, "Give her of the fruit of her hands." (Prov. xxxi. 31.) Reward according to the works which have been done.

Affections and Prayers.

Ah, my Jesus, if now Thou dost wish to pay me according to the works which I have done, no other than hell would be my fate. O God, how many times have I not written the sentence of my condemnation to that place of torments! I thank Thee for the patience which Thou hast had with me in having borne with me for so long. O God, if now I should have to appear at Thy tribunal, what account could I render to Thee of my life? "Enter not into judgment with Thy servant." Ah, Lord, do Thou wait for me a little longer; do not judge me yet. If now Thou shouldst judge me, what would become of me? Wait for me, since that Thou hast shown so many mercies towards me until now; grant me even this; give me a great grief for my sins. I repent, O Sovereign Good, for having so often despised Thee. I love Thee above all things. Eternal Father, pardon me through the love of Jesus Christ, and through His merits, grant me holy perseverance. My Jesus, I hope for all things through Thy Blood.

SECOND POINT.

In conclusion, for the soul to obtain eternal salvation, it must be found to have led a life which was conformable to the life of Jesus Christ. "For whom He did foreknow, He also did predestinate to be conformed to the image of His Son." (Rom. viii. 29.) But it was this which caused Job to tremble. "What shall I do when God riseth up? And when He visiteth, what shall I answer Him?" (Job xxxi. 14.) Philip II. having a servant who told him a lie, reproved him, saying, "Is it thus thou wouldst deceive me?" The man, it is said, returned home, and died of grief. What will the sinner do, and what will He answer Jesus Christ, Who will be his Judge? He will do that which the man in the Gospel did, who having come in not having a wedding-garment, was silent, not knowing what to say. "He was speechless." (S. Matt. xxii. 12.) His own sin will stop his mouth. "The mouth of all wickedness shall be stopped." (Ps. cvii. 42.)

S. Basil observes, that the sinner will then be more tormented by shame, than by the fire itself of hell. "The shame will be more horrible than the fire."

Behold, the Judge will finally pronounce the sentence: "Depart from Me, ye cursed, into everlasting fire." "Oh, what terrible thunder will this be! Oh, how terribly will it resound!" says the Carthusian; so also S. Anselm, "He who does not tremble at so great thunder does not sleep, but is dead." And Eusebius adds, that the fear of the sinners will be so great in hearing their sentence pronounced, that if they could die again, they would do so. S. Thomas of Villanova remarks, that no longer is a place for prayer given, there are no longer intercessors to whom to flee unto. To whom, therefore, can they flee? Perchance to God Whom they have so despised. "Who will deliver you? Perhaps that God Whom you have despised."

O God, exclaims S. Thomas of Villanova, alas! with what indifference do we hear the judgment spoken of, as if the sentence of condemnation did not concern us! And as if we shall not have to be judged! And what folly is it, continues the same Saint, to rest secure in a thing of so much danger! S. Augustine warns thee and says, "Do not say, my brother:" "Will God really send me to hell?" Do not say it, observes the Saint, because even the Jews could not be persuaded that they should be destroyed; and many who have been condemned would never believe that they should be sent to hell; but afterwards the end of their punishment has come! "An end is come, the end is come. . . . . Now will I shortly pour out My fury upon thee, and accomplish My anger upon thee: and I will judge thee according to thy ways." (Ezek. vii. 6-8.) And even thus, observes S. Augustine, will it happen with thee, "The day of judgment will come, and thou shalt find that true, which God has threatened." Now it is in our power to choose the sentence that we hope will be ours. S. Eligius observes, "It is put into our power how we will be judged." And what have we to do? To settle our accounts before the judgment. "Before judgment prepare thee justice." (Ecclus. xviii. 19.) S. Bonaventure observes, that those merchants who are wise, frequently look over and cast up their accounts, so that they may be in no danger of failing. S. Augustine remarks, "That the Judge may be propitiated before the judgment, but not in it." "I long to present myself before thee as judged, and not as to be judged." Let us therefore say to the Lord, as did S. Bernard, My Judge, I desire that Thou shouldst judge and punish me now during life, now that it is the time of mercy, and now that Thou canst pardon me, for after death will it be the time for judgment.

Affections and Prayers.

My God, if I am not reconciled to Thee now, the time will come when I can no longer be reconciled to Thee. But how can I be reconciled to Thee, who so many times have despised Thy friendship for pleasures which have proved to be base and miserable? I have repaid Thy great love with ingratitude. What satisfaction that is worth offering, can a creature give for the offences committed against its Creator? Ah, my Lord, I thank Thee, that Thy mercy has already opened the way for me to become reconciled to Thee and to give Thee satisfaction. I offer to Thee the Blood and the Death of Jesus Thy Son, and behold I see Thy justice already reconciled and satisfied beyond measure. And for this, my repentance is also necessary. Yes, my God, I repent with all my heart because of all the offences I have committed against Thee. Judge me therefore now, O my Redeemer. I abhor, beyond every other evil, the displeasure which I have caused Thee. I love Thee beyond all things with all my heart; and I purpose ever to love Thee, and to die rather than to offend Thee more. Thou hast promised to pardon him who repents; then do Thou judge me now, and do Thou absolve me from my sins. I accept the punishment which I deserve, but restore me to Thy favour, and keep me in it, until I die. Even so do I hope.

CONSIDERATION XXV.

The General Judgment

"The Lord is known to execute judgment." Ps. ix. 16.

FIRST POINT.

IF now we consider well, there is no person in the world more despised than Jesus Christ. We take more account of a peasant than we do of God; because we fear, if we have offended such an one, lest he being filled with wrath, should avenge himself; but we commit offences against God over and over again as if God were not able to avenge Himself whenever it pleases Him so to do. "Which said unto God, Depart from us: and what can the Almighty do for them?" (Job xxii. 17.) But therefore it is that the Redeemer has appointed a day which will be the day of general judgment, called, even in Holy Scripture, "The day of the Lord," in which Jesus Christ will be known to be that Sovereign Lord, Who indeed He is. "The Lord is known to execute judgment." (Ps. ix. 16.) Hence such a day is no longer called a day of mercy and pardon, but "a day of wrath, a day of trouble and distress, a day of wasteness and desolation, a day of darkness and gloominess." (Zeph. i. 15.) Yes, for then will the Lord very justly redeem to Himself the honour which sinners during this life have sought to deprive Him of. Let us try to imagine in what way the judgment of that great day will come to pass.

Before the Judge shall come, "there shall go a fire before Him." (Ps. xcvii. 3.) Fire shall come from heaven which will burn the earth, and all the things of the earth, "The earth also and the works that are therein shall be burned up." (2 S. Pet. iii. 10.) So that palaces, churches, towns, cities, kingdoms, all, will become a pile of ashes. This house, all polluted as it is with sin, will be purged with fire. Behold the end which all the riches, the pomps, and the pleasures of this world will have. For those who are dead, the trumpet will sound, and they will all arise. "For the trumpet shall sound, and the dead shall be raised." (1 Cor. xv. 52.) S. Jerome observes, "As often as I reflect upon the day of judgment, I tremble: that trumpet seems ever to resound in my ears, Arise, ye dead, and come to judgment." At the sound of that trumpet the beautiful souls of the Blessed, will descend to be united to their bodies with which they have served God in this life; but the miserable souls of the lost will ascend from hell, to be united to those accursed bodies with which they have offended God.

Oh, what a difference will there be, then, between the bodies of those who are Blessed and the bodies of those who are lost. The Blessed will appear beautiful, lovely, and more resplendent than the sun. "Then shall the righteous shine forth as the sun." (S. Matt. xiii. 43.) O happy he, who in this life knows how to mortify his flesh by refusing to it pleasures that are forbidden; and who, in order to keep it more under control, refuses it even the lawful pleasures of the senses, and ill-treats it as the saints have done! Oh, what happiness will he derive from it at that time!

On the other hand, the bodies of the lost, will appear deformed, black, and offensive. Oh, what anguish will the lost soul feel upon being united to its body! The soul will exclaim, "Accursed body, in order to please thee I am lost." And the body will reply, "Accursed soul, when thou hadst reason in thy power, wherefore didst thou grant me those pleasures which have caused both thee and me to be lost for all eternity?"

Affections and Prayers.

Ah, my Jesus and my Redeemer, Thou Who one day will be my Judge, do Thou pardon me before that day shall arrive. "Cast me not away from Thy presence." (Ps. li. 11.) Now Thou art a Father to me, and as that Father do Thou receive into Thy favour a son who returns repentant to Thy feet. My Father, I ask pardon from Thee. I have offended Thee unjustly, I have left Thee wrongfully. Thou didst not deserve to be treated as I have treated Thee. I repent and I grieve with all my heart. Pardon me. "Cast me not away from Thy presence," (Ps. li. 11). Do not turn away Thy face from me; do not drive me from Thee as I deserve that Thou shouldst. Remember the Blood which Thou hast shed for me, and have mercy upon me. My Jesus, I desire no other Judge than Thee.

S. Thomas of Villanova said, "I willingly submit to the judgment of Him Who died for me, and that I might not be condemned, suffered Himself to be condemned to the cross." And before him, S. Paul said, "Who is he that condemneth? It is Christ that died . . . . for us." (Rom. viii. 34.) My Father, I love Thee, and for the time to come, I wish never more to leave Thy feet.

Do Thou forget the wrongs which I have committed against Thee, and give me a great love towards Thy goodness. I desire to love Thee more than I have sinned against Thee, but if Thou dost not help me, I am unable to love Thee. Help me, my Jesus; make me live a life ever grateful to Thy love, so that in that day I may be found in the valley, amongst the number of Thy lovers.

Second Point.

When all those who are dead shall have arisen, it shall be intimated to them by the angels that they must all go to the Valley of Jehoshaphat, there to be judged, "Multitudes, multitudes in the valley of decision: for the day of the Lord is near." (Joel iii. 14.) Then when all are assembled there, the angels shall come, and shall separate the wicked from the just, "The angels shall come forth and sever the wicked from among the just." (S. Matt. xiii. 49.) The just will remain on the right hand, and the wicked will be banished to the left hand. What anguish it would cause any one to be expelled from society or from the Church. But how much greater anguish will it cause that one who is expelled from the company of the saints? How, think you, the wicked will be confounded when the just being separated, they will be abandoned? S. Chrysostom observes, that if those who are condemned should have no other punishment, this confusion alone would be enough to constitute a hell. The son shall be separated from the father, the husband from the wife, the master from the servant. "The one shall be taken, and the other left." (S. Matt. xxiv. 40.) Tell me, my brother, which place thou thinkest will then be thine? Dost thou wish to be found on the right hand? Then leave the life which leads thee to the left.

Now in this life princes and rich ones are esteemed fortunate, and the saints who live in poverty and humility are despised. Oh, faithful ones who love God, do not grieve upon seeing yourselves so despised and afflicted in this earth! "Your sorrows shall be turned into joy." (S. John xvi. 20.) Then you will be called the truly fortunate, and you will have the honour of being declared one of those who belong to the court of Jesus Christ. Oh, how great will appear many of the saints, some of whom were branded as apostates, others treated as if mad, others renouncing high positions to die in prisons. Oh, what honours, then, will so many martyrs possess who have been ill-treated by their executioners. "Then shall every man have praise of God." (1 Cor. iv. 5.) And, on the other hand, what a horrible spectacle will Herod, Pilate, and Nero make, and many others who were great ones of the world, but were afterwards for ever lost. Oh, lovers of the world, in the Valley, in the Valley I am expecting you. There, without doubt, you will change your feelings. There, you will weep over your folly. Miserable ones, who, in order to make a short appearance upon the stage of this world, will afterwards have to act the part of the lost, in the tragedy of judgment. The elect, therefore, will be placed on the right hand; nay, for their greater glory, according to S. Paul, they will be raised in the air beyond the clouds, to go with the angels to meet Jesus Christ Who will come from heaven. "We . . . . shall be caught up together with them in the clouds to meet the Lord in the air." (1 Thess. iv. 17.) And the condemned, like so many goats destined to the slaughter, shall be confined upon the left hand to await their Judge, Who will make a public condemnation against all His enemies.

But, behold the heavens are opening, and the angels are coming to assist at the judgment, and are bearing the tokens of the passion of Jesus Christ. S. Thomas remarks, saying, "When the Lord comes to judgment, the sign of the Cross and other marks of His Passion will be seen." Especially will the Cross appear: "And then shall appear the sign of the Son of Man; and then shall all the tribes of the earth mourn. (S. Matt. xxiv. 30.) Cornelius à Lapide observes, "Oh, how sinners will then weep upon seeing the Cross, even those sinners who, during life, esteemed their eternal salvation of so little value, which salvation cost the Son of God so much." Then declares S. Chrysostom, "The nails will complain of thee, the wounds will speak against thee, the Cross of Christ will proclaim against thee." The holy apostles, with all their imitators, will act as assessors at this judgment, who, together with Jesus Christ, will judge the nations. "They shall shine . . . . they shall judge nations." (Wisd. iii. 7, 8.) Finally, the Judge Himself shall come upon a throne of power and light. "And they shall see the Son of Man coming in the clouds of heaven with power and great glory." (S. Matt. xxiv. 30.) "Before their face the people shall be much pained." (Joel ii. 6.) The sight of Jesus Christ will console the elect, but to the wicked it will bring more anguish than hell itself. S. Jerome thought that, to the lost the punishments of hell will be easier to bear than the presence of the Lord.

S. Teresa said, "My Jesus, do Thou give me every anguish, but do not suffer me to behold Thy face wrathful against me at that day." And S. Basil, "This confusion surpasses all pain." Then will come to pass what S. John predicted, that the lost will pray to the mountains to fall upon them and to hide them from the sight of the angry Judge, and will say "to the mountains and rocks, Fall on us, and hide us from the face of Him that sitteth on the throne, and from the wrath of the Lamb." (Rev. vi. 16.)

Affections and Prayers.

O my dear Redeemer, O Lamb of God, Who didst come into the world—not indeed to punish, but to pardon sins. Ah! do Thou pardon me quickly, before that day shall come in which

Thou wilt have to be my Judge. At that time the sight of Thee, Thou Lamb of God, Who hast had so much patience with me, in bearing with me, would be the hell of hells if I should be lost. Ah, I repent, pardon me quickly; draw me with Thy merciful hand from the precipice where I have fallen, through my sins. I repent, O Sovereign Good, for having offended Thee, and for having offended Thee so much. I love Thee, my Judge, Who hast loved me so much. Ah, through the merits of Thy death, bestow such a grace upon me as may change me from a sinner into a saint. Thou hast promised to hear those who pray to Thee: "Call unto me, and I will answer thee." (Jer. xxxiii. 3.) I ask Thee not for earthly goods; I ask for Thy grace, Thy love, and for nothing else. Hear me, my Jesus, through that love which Thou didst bear me, dying for me upon the Cross. My beloved Judge, I am the guilty one, but I am the guilty one who loves Thee more than he loves himself. Do Thou have mercy upon me.

Third Point.

But behold the judgment already begins. The trials are brought on; that is to say, the conscience of each one is disclosed. "The judgment was set, and the books were opened." (Dan. vii. 10.) In the first place, the devils will be the witnesses against the wicked, who will say, according to S. Augustine, "Most just God, adjudge him to be mine who was unwilling to be Thine." In the second place, their own consciences will be witnesses against them: "their conscience also bearing witness." (Rom. ii. 15.) Moreover, the very walls of that house in which the sinner has offended God will be witnesses against them, and shall cry for vengeance, "For the stone shall cry out of the wall." (Hab. ii. 11.) Finally, the Judge Himself shall be a witness against them, Who has been present at the time that all the offences have been committed against Him. "Even I know, and am a witness, saith the Lord." (Jer. xxix. 23.) S. Paul says, that then the Lord "will bring to light the hidden things of darkness." (1 Cor. iv. 5.) He will make known to all men the most secret and shameful sins of the wicked which have been unknown during life : "I will discover thy skirts upon thy face." (Nahum iii. 5.)

The Master of the Sentences, with others, considers that the sins of the elect will not then be manifested, but be hidden, according to what David said, "Blessed is he whose unrighteousness is forgiven, and whose sin is covered." (Ps. xxxii. 1.)

On the contrary, S. Basil tells us, that the sins of the wicked shall be seen by all at a glance, as in a picture. S. Thomas observes that if, in the Garden of Gethsemane, when Jesus Christ said, "I am He," all the soldiers who were come forth to take Him went backward and fell to the ground, what will it be when He, sitting as a Judge, shall say to the lost, "Behold, I am He Whom thou hast so much despised?" What will He do, when about to judge, who so did, being judged?

But let us hasten on to the sentence. Jesus Christ will, in the first place, turn towards the elect, to whom He will address these sweet words, "Come, ye blessed of My Father, inherit the kingdom prepared for you from the foundation of the world." (S. Matt. xxv. 34.) Will it not be, indeed, great joy to hear the Judge exclaim, "Come, ye blessed children, come to the kingdom; no longer will there be any trouble for you; no longer any fear. Already you are, and ever will be, safe for ever. I bless the Blood which I once shed for you, and I bless the tears which you have shed because of your sins; let us quickly enter Paradise, where we shall be together for all eternity." And thus, singing Alleluias, the righteous will enter heaven in triumph, to possess, to praise, and to love God for all eternity.

On the other hand, the lost, turning to Jesus Christ, will say to Him, "And we, poor miserable ones that we are, what are we to do?" The Eternal Judge will then say, "Since you have renounced and despised My grace—Depart from Me, ye cursed, into everlasting fire." (S. Matt. xxv. 41.) Depart from Me, for never more do I wish to see you, neither to hear of you. Go, and go accursed, since you have despised My Blessing." And where, Lord, are the miserable ones to go? "Into everlasting fire." Into hell, to burn in the soul and in the body. And for how many years, and for how many ages? "Into everlasting fire," even for all eternity, whilst God shall be God. After this sentence, observes S. Ephraim, the wicked shall be bid farewell by the angels, by the saints, and by their relations. Farewell, ye just; farewell, O Cross; farewell, heaven; farewell, fathers and children; for we shall behold you never more.

And so, in the middle of the valley, a great pit will be opened, where the devils and the lost will fall together, who will hear, O God, those doors to shut behind them which will never open more. Never, never more, through all eternity. Oh, accursed sin, to what a wretched end wilt thou one day lead so many wretched souls? Oh unhappy souls, for whom this wretched end is being preserved!

Affections and Prayers.

Ah, my Saviour and God, what will be the sentence concerning me in that day? If now, my Jesus, Thou shouldst demand an account of my life, what answer could I make, except to tell Thee that I deserve hell a thousand times over? Yes, it is true, my dear Redeemer, I do deserve hell a thousand times; but Thou knowest that I love Thee, and that I love Thee more than I love myself; and for the offences which I have committed against Thee, I feel so grieved that it would please me more to have suffered every evil rather than to have displeased Thee. Thou didst condemn, O my Jesus, those sinners who were obstinate in their sins, but not those who repented, and wished to love Thee. Behold me at Thy feet repentant; make me to feel that Thou has pardoned me. But already dost Thou make me hear by the prophet, "Turn ye unto Me, ... and I will turn unto you." (Zech. i. 3.) I leave everything, I renounce all the pleasures and the wealth of the world, and I turn and embrace Thee, my loved Redeemer. Ah, receive me into Thy heart, and there inflame me with Thy holy love; inflame me so much that I may never more think of becoming separated from Thee. My Jesus, save me, and may my eternal happiness be ever spent in loving and in praising Thy mercy. "My song shall be always of the loving-kindness of the Lord." (Ps. lxxxix. 1.)

CONSIDERATION XXVI

Of the Pains of Hell

"And these shall go away into everlasting punishment." S. Matt. xxv. 46.

First Point.

THE sinner, when he sins, commits two evils: he leaves God, the highest good, and he turns over to the creature. "My people have committed two evils: they have forsaken me the fountain of living waters, and hewed out cisterns, broken cisterns, that can hold no water." (Jer. ii. 13.) Since, then, the sinner turns to the creature, with a loathing at God, by those very creatures he shall be justly tormented in hell, by the fire and by demons; and this forms the pain of the senses. But since his greatest guilt, in which the sin consists, lies in his turning away from God, so the chief punishment, and that which will make hell, will be the pain of loss; that is, the pain of having lost God.

Let us consider, in the first place, the pain of the senses. It is an article of faith that there is a hell. This prison is reserved in the middle of the earth for the punishment of the rebels against God. What is this hell? It is a place of torments. "This place of torment," (S. Luke xvi. 28), as the condemned glutton called hell. A place of torments, where all the senses and the powers of the condemned will each have their especial torment; and in proportion as one sense has especially offended God, so also will be its peculiar punishment. "That wherewithal a man sinneth, by the same also shall he be punished." (Wisd. xi. 16.) "How much she hath glorified herself, and lived deliciously, so much torment and sorrow give her." (Rev. xviii. 7.) The sight will be tormented with darkness. "The land of darkness, and the shadow of death." (Job x. 21.) What compassion should we feel for a poor man who remained shut up in a dark pit for the remainder of his life, for forty or fifty years! Hell is a pit, shut in on every side, in which no ray of the sun or any other light will ever enter. "Man . . . . shall never see light." (Ps. xlix. 20.) The fire which enlightens on earth, in hell will be altogether dark. "The voice of the Lord divideth the flames of fire." (Ps. xxix. 7.) Which expression S. Basil explains, of the Lord dividing the fire from the light, so that it will suffice to burn only, and not to illuminate; or as Albert the Great expresses it, "He will divide the glowing from the heat." The very smoke which leaves this fire will form that "blackness of darkness," which S. Jude says is reserved for ever for the wicked. (S. Jude 13.) S. Thomas Aquinas says, that there will be reserved for the wicked, light, "as much as suffices for men to see those things which torment them." They will see in that glimmer of light the ugliness of the other reprobates, and of the demons, who, to frighten them the more, will assume horrible forms.

The sense of smell will be tormented. What torment would it be, to be shut up in a room with a putrid corpse? "Their stink shall come up out of their carcases." (Isa. xxxiv. 3.) The lost will have to remain in the midst of so many millions of other lost ones, alive as to pain, but corpses from the odour which they emit.

But some foolish one may say, "If I go to hell, I shall not be alone." Wretched one! By how many the more there are in hell, by so much the more will they suffer. As S. Thomas Aquinas says, "There the society of the wretched will not lessen, but increase the misery;" they will suffer all the more, I say, from the smell, the cry, the confinement; since in hell they will be upon each other like sheep are penned up together in the winter time. "They live in hell like sheep." (Ps. xlix. 14.)

Nay more, they will be as grapes, pressed under the press of the wrath of God. "He treadeth the winepress of the fierceness and wrath of Almighty God." (Rev. xix. 15.) They shall have from this also the pain of fixedness. "They shall be as still as a stone." (Exod. xv. 16.) Thus the lost, as they fall into hell at the last day, so will they remain without ever changing their place, and be unable to move either foot or hand, whilst God shall be God.

The sense of hearing will be tormented with the ceaseless howling and wailing of those poor desperate ones. The demons will make continual dins. "A dreadful sound is in his ears." (Job xv. 21.) What pain this, when one wishes to sleep, to hear the continual moaning of the sick, the barking of a dog, or the crying of an infant? Unhappy lost ones! who are condemned to ever hear for all eternity, the groans and cries of those who are tortured.

The appetite will be tormented by hunger; the lost ones will experience a rabid hunger, "grin like a dog, ... and grudge if they be not satisfied." (Ps. lix. 14, 15.) But they shall not have a crumb of bread.

The thirst will be so great, that all the water of the sea would not suffice for it; nevertheless, they shall not have one drop. The rich man asked for one drop, but this he has not yet had, and will never have it—never.

Affections and Prayers.

Ah, my Lord, behold at Thy feet one who has made small account both of Thy grace and of Thy chastisements. Poor me; if Thou, my Jesus, hadst not had pity upon me, for how many years should I have been in that fearful furnace, where truly are now burning so many like myself. Oh, my Redeemer, how is it, that whilst thinking upon this I do not burn with Thy love? How shall I ever be able to think of offending Thee anew? Oh, may it never be, my Jesus Christ; grant me rather to die a thousand deaths. Since Thou hast begun, finish the work. Thou hast delivered me from the ruin of my many sins, and with so great love, Thou hast called me to love Thee. Ah, grant now that this time which Thou hast given me, I may spend wholly for Thee. How would the lost desire one day, nay, one

… the same man shall he be
… how much he hath glorified
… so much torment and sorrow give
… will be tormented with dark-
… the shadow of death."
… compassion should we feel for a poor man
… remainder of his
… shut in on every
… any other light will ever
… and never see light." (Ps. xlix. 20.)
… will be altogether dark.
… flames of fire." Ps.
… expression St. Basil explains, of the Lord
… so that it will suffice to burn
… or as Albert the Great expresses
… from the heat." The very
… that "blackness of dark-
… is reserved for ever for the wicked.
… Thomas Aquinas says, that there will be re-
… as much as suffices for men to
… them." They will see in that
… and of the
… will assume horrible

Nay more, they will be as grapes, pressed under the press o[illegible] wrath of God. "He treadeth the winepress of the [illegible] wrath of Almighty God." (Rev. xix. 15.) They shall have [illegible] also the pain of fixedness. "They shall be as st[illegible]" (Exod. xv. 16.) Thus the lost, as they fall into hell [illegible] so will they remain without ever changing their p[illegible] unable to move either foot or hand, whilst God shall [illegible]

The sense of hearing will be tormented with the ceas[illegible] howling and wailing of those poor desperate ones [illegible] will make continual dins. "A dreadful sound [illegible]" (Job xv. 21.) What pain this, when one wishes to sleep [illegible] the continual moaning of the sick, the barking of [illegible] crying of an infant? Unhappy lost ones! who are [illegible] to ever hear for all eternity, the groans and cries [illegible] are tortured.

The appetite will be tormented by hunger [illegible] experience a rabid hunger, "grin like a [illegible] if they be not satisfied." (Ps. [illegible] have a crumb of bread.

The thirst will be so great, that [illegible] not suffice for it; neverthe[illegible] The rich man asked for one [illegible] and will never have it—ne[illegible]

Ah, my [illegible] account both [illegible] if Thou, my Jes[illegible] [illegible]rs should [illegible] now [illegible] hour of the time which Thou hast granted to me; and I, what shall I do? Shall I continue to spend it on things which displease Thee? No, my Jesus! do not allow this by the merits of that Blood which hitherto has delivered me from hell. I love Thee, O Highest Good; and because I love Thee, I repent of having offended Thee. I desire to offend Thee no more, but ever to love Thee. Grant that I may obtain the gift of perseverance and of Thy holy love.

Second Point.

The punishment which most torments the senses of the lost, is the fire of hell which torments the touch. "The vengeance of the ungodly is fire and worms." (Ecclus. vii. 17.) Therefore it is, that the Lord makes special mention of it in His description of the judgment. "Depart from Me, ye cursed, into everlasting fire." (S. Matt. xxv. 41.) Even in this life, the pain which is caused by fire is sharper than any other; but there is so much difference between this pain and that which will be caused by the fire of hell, that S. Augustine tells us, the pain we suffer here would seem to be but painted. And S. Vincent Ferrer observes, that in comparison to that fire, our fire is but cold. The reason is, that our fire is made for our use; but the fire of hell is created by God on purpose to punish. Tertullian observes that the fire which is for human use, is very different from the fire which serves for the judgment of God. The wrath of God kindles that avenging fire. "A fire is kindled in Mine anger." (Jer. xv. 14.) Therefore, by Isaiah, the fire of hell is called the spirit of burning. "When the Lord shall have washed away the filth . . . . by the spirit of burning." (Isa. iv. 4.) The lost shall not only be sent to the fire, but into the fire. "Depart from Me, ye cursed, into everlasting fire." So that the miserable ones will be surrounded with fire, like wood in a furnace. The lost will find themselves, with an abyss of fire beneath, an abyss of fire above, and an abyss of fire around them. If they touch anything, if they see, if they breathe, it is only fire that they touch, see, and breathe. They will be in the fire as a fish is in the water. But not only will this fire remain, surrounding those who are lost, but it will even enter within them to torment them. The body will become all fire, so that the bowels within will burn; the heart within the breast will burn; the brain within the head will burn; the blood within the veins; even the marrow within the bone—every lost one will become in himself a furnace of fire. "Thou shalt make them like a fiery oven." (Ps. xxi. 9.)

There are some who cannot endure to walk along a road dried up by the sun, or to remain in a close room with a brasier; neither can they endure a spark that may chance to fly from a candle; and yet they do not fear that fire which devours, as Isaiah inquires, "Who among us shall dwell with the devouring fire?" (Isa. xxxiii. 14.) As a wild beast devours a young kid, even so does the fire of hell devour the lost; it devours them, but without causing them to die. S. Peter Damian, speaking to the incontinent, observes, Continue to please thy flesh, for a day will come, when thy lewdness will become as pitch within thy bowels, which will cause the flame which will burn thee in hell to be more great and more tormenting. S. Jerome adds, that this fire will bring with it all the torments and pains which are suffered in this life—pains in the side, in the head, in the bowels, in the nerves. The pain of cold will also be felt in this fire. "Drought and heat consume the snow waters." (Job xxiv. 19.) But let it be ever understood, that all the pains which are endured in this life are but as a shadow, as S. Chrysostom remarks, when compared to the pains of hell, "Imagine fire, imagine the knife; what are these things but shadows compared with these torments?"

The powers belonging to the mind will also bring their own torment. The lost one will be tormented by memory, in remembering the time which he once had during this life in order to become saved, but which he has spent in causing his soul to be lost, and in remembering the graces which he received from God, but which he has never been willing to make use of. He will also be tormented by the intellect, in thinking of the great good which he has lost—paradise and God; and that for this loss there is no longer any remedy. He will be tormented by the will, by seeing that every thing which he may ask for, will be for ever denied to him. "The desire of the ungodly shall perish." (Ps. cxii. 10.) The wretched one will never have that which he desires, but will ever have that which he abhors, which will be his eternal sufferings. He would wish to escape from the torments, and to find peace; but he will be tormented for ever, and will never more find peace.

Affections and Prayers.

Ah, my Jesus, Thy Blood and Thy death are my hope. Thou didst die to free me from eternal death. Ah, Lord, and who has ever shared more of the merits of Thy Passion than I, miserable one that I am, who have so often deserved hell? Ah, no longer do Thou allow me to live ungrateful for the graces which Thou hast bestowed upon me. Thou hast freed me from the fire of hell, because Thou didst not wish me to burn in that fire of torment, but Thou didst wish that I should burn with the sweet fire of Thy love. Help me, therefore, so that I may comply with Thy desire. If now I were in hell, I could never love Thee more, but since I can love Thee, I wish to love Thee. I love Thee, O Thou Infinite Goodness, I love Thee, my Redeemer, Who hast loved me so much. How could I live so long forgetfully of Thee! I thank Thee that Thou hast never been forgetful of me. If Thou hadst been forgetful of me, I should either be in hell now, or I should not feel any grief because of my sins. This grief which I feel in my heart for having offended Thee, the desire which I feel to love Thee as I ought to do, are the gifts of Thy grace, which is still aiding me. I thank Thee for it, my Jesus. I hope for the future to give the life which may remain to me to Thee. I renounce all things. I only wish to think of serving Thee and pleasing Thee. Do Thou ever remind me of the hell which I have deserved, and of the graces which Thou hast bestowed upon me, and do not allow me ever to turn away from Thee, and to condemn myself to that pit of torments.

Third Point.

But all these pains are as nothing compared with the anguish we shall feel at our loss. The darkness, the smell, the cries, the fire, and the pain do not make hell; it is the anguish at having lost God which makes hell. S. Bruno observes, "Let torments be added to torments, so that they are not deprived of God." And S. Chrysostom, "If thou hast spoken of a thousand hells, thou hast said nothing equal to the grief of this." And S. Augustine adds, that if the lost could enjoy the sight of God, they would feel no punishment, and hell itself would be turned into heaven.

In order to understand somewhat of this punishment, let us suppose some one were to lose a gem, for example, which might be worth a hundred crowns, he would be very sorry; but if it were worth two hundred crowns, he would be doubly sorry, and if four hundred, he would be still more sorry; in short, as the value of the thing which is lost increases, so does the sorrow for the loss increase. And what good is it that the wicked will have lost? An Infinite Good, even God; and therefore, S. Thomas tells us, it is, that they certainly feel an infinite sorrow. "The pain of the lost is infinite, since it consists of the loss of Infinite Good." This punishment now, is the only one feared by the saints. S. Augustine observes, "This is punishment for those who love, not for those who despise." S. Ignatius Loyola also says, "Lord, I can endure every punishment, but I cannot bear to be deprived of Thee." But sinners never conceive of this pain, who are contented to live months and years without God, because the miserable ones are living in the midst of darkness. In death they will know the great good which they are now losing. The soul, in departing from this life, directly understands that it was created for God; as S. Antoninus teaches, "The mind separated from the body understands God to be the Highest Good, and that it was created for Him." Therefore, directly, the soul rushes forward to go and to embrace its Sovereign Good; but remaining in sin, it will be driven away by God. If a dog sees a hare, and the dog is held by a chain, what strength does he not use to break the chain, and to go and seize his prey? The soul, in being separated from the body, is naturally drawn to God; but sin divides it from God, and sends it far away to hell: "Your iniquities have separated between you and your God." (Isa. lix. 2.)

Hell, therefore, consists entirely in that first word of the condemnation, "Depart from me, ye cursed." Jesus Christ will say to them, "Go, I do not wish you to see My face any more." S. Chrysostom says, "If one conceives of a thousand hells, nothing is expressed that is comparable to being deprived of Christ." When David condemned Absalom never again to appear before him, this punishment was so great to Absalom that he answered, "Now, therefore, let me see the king's face; and if there be any iniquity in me, let him kill me." (2 Sam. xiv. 32.) Philip the Second said to a nobleman whom he observed to be irreverent in Church, "Never again appear before me." The punishment was so great to the nobleman, that he is reported to have died of grief. What will it be when God shall intimate to the sinner at the time of death, Depart, for I never wish to see thee more? "I will hide My face from them, and they shall be devoured, and many evils and troubles shall befall them." (Deut. xxxi. 17.) Jesus Christ will say to the lost in that Last Day, "You are no longer Mine, I am no longer yours." "Call his name Lo-ammi, for ye are not My people, and I will not be your God." (Hosea i. 9.)

What a trouble it is to a son when his father dies, or to a wife when her husband dies, to say, My father, or my husband, I shall never see thee again. Ah, if we could now hear a lost soul weeping, and if we were to ask, Wherefore, soul, dost thou weep so much? this would be the only answer it would make, I weep because I have lost God, and I shall never more behold Him. Were the miserable soul at least able to love its God in hell, and to resign itself to His will—but no, if it could do that, hell would not be hell. The unhappy one is unable to become resigned to the will of God, because he is become an enemy to the Divine will. Neither can he love his God any longer, but he hates Him, and will hate Him for ever; and this will be his hell—to know that God is a Sovereign Good, and to feel obliged to hate God at the same time that he knows God is worthy of infinite love. The lost one will hate and will curse God, and cursing God, he will curse even the benefits which God has bestowed upon him—creation, redemption, the Sacraments, especially that of baptism, repentance, and above all, the most Holy Eucharist. He will hate all the angels and the saints, but especially his own guardian angel; and chiefly will he curse the three Divine Persons; and amongst these three the Son of God particularly, Who one day suffered death for his salvation, cursing His Wounds, His Blood, His Pains, and His Death.

Affections and Prayers.

Ah my God, Thou art therefore my Highest Good, my Infinite Good; and have I so often lost Thee voluntarily? I know that by sinning, I gave Thee great displeasure, and that I was losing Thy grace; and yet have I done it? Ah, but if I did not behold Thee, O Son of God, nailed to the Cross dying for me, I should no longer have courage to ask Thee and to hope for pardon from Thee. Eternal Father, look not upon me, but look upon that Beloved Son Who begs mercy from Thee for me; hear Him, and pardon me. I ought now to be in hell, and for so many past years, without any hope of being able to love Thee again, and of regaining Thy lost favour. My God, I repent beyond every other evil for the offence which I have committed against Thee, of renouncing Thy friendship and despising Thy love, for the miserable pleasures of this world. Oh, would that I had rather died a thousand times over! How could I be so blind and so mad? I thank Thee, my Lord, that Thou dost give me time to amend my evil doings. Since it is through Thy mercy that I am not in hell, and through Thy mercy that I am able to love Thee, my God, I do wish to love Thee. I do not wish any longer to defer being converted entirely to Thee. I love Thee, Thou Infinite Goodness, I love Thee, Who art my Life, my Treasure, my Love, my All.

Ever remind me, O Lord, of the love which Thou hast borne for me, and of the hell where I ought now to be; so that this thought may ever kindle a desire in me, to perform acts of love to Thee, and ever to tell Thee that I love Thee.

CONSIDERATION XXVII

The Eternity of Hell

"And these shall go away into everlasting punishment." S. Matt. xxv. 46.

FIRST POINT.

IF hell were not eternal it would not be hell; for that pain which does not last long, is not very great. One sick person has an abscess lanced, and another has a gangrene cauterised; the pain is great, but in a little while after the operation is completed, the pain is not very great. But what would the pain be if that cutting and that cauterising lasted for a week, or for an entire month? When a pain lasts for a long time, even should it be a very light one, such as the eye-ache or a swelling, it becomes unbearable. But why do I speak of pain? For a comedy or a concert that lasted over long, even for a day, would not be borne for weariness; how would it be if it lasted for a month or for a year? What then will hell be? in which it is not the hearing of the same comedy or music, or the suffering the eye-ache, or the swelling; nor is it suffering the torture of the lancing alone, or of the red-hot iron, but there will be all torments, all pains—and for how long? Through all eternity, "Shall be tormented day and night, for ever and ever." (Rev. xx. 10.) The belief in this eternity, is an article of faith; it is not only a certain opinion, but is a truth witnessed to us by God in many places of Holy Scripture: "Depart from me, ye cursed, into everlasting fire." (S. Matt. xxv. 41.) "And these shall go away into everlasting punishment." (S. Matt. xxv. 45.) "Who shall be punished with everlasting destruction." (2 Thess. i. 9.) "Every one shall be salted with fire." (S. Mark ix. 48.) As salt preserves things, so the fire of hell, in the very time in which it torments the lost, performs the office of salt, preserving life to them. S. Bernard says, "There the fire consumes, that it may always, preserve."

Now, what madness would it be of any one, who, to obtain one day of pleasure should condemn himself to be shut up in a pit some twenty or thirty years. If hell were to last a hundred years; why do I say a hundred?—if it should not last more than two or three years, still it would be great madness for a moment of vile pleasure to condemn oneself to two or three years of burning. But it does not treat of thirty, of a hundred, of a thousand, or of a million years, but of eternity; it is a question of suffering for ever, the same torments, which will never end, never be lightened even for a moment. The saints, therefore, had reason, whilst they were in this life, and even in danger of being condemned, to weep and to tremble. The blessed Isaiah although living in the desert in fasting and penitence, wept, saying, "Alas, unhappy me, for I am not yet delivered from the fire of hell."

Affections and Prayers.

O my God, hadst Thou sent me to hell, as truly many times I have deserved to be sent, and Thou through Thy pity hadst afterwards delivered me from it, how greatly would I have remained indebted to Thee? and from thenceforth what a holy life I should have begun to live? Now that with still greater mercy Thou hast preserved me from falling into it, what shall I do? Shall I turn again and offend and provoke Thee to scorn, in order that Thou mayest properly send me to burn in that prison of Thy rebels, where so many indeed truly burn for less sins than mine? Oh, my Redeemer, so have I acted in time past; instead of serving Thee in the time which Thou hast given me to weep over my sins, I have spent it in still further provoking Thee to anger. I thank Thy infinite goodness that has borne with me so long; if it had not been infinite, how could it ever have so borne with me? I thank Thee for having with so great patience waited for me till now, and I thank Thee especially for the light which Thou now givest me, by which Thou teachest me to know my madness, and the wrong that I have done in insulting Thee by my many sins. My Jesus, I detest them, and I repent with my whole heart; pardon me by Thy Passion, and so assist me by Thy grace, that I may never offend Thee more. Justly now I ought to fear, that after another deadly sin Thou wilt abandon me. Oh, my Lord, I pray Thee, place before my eyes this just fear whenever the devil may tempt me to offend Thee again. My God, I love Thee, never will I lose Thee any more. Assist me by Thy grace, so that I may never more lose Thee.

Second Point.

He who once enters hell shall never leave it for all eternity. This thought made David tremble, and say, "Neither let the deep swallow me up, and let not the pit shut her mouth upon me." (Ps. lxix. 15.) When the lost one has fallen into that pit of torment, the pit closes its mouth and opens it no more. In hell there is a door of entrance, but no door of exit; so Eusebius Emissenus says "there will be a descent, but no ascent," and he explains the Psalmist's words, "let not the pit shut her mouth upon me," (Ps. lxix. 15), as implying, that the pit, when it has received the wicked, is closed above and opened below. As long as the sinner lives, he can ever hold to the hope of a remedy; but if he shall be caught by death whilst in sin, all hope for him will be ended. "When a wicked man dieth, his expectation shall perish." (Prov. xi. 7.) The lost, at least might be able to flatter themselves with this false hope, and so find some alleviation for their despair. That poor wounded one, confined to his bed, whom the physicians have despaired of being able to cure, yet flatters and consoles himself by saying, "Who knows, but that I may yet find some physician or some remedy to cure me?" That wretched one, condemned to the galleys for life, even comforts himself by saying, "Who knows, whether I shall succeed and free myself from these chains?" At least, I say, the lost might be able to say similarly, "Who knows, whether one day I shall leave this prison?" and so might be able to deceive themselves with this false hope. No. In hell there will be no hope, either true or false; no "*Who knows?*" "I will set before thee the things that thou hast done." (Ps. l. 21.) The lost one will ever see his condemnation written before his eyes, that he must ever remain and weep in that pit of punishment. "Some to everlasting life, and some to shame and everlasting contempt." (Dan. xii. 2.) Whence the lost not only suffer what they endure every moment, but they suffer in every moment the pain of eternity, saying, "That which I now suffer I have to suffer for ever;" as Tertullian says, "They bear the burden of eternity." Let us pray, then, to the Lord S. Augustine's prayer, "Here, burn Thou; here, cut Thou; here, spare not, that Thou mayest spare in eternity." The punishments of this life pass away. "Thine arrows went abroad." (Ps. lxxvii. 17.) But the chastisements of the other life never pass away. Let us fear these; let us fear that thunder, "the voice of Thy thunder," (Ps. lxxvii. 18); the thunder of eternal condemnation which will come forth from the mouth of the Judge in His judgment against the reprobate, "Depart from Me, ye cursed, into everlasting fire." (S. Matt. xxv. 41.) "I, the Lord, have drawn forth My sword out of his sheath: it shall not return any more." (Ezek. xxi. 5.) The punishment in hell will be great; but that which ought to terrify us the more, is, that it will be irrevocable.

But how, the hapless one will say, what justice is this? to punish a sin which lasts for a moment with an eternal punishment? But how, I reply, can a sinner dare, for a momentary pleasure, to offend a God of infinite majesty? Even according to human justice, says S. Thomas Aquinas, the punishment is not measured according to the duration of the sin, but according to its nature. "It is not because murder is committed in a moment that it is punished with a momentary punishment." For one deadly sin, one hell is little; but one offence against infinite majesty demands an infinite punishment. S. Bernardine of Sienna observes, "In every deadly sin, infinite injury is inflicted upon God, which demands, therefore, an infinite punishment." But as, perhaps, the creature is not capable of infinite punishment as to intensity, suggests S. Thomas, so God justly makes it infinite, as to extension.

Moreover, this punishment must be necessarily eternal; first, since the condemned cannot make any further satisfaction for their guilt. In this life the penitent sinner is able to make so much satisfaction, as the merits of Jesus Christ are applied to him. But the lost one is shut out from these merits, so that he cannot any more appease God; and as his sin is eternal, so also is his punishment. "It cost more to redeem their souls; so that he must let that alone for ever." (Ps. xlix. 8.) Hence, says Belluacensis, "Sin will be ever punished there, and never expiated;" as S. Augustine observes, "There, the sinner is not able to repent;" therefore the Lord will ever remain angry with him. "The people against whom the Lord hath indignation for ever." (Mal. i. 4.) Moreover, the condemned, even should God wish to pardon them, cannot be pardoned, for their will will be stubborn and confirmed in its hatred against God. Innocent III. said, "The reprobate will not be humbled, but in them the malignity of hatred will increase.". S. Jerome writes of the lost, "They are insatiable in the desire of sinning." Whence the wound of the condemned is desperate, since it refuses even to be healed. "Why is my pain perpetual, and my wound incurable, which refuseth to be healed?" (Jer. xv. 18.)

Affections and Prayers.

So, my Redeemer, if I were now condemned as I have deserved to be, I should be obstinate in my hatred of Thee, my God, Who hast died for me. O God! and what a hell it would be to hate Thee, Who hast so greatly loved me, and Who art Infinite Perfection, Infinite Goodness, worthy of infinite love? So, were I now in hell, should I not be in that unhappy state in which I should no longer desire the pardon which Thou offerest to me? My Jesus, I thank Thee for the pity which Thou hast had towards me; and since now I am able to obtain pardon and to love Thee, I desire to be pardoned and to love Thee. Thou offerest me pardon, and I ask it of Thee, and I hope for it through Thy merits. I repent of all the offences which I have committed against Thee, O Infinite Goodness, and do Thou pardon me. I love Thee with all my heart. Ah, Lord, and what evil hast Thou done me that I should hate Thee as my enemy for ever? What friend have I had ever, who has both done and suffered for me as Thou hast, O my Jesus? Ah, suffer me not to fall again under Thy displeasure, and to lose Thy love; grant that I may rather die than this utter ruin should befall me. O shelter me under the mantle of Thy protection, and do not suffer me again to rebel against Thee.

THIRD POINT.

Death is the thing which is most feared by sinners whilst they are in this life; but when they are in hell, it will be the thing which is most desired. "In those days shall men seek death, and shall not find it; and shall desire to die, and death shall flee from them." (Rev. ix. 6.) When, as S. Jerome wrote, "O death, how sweet thou wouldst be to those to whom thou hast been so bitter." David says of the condemned, "Death gnaweth upon them." (Ps. xlix. 14.) S. Bernard explains, that as the sheep feeding upon the grass consume the blades and leave the roots; so death feeding upon the lost, kills them every moment, but leaves them life, that it may continue to kill them with pain for ever. S. Gregory says, that the condemned "delivered up to the avenging flames, will ever die." If one dies, killed by grief, every one pities him; the condemned one will have at least some one to pity him. No, the wretched one dies through grief every moment; but he neither has, nor will have, any one to compassionate him. Zeno the Emperor, confined in a dungeon, cried out, "Unclose to me for compassion's sake." No one was mindful of him, whence he was found dead, having despaired, since he had eaten the very flesh itself of his arms. S. Cyril of Alexandria says that the lost "lament, and no one rescues them; they weep, and no one compassionates them."

And this their misery, how long will it last? For ever and ever. Poor Judas! truly eighteen hundred years have passed since he has been in hell, and his hell is even now at its beginning. Poor Cain! he has been in the flames for five thousand eight hundred years, and his hell is only at its beginning. If a devil could be asked how long he has been in hell, he would answer, "Yesterday!" and if it was answered, "Hast thou not been condemned more than five thousand years?" he would reply, "Oh, if thou knewest what it is to say eternity, thou wouldst understand perfectly, that by comparison, five thousand years are but as a moment." If an angel were to say to one of the lost, "Thou shalt leave hell, but not until as many ages have passed away as there are drops of water, leaves on the trees, and grains of sand on the sea-shore," he would rejoice more than a beggar would on hearing the news that he was made rich. Yes! since all these ages will pass away, should they be multiplied an infinite number of times, and hell will be ever at its beginning. Every lost one would gladly make this compact with God, "Lord, increase my pain as much as Thou wilt; cause it to last as long as Thou pleasest: put a limit to it, and I am content." But no, for this limit will never be; the trumpet of Divine justice will sound out in hell nothing but "for ever, for ever;" "never, never."

The lost will ask of the devils, "Watchman, what of the night?" (Isa. xxi. 11.) When does it end? and when will these trumpets, these cries, this stench, these flames, these torments finish? Then it will be answered to them, "Never!" "never!" How long will they last? "For ever;" "for ever." Ah, Lord, give light to the many blind who, when urged not to lose themselves, reply, "If at last I go to hell, patience." O God, they have not patience to bear a little cold; to remain in an over-heated room; to endure a blow; and hereafter, will they have patience to abide in a sea of fire, to be trampled upon by devils, and to be abandoned by God and by all, for eternity?

Affections and Prayers.

Ah! Father of mercies, Thou dost not abandon those who seek Thee. "Thou, Lord, hast never failed them that seek Thee." (Ps. ix. 11.) I, in the past time, have often turned away from Thee, and Thou hast not abandoned me; do not abandon me, now that I seek Thee. I repent, O Highest Good, of having so lightly esteemed Thy grace, that I have bartered it away for a mere nothing. Behold the wounds of

Thy Son; hear their cry; they beseech Thee to pardon me: do Thou pardon me. And Thou, my Redeemer, bring ever to my remembrance, the pains which Thou hast suffered on my behalf; the love that Thou hast borne me; and my ingratitude, through which so many times I have deserved hell; that so I may ever bewail the insults I have offered Thee, and may ever burn with Thy love.

Ah! my Jesus, how shall I not burn with Thy love, when I think that for so many years I ought to be burning in hell, and then to burn for all eternity; and that Thou hast died to liberate me, and with so great compassion hast delivered me? Were I in hell, I should now hate Thee, and be compelled to hate Thee for ever; but now I love Thee, and I desire to love Thee for ever. This I hope for, through Thy Blood. Thou lovest me, and I also love Thee; and Thou wilt ever love me if I leave Thee not. Ah, my Saviour, save me from the disgrace of leaving Thee, and then do with me as Thou wilt. I deserve every chastisement, and I accept it, that Thou mayest deliver me from the chastisement of being deprived of Thy love. O Jesus, my Refuge, how often have I condemned myself to hell, and Thou hast delivered me. Ah, deliver me from sin, which alone can deprive me of the grace of God, and carry me downwards to hell.

CONSIDERATION XXVIII

The Remorse of the Lost

"Where their worm dieth not." S. Mark ix. 46.

First Point.

BY the worm that does not die, S. Thomas Aquinas thinks, is signified, that remorse of conscience by which the lost will be eternally tormented in hell. The remorse will be manifold, with which conscience will gnaw the heart of the reprobate; but three forms of it will be the most afflicting—first the thought of the little for which they are lost, then the little that was required for their salvation, and lastly the great good which they have lost.

The first sting, then, which the lost one will have, will be the thought, for how little he is lost. After Esau had eaten of that pottage of lentils, for which he had sold his birthright, Holy Scripture says, that, through grief and remorse, "He cried with a great and exceeding bitter cry." (Gen. xxvii. 34.) Oh, how the lost will howl and roar when he thinks that for a few momentary and hurtful gratifications he has lost an eternal kingdom of joy, and has to see himself eternally condemned to a perpetual death. Whence he will weep much more bitterly than Jonathan did when he found himself condemned to death by Saul, his own father, for having eaten a little honey, "I did but taste a little honey, ... and lo, I must die. (1 Sam. xiv. 43.)

Oh, God, what a punishment will it be for the condemned to

bear, to see men the cause of their own condemnation? At the present, what does our past life seem to us but a dream, a moment? Now, what will appear to those in hell the fifty or sixty years of the life which they have lived on this earth, when they find themselves in the abyss of eternity, in which a hundred or a thousand millions of years having passed—it will be seen that their eternity then begins? But why do I say fifty years of life, all, perhaps, passed in pleasure? And does the sinner by chance, who lives without God, ever delight in his sins? How long do the pleasures of sin last? They endure but moments, and all the rest of the time in which the sinner lives out of the grace of God, is a time of pains and torments. Now, what indeed will these moments of pleasure appear to the poor condemned one, and what in particular that last moment and last sin, through which he was lost? Then he will say, 'for a wretched animal pleasure that endured but for a moment, and which, as soon as possessed, disappeared as the wind, I shall have to continue to burn in this flame despised and abandoned by all, whilst God shall be God for all eternity.

Affections and Prayers.

Lord, enlighten me, that I may know the wrong which I have committed in offending Thee and the eternal punishment which I have deserved on this account. My God, I feel great sorrow for having offended Thee, but this sorrow consoles me: If Thou hadst sent me to hell as I deserved, this remorse would have been the hell of my hell, the thinking for how little I had condemned myself; but now this remorse consoles me, since it gives me the courage to hope for pardon from Thee, Thou Who hast promised to pardon those who repent. Yes, my Lord, I repent of having outraged Thee. I embrace this sweet grief, I even pray Thee to increase it, and to preserve it in me till death, that so I may ever weep bitterly over the displeasure that I have caused Thee. My Jesus, pardon me. O my Redeemer, Who, though having pity upon me, hadst no pity for Thyself, condemning Thyself to die of grief to liberate me from hell, have pity upon me. Grant, then, that the remorse of having offended Thee may keep me ever sorrowful, and at the same time may inflame me wholly with love of Thee, Who has so greatly loved me, and Who hast with so much patience borne with me, and Who now, instead of chastising me, encirclest me with light and grace. I thank Thee for these, O my Jesus. I love Thee: I love Thee more than myself, I love Thee with my whole heart. Thou knowest not how to despise one who loves Thee. I love Thee. "Cast me not away from Thy presence." Receive me, then, into Thy grace, and suffer me not again to lose Thee. O my Jesus, accept me as Thy servant and bind me to Thyself; pardon me, give me Thy love and the grace of perseverance until death.

SECOND POINT.

S. Thomas Aquinas says that the lost "will chiefly grieve that they have been condemned for nothing, and yet most easily they could have obtained eternal life." *The second remorse* of conscience will be the thought, of how little was required to obtain salvation. The greatest torment in hell to the lost soul will be the thought, for what trifles it has lost itself, and how little there was to do that it might have been saved. Then will the soul say: "Had I mortified myself by not looking at that object; had I conquered that undue deference to human opinion; had I fled from that temptation, that companion, that assembly, I should not have been condemned. If I had confessed every week, been diligent in the discharge of my religious duties, and read daily such a spiritual book; had I commended myself to Jesus Christ, I should not have become a lapsed one. Very often I resolved to do all this, but I did not carry out my resolution, or, at least, I began to do so, and I failed; and so I am lost."

The examples which he will have had of other holy friends and companions will increase his remorse, and the good gifts which God has granted to him for salvation will increase it still further; the gifts of nature likewise, of good health, of fortune, of ability, which the Lord had given to employ well, and to make him holy; gifts, moreover, of grace, so great lights, inspirations, calls, and so many years granted to remedy the sin; but he will see that, in that miserable state at which he has now arrived, there is no more time for remedy. He will hear the angel of the Lord "stand upon the sea, and sware by Him that liveth for ever . . . . that there should be time no longer." (Rev. x. 5, 6.) Oh, what cruel daggers will be all these graces which have been received in the heart of the poor condemned one, who will then see that the time for repairing his eternal ruin is past. The soul will say then, weeping with its other desperate companions, "The harvest is past, the summer is ended, and we are not saved." (Jer. viii. 20.) He will cry, "Oh! if the labours which I have borne for my condemnation I had spent for God, I should have become a great saint; and now, what remains for me but remorse and pains, which will torment me for ever?" Ah, this thought will torment the condemned more than the fire and the other torments of hell—I might have been for ever happy, and now I must be for ever miserable.

Affections and Prayers.

Oh, my Jesus, and how is it that Thou hast been able to bear with me so long? I have so often turned away from Thee, and Thou hast not ceased to come nigh me. I have often offended Thee, and Thou hast turned again and pardoned me. Alas! give me a portion of the grief which Thou didst feel in the Garden of Gethsemane for my sins, which then made Thee to sweat blood. I repent, my dear Redeemer, of having so evilly repaid Thy love. O my cursed pleasures, I detest and loathe you; ye made me forfeit the grace of my Lord. My beloved Jesus, now I love Thee above all things, and I renounce all unlawful gratifications; I purpose rather to die a thousand deaths than to offend Thee more. Ah, by that affection with which Thou hast loved me on the Cross, and hast offered Thy Divine life for me, give me light and strength to resist temptations, and to have recourse to Thy aid when I am tempted. O Lord, grant me holy perseverance, and the grace never to separate myself again from Thy holy love.

Third Point.

The third remorse of the condemned will be to see the great good which they have lost. S. Chrysostom says "they will be tormented more by heaven than by hell;" for that which will afflict them chiefly in all eternity, will be to see that they have lost heaven and the Highest Good, that is God; not indeed through any evil providence, or by the evil designs of others, but by their own fault. The soul will see that it was created for heaven; that God had given to it the choice of procuring either life or death. "Before man is life and death, and whether him liketh shall be given him." (Ecclus. xv. 17.) So it will see that it was in its hand, if it willed, to render itself eternally happy; and it will see that of itself it has chosen to cast itself into that gulf of torment, from which it will never be able to escape, nor will any one else be able to procure its freedom. It will see, amongst the saved, so many of its companions who were placed in the same, or perhaps in greater danger from sin, but who had the knowledge to restrain themselves, or to commend themselves to God; or, albeit if ever they fell, since they had the wisdom to arise and give themselves to God, they were saved. But this lost one, since he willed not to put an end to sin, has come unhappily to his end in hell, in that sea of torments, without the hope of being able to better himself further.

My brother, if in past time you even have been so foolish as to have willed to lose heaven and God for some wretched pleasure, procure a remedy now that there is time. Do not choose to continue to be so foolish. Tremble lest you should have to weep over your disgrace in eternity. Who knows whether this consideration which you are now reading may be the last call that God will give you. Who knows but that if now you do not change your life, at that other deadly sin which you may commit, the Lord will abandon you, and for this afterwards send you to suffer eternally amidst that crew of foolish ones who are now in hell, and are confessing their error. "Therefore we have erred;" but they confess it, being desperate, seeing that there is no longer any remedy for their error. When the devil tempts you to sin anew, think of hell, and have recourse to God; the thought of hell will deliver you from hell. "Remember the end, and thou shalt never do amiss." (Ecclus. vii. 36.) For the thought of hell will make you fly to God.

Affections and Prayers.

Ah, my Highest Good! how often have I lost Thee for nought, and have deserved to lose Thee for ever! But it comforts me to think of that which the Psalmist says, "Let the heart of them rejoice that seek the Lord." (Ps. cv. 3.) I ought not, therefore, to despair of recovering Thee, my God, if I seek Thee with the heart. Yes, my Saviour, I now yearn after Thy grace more than for any other good. I am content to be deprived of all things, even of life, rather than to be deprived of Thy love. I love Thee, my Creator, above all things; and because I love Thee, I repent of having offended Thee. My God, do Thou quickly pardon me who am lost and despairing; and grant that I may find Thee, for I desire to never lose Thee again. If Thou receivest me again to Thy friendship, I desire to lose all things, and to give up myself to Thy love alone; and this I hope for, from Thy compassion. Eternal Father, hear me, for the love of Jesus Christ. Pardon me, and give me grace never to separate myself from Thee again; for if I willingly lose Thee again, I ought to tremble justly, lest Thou abandon me. O Jesus! O peace-maker of sinners! grant me to have peace with God, and then hold me fast under Thy mantle, so that I may never again lose Thee.

CONSIDERATION XXIX

Of Heaven

"Your sorrow shall be turned into joy." S. John xvi. 20.

First Point.

LET us now endeavour to endure patiently the afflictions of this life, offering them to God in union with the pains which Jesus Christ endured for our sakes, and let us encourage ourselves with the hope of paradise. All these afflictions, sorrows, persecutions, and fears, will one day come to an end; and when we are saved they will become joys and pleasures for us in the kingdom of the blessed. Even thus does the Lord encourage us, "Your sorrow shall be turned into joy." Let us, therefore, reflect to-day somewhat upon paradise. But what can we say of this paradise, if the saints who had more knowledge than we, were unable to make us understand the joys which God has in store for His faithful servants, and David could only express his praise of it by saying, that paradise is a rest which is very desirable, "Oh, how amiable are Thy dwellings, Thou Lord of Hosts." (Ps. lxxxiv. 1.) But thou, at least, my holy Paul, thou who hadst the happy chance of being ravished at the sight of heaven, "caught up into paradise," tell us something of what thou hast seen. No, says the Apostle, it is not possible to explain what I have seen. The delights of paradise are "unspeakable words, which it is not lawful for a man to utter." (2 Cor. xii. 4.) They are so great that they cannot be described unless they are enjoyed. I can tell you nothing more, says the Apostle, than that "eye hath not seen, nor ear heard, neither have entered into the heart of man the things which God hath prepared for them that love Him." (1 Cor. ii. 9.) No man on earth has ever seen, or heard, or understood, the joys, the harmonies, the pleasures which God has prepared for those who love Him.

We are unable to understand the joys of paradise, because we have no conception but of the joys of this earth. If horses were capable of reasoning, and they knew that their master had prepared a grand banquet, they would imagine that it could consist of nothing else but of good hay, oats, and barley, because horses have no notion of food except such as this. Even thus do we form notions of the joys of paradise. It is beautiful to see, on a summer's night, the sky all glittering with stars; and how delightful, in the time of spring, to stand on the sea-coast when the sea is calm, so that the rocks within can be seen all covered with seaweed, and the fishes which glide nimbly by; and it is very delightful to be in a garden full of fruit trees and flowers, surrounded by running fountains, and with birds which fly about and sing as they fly. Some might say, "Oh, what a paradise!" What a paradise? Do you say, What a paradise? Very different are the joys of paradise. In order to understand something, although obscurely, of paradise, let us remember that the Omnipotent God is there, Who is ever engaged in delighting the souls which love Him. S. Bernard says, Dost thou wish to know what there is in paradise? "There is nothing that thou wouldst not have, but everything that thou wouldst have, there."

O God, what will the soul say upon entering into that blessed kingdom! Let us imagine that some young girl and some youth, who, having consecrated themselves to the love of Jesus Christ, are dying; the hour of death having arrived, the spirit quits this earth. The soul is presented before the judgment-seat, the Judge embraces her, and makes known to her that she is saved. Her guardian angel comes to meet her and rejoices with her; she thanks the angel for the assistance given to her, and the angel then says, "Take courage, beautiful soul, rejoice, for thou art now saved. Come and see the face of thy Lord." Behold, the soul now passes through the clouds, the heavens, and the stars. She enters heaven. O God, what will she say when she enters for the first time that blessed country, and when she looks for the first time upon that city of delights? The angels and the saints will come to meet her, and they will welcome her with shouts of joy. What consolation she will have in meeting again those relations or friends who entered paradise before her. The soul will then wish to kneel before them and to worship them, but they will say to her, "See thou do it not, for I am thy fellow-servant." (Rev. xxii. 9.) Then the soul will be led to Jesus, Who will receive her as His spouse, and will say to her, "Come with Me from Lebanon, My spouse." (Cant. iv. 8.) Rejoice greatly, My spouse, all thy tears, griefs, and fears are now for ever ended, receive the everlasting crown which I have obtained for thee by My Blood. Jesus Himself will then lead her to receive the blessing of His Divine Father, Who, embracing her, will bless her, saying, "Enter thou into the joy of Thy Lord." (S. Matt. xxv. 21.) And He will bless her with the same beatitude which He Himself enjoys.

Affections and Prayers.

Behold, my God, at Thy feet one ungrateful, who was created by Thee for heaven, but who, often for miserable pleasures, has renounced it to Thy face, and has chosen to be condemned to hell. But I hope that even now Thou hast forgiven all the injuries that I have done, of which I repent over and over again, and will continue to repent until death. I desire that Thou ever wouldst renew my pardon. But, O my God, although Thou hast already pardoned me, it will yet be ever true that I had no disposition to embitter Thee, my Redeemer, Who, to bring me to Thy kingdom, hadst given Thy life. But may Thy compassion, O my Jesus, be ever praised and blessed, that with so great patience hast borne with me, and in place of chastisements hast increased toward me graces, lights, and calls. I see, my dear Saviour, that Thou didst will my special salvation, and in Thy country to love Thee eternally, but Thou desirest that first I should love Thee on earth. Yes, I will love Thee, and this, even were there no heaven, while I live, with all my soul and with all my might. It is enough for me to know that Thou, my God, desirest to be loved by me. My Jesus, assist me with Thy grace and do not abandon me. My soul is eternal; therefore, it is certain that for ever either I must love Thee or hate Thee. No, I will love Thee for ever, and I will love Thee much in this life and in the next. Dispose of me as it pleaseth Thee, chasten me here as Thou wilt, but do not deprive me of Thy love, and afterwards do with me as it may please Thee. My Jesus, Thy merits are my hope. I place all my trust in Thy intercession. Thou didst deliver me from hell when I was in sin; now that I desire Thee, do Thou save me and make me holy.

SECOND POINT.

When the soul shall have entered into the beatitude of God, "There shall in no wise enter into it anything that defileth." (Rev. xxi. 27.) There will be no more trouble. "God shall wipe away all tears from their eyes; and there shall be no more death, neither sorrow, nor crying, neither shall there be any more pain: for the former things are passed away. And He that sat upon the throne said, Behold, I make all things new." (Rev. xxi. 4, 5.)

In heaven there is no more weakness, nor poverty, nor trouble; no longer any succession of day and night, nor of cold and heat; there, it is perpetual day, ever serene; a continual spring, ever delicious. There will be there no more persecutions, or envyings. All will love tenderly, and each one will rejoice in the good of the other as if it were his own. There are no more fears, since the soul, confirmed in grace, can no longer sin and lose its God. "Behold, I make all things new." All are new, and are consoling and satisfying. "There is everything that one can desire." There, shall the sight be satisfied by gazing at that city. "The perfection of beauty." (Lam. ii. 15.) What delight would it be to behold a city, where the pavement of its streets would be of crystal, the palaces of silver with ceilings of gold, and the whole adorned with festoons of flowers? Oh! how much more beautiful will be the heavenly city! What will it be to behold those citizens clad in royal robes, since all are kings; as S. Augustine said, "As many citizens, so many kings." What will it be then to see the Divine Lamb, the Spouse Jesus! The sense of smell will be satisfied with the odours of heaven; the sense of hearing by celestial harmonies. What will it be to hear all the saints and angels singing in chorus the glories of God! "They will be always praising Thee." (Ps. lxxxiv. 4.) In short, all the delights are there that can possibly be desired.

But these delights now mentioned are the lesser blessings of heaven. The good which makes heaven is the Highest Good, which is God. S. Augustine says that "all which we look for are two syllables, Deus, God." The reward which the Lord promises us does not consist only in the beauties, the harmonies, and the other joys of that blessed City, for the chief reward there is GOD HIMSELF, that is, to see and to love God face to face. "I am . . . . thy exceeding great Reward." (Gen. xv. 1.) S. Augustine says, That if God were to show Himself to the lost, immediately hell itself would be changed into a pleasant paradise; and he continues, That if a departed soul did choose between seeing God and abiding in the punishments of hell, and not seeing God and being liberated from it, "it would rather choose to see God and to be in these pains."

This joy of seeing and loving God face to face cannot be understood by us in this life, but we can infer something of what it is like, knowing that this Divine love is so sweet, that even in this life it has lifted from earth the souls of the saints. The holy martyrs, through its sweetness, were joyous in the midst of their very torments. S. Augustine records, that S. Vincent, whilst he was being tortured, so spake that "it seemed one who suffered, and another who spoke." S. Laurence, whilst on a gridiron, scorned the tyrant, "Turn me and eat me." Yes, says S. Augustine, because S. Laurence, inflamed with this fire of Divine love, did not feel the burning. Moreover, how sweet it proves to a sinner in this life, even the weeping over his sins. Whence S. Bernard says, "If it be so sweet to weep for thee, what must it be to rejoice for thee?" What sweetness then does not the soul experience, to whom in prayer is disclosed by a ray of light, the

Divine goodness, the mercies experienced, and the love which has been and still is shed upon it, by Jesus Christ. And although in this life we see not God as He really is, for we see Him but obscurely. "Now we see through a glass, darkly; but then face to face." (1 Cor. xiii. 12.) At this present time we have a bandage before our eyes, and God is hidden under the veil of faith, and He allows us not to see Him. But what will it be, when the bandage is taken away from the eyes and the veil is raised, and we can see God face to face? Then shall we see how lovely, how glorious, how just, how perfect, how amiable, how loving He is.

Affections and Prayers.

Oh, my Highest Good, I am that miserable one who has turned away from Thee, and has renounced Thy love, so that I am not worthy either to see Thee or to love Thee. But Thou art He, Who through compassion for me, hadst no compassion upon Thyself, but condemnedst Thyself to die of shamed grief upon the accursed tree. Thy death, indeed, gives me hope that one day I shall see and enjoy Thy face, and then I shall love Thee with all my strength. But now that I stand in danger of losing Thee for ever, now that I find that I have already lost Thee through my sins, what shall I do in the life which remains to me? Shall I continue to offend Thee? No, my Jesus, I detest with entire hatred the offences which I have committed. It grieves me in the greatest degree that I have injured Thee, and I love thee with all my heart. Wilt Thou cast away from Thee a soul which repents and loves Thee? No, truly I know what Thou hast said—that Thou knowest not how, my loved Redeemer, to cast away any one who comes as a penitent to Thy feet. "Him that cometh unto Me, I will in no wise cast out." (S. John vi. 37.) My Jesus, I leave all and turn to Thee, and embrace Thee, and unite Thee to my heart. Do Thou embrace me, and unite me to Thy heart. I dare so to speak, since I speak to and treat with Infinite Goodness. I speak to that God who willed to die for my sake. My Beloved Saviour, give me hope in Thy love.

Third Point.

In this life the greatest pain that can afflict the souls who love God, and who are desolate, is the fear that they do not love, and are not loved by God. "No man knoweth either love or hatred by all that is before them." (Eccles. ix. 1.) But in heaven the soul is certain that it loves God, and that it is loved by God, and it sees that it is happily lost in the love of its Lord; and that God holds it in His embrace as if it were a dear child; and it sees that this love will not be dissolved even in eternity. The better knowledge that it will then acquire, will increase the blessed flames of that love which led God to become man, and to die for us, of that love which instituted the Holy Communion, in which God becomes the food of worms. The soul will then see distinctly even all the graces which God has given to it—in liberating it from so great temptations, and the dangers of being lost; and then it will see that those tribulations, weaknesses, persecutions, and losses, which it called the punishments and chastenings of God, were all of love, and that they came by Divine providence to conduct it to heaven. It will see particularly the patience that God had in bearing with so great sins, and the long-sufferings that He has exercised in giving it so many lights and so many calls of love. It will see there, from that blessed mountain, so many souls condemned to hell for less sins than its own; and it will see itself saved, in possession of God, and secure of never losing that Highest Good for all eternity.

For ever then will that blessed soul, enjoy that happiness which, through all eternity, at every moment will be for ever new, as if that moment was the first in which it enjoyed it. It will ever enjoy that happiness and will ever obtain it; ever thirsting and ever satisfied; ever satisfied and ever thirsting. Yes, since the desire of heaven brings no pain, and the fulfilment of it brings no weariness. In short, as the lost are vessels of wrath, so the blessed are vessels of joy. S. Teresa says that, even in this world, when God brings a soul into "the banqueting house," where it partakes of this Divine love, He renders it so happily inebriated, that it loses the affection for all earthly things. But in entering heaven, as David says, how much more perfectly shall it "drink of Thy pleasures as out of the river." (Ps. xxxvi. 8.) It will happen then, that the soul, beholding so openly, and embracing the highest good, will remain so inebriated with love, that delightfully it will lose itself in God; that is, will perfectly forget itself, and will not think of anything else from that moment than to love, praise, and bless that Infinite Good which it possesses.

When, therefore, the crosses of this life afflict us, let us comfort ourselves, and bear them patiently with the hope of heaven. S. Mary of Egypt being asked at the end of her life how she had been able to endure living so many years in that desert, answered, "In the hope of heaven." Let us also, when we find ourselves straightened by the miseries of this present life, raise our eyes to heaven, and console ourselves by sighing and saying, "Heaven, heaven." Let us consider that if we are faithful to God, shall end one day, all these pains, miseries, and fears, and we shall be received into that blessed country, where we shall be fully happy, whilst God shall be God. Behold, the saints are expecting us; and Jesus stands with a crown in His hand to make us kings of that eternal kingdom.

Affections and Prayers.

My beloved Saviour, Thou hast taught me to pray, "Thy kingdom come." Thus now do I pray to Thee, may Thy kingdom come in my soul, that Thou mayest wholly possess it, and that it may possess Thee, the Highest Good. O my Jesus, Thou hast spared nothing to save me, and to gain my love; save me, therefore, and may it be my salvation to love Thee for ever in this life and in the next. I have so often turned away from Thee, and with all this Thou causest me to know that Thou wilt not disdain to embrace me in heaven through all eternity with as great love as if I had never caused Thee offence. And knowing this, shall I be able to love any other save Thee, seeing that Thou desirest to give me heaven, after I have so often deserved hell? Ah, my Lord! that I had never offended Thee! Oh, if I could be reborn, I would ever love

Thee! But what is done is done. Now, I can do no more than give to Thee that portion of life which remains to me. Yes, I give it all to Thee; I consecrate it all to Thy love. Depart from my heart, ye worldly affections; give place to my God, Who desires to possess it wholly. Yes, possess me altogether, O my Redeemer, my Love, my God. From this day forward I would only think how I can please Thee. Aid me with Thy grace; this I hope for through Thy merits. More and more increase in me Thy love, and the desire to please Thee. Heaven, heaven! When will it be, O Lord, that I shall see Thee face to face, and shall embrace Thee, without the fear of ever having to lose Thee. Ah, my God, hold Thy hand over me, so that I shall no more offend Thee. Help me, O my Jesus! suffer me not to lose myself, and to stand afar off from Thee.

CONSIDERATION XXX

Of Prayer

"Ask, and it shall be given you; . . . . for every one that asketh receiveth."
S. Luke xi. 9, 10.

FIRST POINT.

NOT only in this, but in many other places in the Old and New Testaments, God promises to hear those who pray to Him. "Then call thou, and I will answer." (Job xiii. 22.) "He shall call upon Me, and I will answer him." (Ps. xci. 15.) Call upon Me, and I will deliver thee from danger. "If ye shall ask anything in My Name, I will do it." (S. John xiv. 14.) Whatsoever shall be asked through My merits I will grant. "Ye shall ask what ye will, and it shall be done unto you." (S. John xv. 7.) Seek what you will, it is enough that you seek, and it shall be granted to you. And so in many other passages. Therefore Theodoret says, that "Prayer, although it is one thing, can obtain all things." S. Bernard says, that when we pray He "will give us either what we desire, or what He knows to be more profitable for us." Therefore, the prophet encourages us to pray, assuring us that God is all compassion towards those who call upon Him for help. "For Thou, Lord, art good and gracious, and of great mercy unto all them that call upon Thee." (Ps. lxxxvi. 5.) And still more does S. James encourage us, by saying, "If any of you lack wisdom, let him ask of God, Who giveth to all men liberally, and upbraideth not." (S. James i. 5.) This same

Apostle says, that when the Lord is supplicated, He opens His hand and gives us more than we ask of Him. "Who giveth to all men liberally, and upbraideth not." Neither does He reprove us for the displeasure we have caused Him; for when we pray to Him, He seems to forget all the offences we have committed against Him.

S. John Climacus says, that prayer in a certain way forces God to grant us what we seek. "Prayer is a holy violence done to God." But it is a violence which is dear to Him, and desired by Him of us. "This violence is pleasing to God," as Tertullian wrote. Yes, because, as S. Augustine remarks, God "desires more to bestow His benefits than we desire to receive them." And the reason of this is, that God of His own nature is infinite goodness, as writes S. Leo; and therefore He desires most ardently to impart to us His blessings. Thence it is that S. Mary Magdalene of Pazzi says, that God is almost under an obligation to that soul which prays to Him, since in this manner the way is open to Him to gratify the desire which He has of bestowing His favours upon us. And David says that this kindness of the Lord, in listening directly to those who pray to Him, proved to him that He was his true God. "Whensoever I call upon Thee, then shall my enemies be put to flight: this I know; for God is on my side." (Ps. lvi. 9.) Some people unjustly complain, observes S. Bernard, that the Lord is failing them; much more justly might the Lord complain that many are failing Him, ceasing to come and seek His grace. "And it seems to have been exactly of this that the Redeemer one day complained to His disciples, "Hitherto have ye asked nothing in My Name; ask, and ye shall receive." (S. John xvi. 24.) Do not complain of Me, He seems to have said, if you have not been fully happy, complain of yourselves for not having asked Me for My favours; from henceforth ask Me for them and you shall be satisfied.

From this the monks of old concluded, in their conferences, that there was no exercise more profitable to the salvation of their souls than evér to be praying, and saying, "Lord, help me." The venerable Father Paul Segneri said of himself, that in his meditations he at first cultivated emotion; but afterwards, knowing the great efficacy of prayer, he tried as much as he could, to occupy himself in prayer. May we ever do the same. We have a God Who loves us so much, and Who is so anxious for our salvation, and Who is for this reason ever ready to hear those who pray to Him. The princes of the world, says S. Chrysostom, give audience to few; but God is pleased to grant audience to every one who desires it.

Affections and Prayers.

Eternal God, I adore Thee, and thank Thee for the many benefits which Thou has granted to me; for having created and redeemed me through Jesus Christ; for having made me a Christian; for having waited for me when I remained in sin; and for having so often forgiven me. Ah, my God, I should never have offended Thee, if in the time of temptation I had prayed to Thee for help. I thank Thee for the light by which Thou makest me now to understand, that my salvation depends entirely upon my praying to Thee, and upon my asking for Thy help. Behold, I now ask of Thee, in the Name of Jesus Christ, to make me very sorry for my sins; to give me strength to persevere in Thy grace; to give me a peaceful death, and afterwards to make me a partaker of Paradise; but, above all, I entreat Thee for the highest gift of Thy love, and for a most complete submission to Thy most holy will. I know, indeed, that I am unworthy of these Thy mercies, but Thou hast promised them to those who seek them through the merits of Jesus Christ, and through the merits of Jesus Christ I entreat and I hope for these Thy mercies.

Second Point.

Let us consider, moreover, the necessity of prayer. S. Chrysostom says, that, as the body is dead without the soul, even so is the soul dead, without prayer. He says likewise, that as water is necessary to plants to prevent them from being dried up, even so is prayer necessary to prevent us from being lost. "We need prayer not less than the trees do water." God desires that we should all be saved. "Who will have all men to be saved." (1 S. Tim. ii. 4.) He does not will that any should be lost. "The Lord is not slack concerning His promise, as some men count slackness; but is longsuffering to us-ward, not willing that any should perish, but that all should come to repentance." (2 S. Peter iii. 9.) But He wishes us to ask Him for the grace which is necessary for our salvation, seeing that, on the one hand, we are not able to keep the Divine commands, and to save ourselves, without the actual help of the Lord; and, on the other hand, He will not, ordinarily speaking, give us His grace unless we ask for it. Therefore the Fathers of old said, that God does not impose impossible precepts upon us, seeing that He either gives us relative and efficient grace to observe them, or else He gives us the grace to ask Him for that efficient grace. S. Augustine teaches, that, excepting the primary graces, such as the call to faith or to repentance, the other graces, and especially the grace of final perseverance, God does not grant, except to those who pray for them. "It holds good, that some things God grants without prayer, as the beginning of faith; whilst others have been prepared only for those who pray, such as final perseverance."

From this, theologians conclude, with S. Basil, S. Augustine, S. Chrysostom, S. Clement of Alexandria, and others, that prayer is absolutely necessary as a means for adults; therefore, without prayer it is impossible for any one to be saved. And this, says the most learned Lessius, ought to be held as an article of faith, "That prayer is necessary for the salvation of adults, as is gathered from the Scriptures."

Holy Scripture is plain upon this subject: "Men ought always to pray." (S. Luke xviii. 1.) "Pray that ye enter not into temptation." (S. Luke xxii. 40.) "Ask, and ye shall receive." (S. John xvi. 24.) "Pray without ceasing." (1 Thess. v. 17.) Now these words, "men ought," "to pray," "ask," according to the general opinion of divines, with that of S. Thomas also, imply a precept which is binding under pain of grievous sin, particularly in three cases: 1. When a man is living in a state of sin; 2. When he is in danger of death; and 3. When he is in great danger of sinning. And divines then generally teach, that he who has not prayed for one month, or two months at the most, cannot be excused from having committed mortal sin. The reason is, because prayer is a means without which we are not able to obtain that assistance which is necessary for our salvation.

"Ask, and ye shall receive." He who seeks obtains, therefore, as S. Teresa says, he who does not seek, does not obtain. And before her, S. James had said, "Ye have not, because ye ask not." (S. James iv. 3.) And especially is prayer necessary to obtain the virtue of continence. "Nevertheless when I perceived that I could not otherwise obtain her except God gave her me. . . . . I prayed unto the Lord and besought Him." (Wisd. viii. 21.) Let us conclude this point. He who prays will certainly be saved, and he who does not pray will certainly be condemned. All those who are saved, were saved by prayer, and all those who are lost were lost through not having prayed; and the knowing that they might so easily have saved themselves by prayer, and that now there is no more time in which to pray, is, and always will be, the great cause of their despair in hell.

Affections and Prayers.

Ah, my Redeemer, and how have I been able to live so forgetful of Thee during the time that is passed? Thou wast prepared to grant me all the favours which I ought to have asked of Thee, expecting only that I should ask for them; but I have thought of gratifying my senses alone, esteeming it of no moment to live without Thy love and Thy favour. O Lord, forget my great ingratitude, and take pity on me; forgive the many times I have sinned against Thee, and give me strength to persevere in well-doing; grant me the grace ever to ask Thee for Thy help, so that I may never more offend Thee, O God of my soul. Do not allow me to be negligent in this respect, as I have been during the time that is passed. Give me light and strength ever to commend myself to Thee, and especially when my enemies again tempt me to offend Thee. Grant me this grace, O my God, through the merits of Jesus Christ, and through the love which Thou bearest for Him. O my Lord, I have offended Thee so often, I would wish to love Thee during the remainder of my life. Give me Thy holy love, and may it ever remind me to seek Thy aid, whenever I may find myself in danger of losing Thee through sin.

THIRD POINT.

Let us consider, lastly, the conditions of prayer. Many pray and do not obtain, because they do not pray aright. "Ye ask, and receive not, because ye ask amiss." (S. James iv. 3.) For our prayers to be heard, in the first place, it is necessary, to pray with humility. "God resisteth the proud, but giveth grace unto the humble." (S. James iv. 6.) God does not grant the prayers of the proud, but, on the contrary, He ever listens favourably to the prayers of the humble. "The prayer of the humble pierceth the clouds : and till it come nigh he will not be comforted : he will not depart till the Most High shall behold." (Ecclus. xxxv. 17.) And this although they may have been sinners during the years that are passed. "A broken and a contrite heart, O God, Thou wilt not despise." (Ps. li. 17.) In the second place, it is necessary to pray with confidence. "Did ever any trust in the Lord, and was confounded." (Ecclus. ii. 10.) For this cause Jesus Christ taught us, that when asking God for His grace we should call Him by no other name than that of Father. "Our Father." Therefore we should pray to Him with that confidence with which a child seeks his father. He therefore who asks with confidence, obtains all that he asks. "What things soever ye desire, when ye pray, believe that ye receive them, and ye shall have them." (S. Mark xi. 24.) And who can fear, says S. Augustine, that what is promised to him by that Truth itself, which Truth is God, can ever come to fail him? "Who can fear to be deceived when Truth promises." Holy Scripture tells us that God is not like unto men, who promise, and then fail in their promise, either because they lie when they make the promise, or else because they afterwards change their minds. "God is not a man, that He should lie. . . . . Hath He said, and shall He not do it?" (Num. xxiii. 19.) And wherefore, adds the same S. Augustine, should the Lord so exhort us to ask for His grace, if He does not intend to grant it to us? "He would not exhort us to ask except He willed to give." With the promise He obliges Himself to grant the favours which we ask of Him. "By promising He made Himself a debtor."

But some one will say: I am a sinner, and on that account do not deserve to be heard. But S. Thomas makes answer that for prayer to obtain the favours which it seeks, it does not depend upon our merits, but upon the Divine compassion, "For every one that asketh receiveth." (S. Luke xi. 10.) The author of the Imperfect Work comments on this, "'Every one,' be he righteous, or a sinner." But in this our Redeemer Himself releases us from every fear, saying, "Verily, verily, I say unto you, Whatsoever ye shall ask the Father in My Name, He will give it you." (S. John xvi. 23.) As if He had said, "Sinners, if you have no merits of your own, I have in my Father's sight; ask them in My Name, and I promise you shall have what you ask." This promise must not, however, be understood to be made concerning temporal favours, such as health, riches, fortune, and the like; because the Lord very often denies these favours to us, seeing, as He does, that they would do hurt to our eternal salvation. S. Augustine says, that "what is profitable for the sick, the physician knows, rather than the patient;" and he also adds, that God "denies to some men in mercy that which He grants to others in wrath." Therefore temporal blessings ought ever to be sought by us on the condition that they may assist our souls. But, on the contrary, spiritual graces, such as forgiveness, perseverance, Divine love, and the like, should be sought for unconditionally by us, with a firm confidence that we shall obtain them, for Jesus Christ says, "If ye then, being evil, know how to give good gifts unto your children: how much more shall your heavenly Father give the Holy Spirit to them that ask Him." (S. Luke xi. 13.)

Perseverance in prayer is necessary before all things. Cornelius à Lapide says, that "the Lord wishes us to be persevering in prayer, even to importunity." And the following passages from Holy Scripture signify the same truth, "Men ought always to pray." (S. Luke xviii. 1.) "Watch ye therefore, and pray always." (S. Luke xxi. 36.) "Pray without ceasing." (1 Thess. v. 17.) These oft-repeated words also signify the same, "Ask, and it shall be given you; seek, and ye shall find; knock, and it shall be opened unto you." (S. Luke xi. 9.) It would have sufficed to say, "Ask;" but no, the Lord wished to make us understand that we ought to become as mendicants who cease not to ask, to urge, and to knock at the door until they receive some charity. And final perseverance is especially a grace which cannot be obtained without continual prayer. This perseverance, says S. Augustine, cannot be merited by us, but by prayer, which, in a certain way, does merit it. Let us then ever pray, and let us never cease to pray, if we wish to be saved. And who is that confessor or preacher who will ever cease to exhort us to prayer, if he desires that our souls should be saved?

Affections and Prayers.

My God, I hope that Thou hast already pardoned me, but my enemies will never cease to fight against me until my death; if Thou dost not help me, I shall be lost. But through the merits of Jesus Christ, I entreat Thee for holy perseverance. "Suffer me not to be separated from Thee." And I entreat the same grace for all those who are now living in Thy love; I am certain that trusting in Thy promise Thou wilt give me the strength to persevere if I continue to ask Thee for it. But I greatly fear lest in temptation I should fail to fly to Thee, and so fall again. I ask Thee, therefore, for grace, so that I may never cease to pray. Grant that in all occasions of falling again into sin I may ever commend myself to Thee, and may call to my aid the most holy Name of Jesus. My God, I purpose and hope to do this if Thou wilt help me with Thy grace. Hear me for the love of Jesus Christ.

CONSIDERATION XXXI

Of Perseverance

"He that shall endure unto the end, the same shall be saved." S. Matt. xxiv. 13.

FIRST POINT.

"IT is of the many to begin, of the few to persevere," writes S. Jerome. Saul, Judas, Tertullian, began well, but they ended badly, since they did not persevere in good. "In Christians, the beginnings are not sought for, but the end," continues the saint; and S. Bonaventure confirms this by saying, "Perseverance alone is crowned;" hence, S. Laurence Justinian calls perseverance "the door of heaven." So that he cannot enter into heaven who cannot find the gate of entrance. My brother, you have at this present time abandoned sin, and may justly hope that you have been pardoned; in this case, you are the friend of God, but know that you are still, not saved. And when will you be saved? When you have persevered even to the end. "He that shall endure unto the end, the same shall be saved." Have you begun the good life? thank the Lord; but S. Bernard warns you, "The reward is promised to those beginning, it is given to those who persevere." It is not enough to run for the prize, but we must run until we obtain it; or, as the Apostle says, "So run that ye may obtain." (1 Cor. ix. 24.)

Now, truly, you have put your hand to the plough, you have begun to live well; but now, ever very much, fear and tremble: "Work out your own salvation with fear and trembling." (Phil.

ii. 12.) Wherefore? Since, if you turn and look back—which God forbid—and go back to your evil life, God will declare you to be excluded from heaven: "No man, having put his hand to the plough and looking back, is fit for the kingdom of God." (S. Luke ix. 62.) Pray for the grace of the Lord, frequent the Holy Communion, make a daily meditation; blessed are you if you have progressed to do thus, and if, so doing, Jesus Christ shall find you, when He comes to judge you. "Blessed is that servant, whom his Lord, when He cometh, shall find so doing." (S. Matt. xxiv. 46.) But do not believe, that now that you have set yourselves to serve God, temptations are either wanting or are at an end. "My son, if thou come to serve the Lord . . . . prepare thy soul for temptation." (Ecclus. ii. 1.) Know that now, more than ever, you ought to prepare yourself for the battle, since your enemies, the devil, the world, the flesh, more than ever will arm themselves to fight against you, to make you lose what you have already gained. Denis the Carthusian says, "By how much any one the more bravely endeavours to serve God, by so much does the adversary rage against him." This is stated in the Gospel according to S. Luke, where it is said, "When the unclean spirit is gone out of a man, he walketh through dry places, seeking rest; and finding none, he saith, I will return unto my house whence I came out. . . . . Then goeth he and taketh seven other spirits more wicked than himself; and they enter in and dwell there: and the last state of that man is worse than the first." (S. Luke xi. 24, 26.) The "unclean spirit," when he is cast out of the soul, finds no rest, and he uses all his energy to return and enter into it; he even calls his companions to his aid;—and if he succeeds in re-entering it, it will quickly be much worse with that soul in its second fall than it was at the first.

Consider, therefore, what arms you have, which will avail to defend you from these enemies, and to preserve you in the grace of God. Against being overcome of the devil, there is no defence save prayer; for S. Paul says, "We wrestle not against flesh and blood, but against principalities and powers." (Eph. vi. 12.) He wishes by this statement to warn us, that we have not strength to resist one so powerful, whence we need help from

God, by which we can do all things. "I can do all things through Christ, which strengtheneth me." (Phil. iv. 12.) So said S. Paul, and so ought to say each one of us. But this help is not given unless it be sought for in prayer. "Ask and ye shall receive." Let us not trust ourselves, then, or our resolutions; for if we put confidence in these, we shall be lost; but when we are tempted of the devil, let us place it in the help of God, commending ourselves to Jesus Christ. This is especially needful when our chastity is tempted, since this temptation is the most terrible of all, and it is that by which the devil gains the most victories. We have not strength in this respect, save from God. We must, therefore, in such temptations, quickly fly to Jesus Christ, and frequently invoke His holy Name. He who so acts shall conquer; and he who acts not thus, shall be overcome.

Affections and Prayers.

"Cast me not away from Thy presence." (Ps. li. 11.) Ah, my God, do not cast me away from Thy presence. I know well that Thou wilt never abandon me if I do not first abandon Thee; but from the experience of my past wisdom, I am fearful of doing this. But, Lord, do Thou give me the strength that I must have to resist hell, which seeks to find me again its slave. I ask it of Thee, for the love of Jesus Christ. Establish, O my Saviour, between Thee and me, a perpetual peace, which will never be broken; and therefore give me Thy holy love. "He that loveth not, ... abideth in death." (1 S. John iii. 14.) But he who loves Thee, is not dead; Thou, O God of my soul, must save me from this unhappy death. I was lost, truly Thou knowest it; it was Thy goodness alone which led me back to my present condition, and I hope to continue in Thy grace. Ah! do not suffer me, my Jesus, by that bitter death which Thou enduredst for me, willingly to turn away and lose myself. I love Thee above all things; and I trust ever to be bound by this holy love, and so being bound, to die; and so being bound, to live for ever.

Second Point.

Let us now consider how it is possible to conquer the world. If the devil be a powerful enemy, the world is a worse one; for if he did not make use of the world and of wicked men, who form the world, he could not obtain the victories that he does. Our Redeemer warns us, not so much to be on our guard against devils as against men. "Beware of men." (S. Matt. x. 17.) Men sin ofttimes more than devils, since the devils flee at prayer and at the invocation of the Name of Jesus; but if evil companions tempt any one to sin, and he answers by some spiritual word, they flee not, but rather the more tempt him, and deride him; they call him a poor creature, one without breeding, one who is fit for nothing; and when they can say nothing else against him, they call him a hypocrite who feigns holiness. And certain weak minds, to escape such reproaches and derisions, miserably associate with these ministers of Satan, and return to the vomit. Be persuaded, my brother, that if you desire to live well, you will have to bear the taunts and revilings of the wicked. "He that is upright in the way is abomination to the wicked." (Prov. xxix. 27.) He who lives badly cannot bear to see those who are living well; and why? Because their life is a continual reproach to him, and therefore he would wish that all should imitate himself, so as not to have that pain of remorse which the good life of others causes him. There is no help for this, says the Apostle, for "all that will live godly in Christ Jesus shall suffer persecution." (2 S. Tim. iii. 12.) All the saints have been persecuted. Who is more holy than Jesus Christ? And the world so persecuted Him even to a bloody death upon the Cross.

There is no help for this, since the precepts of the world are wholly contrary to those of Jesus Christ. That which the world esteems, by Jesus Christ is called folly. "The wisdom of this world is foolishness with God." (1 Cor. iii. 19.) Whilst, on the contrary, the world calls that folly which is esteemed by Jesus Christ. "For the preaching of the Cross is to them that perish foolishness." (1 Cor. i. 18.) But let us comfort ourselves, that if the wicked curse and vituperate us, God blesses and praises us. "Though they curse, yet bless Thou." (Ps. cix. 27.) Is it not enough, perchance, for us to be praised by God, by all the angels, by the saints, and by all good men? Let us leave these sinners to say what they will, and let us persevere in pleasing God, Who is so grateful and faithful to those who serve Him. The more repugnance and contradiction that we experience in doing good, the greater will be our merits and God's pleasure. Let us imagine ourselves to be in the world with none others save God and ourselves. When these wicked ones scoff at us, let us commend ourselves to the Lord, and rather thank God for having given to us that light which He has not given to those miserable ones; and let us pursue our own way. Let us not be ashamed of appearing as Christians, since our blessed Lord protests that "whosoever shall be ashamed of Me and My words, of him shall the Son of Man be ashamed when He shall come in His own glory." (S. Luke ix. 26.)

If we desire to be saved, we must resolve to suffer and to strive; nay, even to do violence to ourselves. "Narrow is the way which leadeth unto life." (S. Matt. vii. 14.) "The kingdom of heaven suffereth violence, and the violent take it by force." (S. Matt. xi. 12.) They who do not force themselves will not be saved. There is no remedy for us since we must go contrary to our rebellious nature, if we wish to follow what is good. We ought especially to endeavour at the beginning to root out every evil, and to acquire every good habit; since when a good habit is formed, it renders the observance of the Divine law, easy, and even sweet. S. Bridget said that he who, in the practice of virtue, with patience and courage, endures the first pricks of the thorns, shall afterwards find the thorns become roses. Attend, therefore, my Christian; Jesus Christ says to Thee now, as he said to the paralytic, "Behold thou art made whole, sin no more, lest a worse thing come unto thee." (S. John v. 14.) Remark what S. Bernard says: "Thou hearest that it is worse to relapse, than to fall." Woe, says the Lord, to those who take hold of the way of God, and then leave it. "Woe to the rebellious children." (Isa. xxx. 1.)

Such as these are punished as rebels against light. "They are of those that rebel against the light." (Job xxiv. 13.) And the punishment of such rebels who have been favoured by God with much light, and who are afterwards unfaithful, will be, to remain blind, and so to finish their lives in their sins. "But when the righteous turned away from his righteousness, ... shall he live? All his righteousness that he hath done, shall not be mentioned; in his trespass and in his sin, ... in them shall he die." (Ezek. xviii. 24.)

Affections and Prayers.

Ah! my God, I have often merited such a punishment, since by means of the light which Thou gavest me I have often left sin, and I have afterwards miserably returned to it again. I thank very much Thy compassion, for not having abandoned me to my blindness, and left me entirely deprived of light, as I deserved. How greatly, then, O my Jesus, am I indebted to Thee, and how very ungrateful should I have been, could I have turned away to fly from Thee. No, my Redeemer. "My song shall be always of the loving-kindness of the Lord." (Ps. lxxxix. 1.) I hope, during the remainder of my life, and through all eternity, ever to sing and to praise Thy great mercy, by ever loving Thee, and not finding myself at any time deprived of Thy grace. The ingratitude which in time past I have shown to Thee, and which above every evil I detest and abhor, makes me ever to weep, and to weep bitterly, for the injuries which I have done to Thee, and to kindle in me fresh love towards Thee, Who, after the many offences which Thou hast received from me, hast given to me such great grace. Yes, I love Thee, O my God, worthy of infinite love; and from this day forwards, Thou shalt be my only Love: my only Good. O Eternal Father, I ask Thee for final perseverance in Thy grace and in Thy love, through the merits of Jesus Christ, and I truly know that Thou wilt grant it me as often as I ask for it. But who can assure me that I shall attend to ask of Thee this perseverance: therefore, my God, I ask for perseverance, and for grace ever to ask for it.

THIRD POINT.

We come to the third enemy, which is the worst of all, that is the flesh; and let us see how we must defend ourselves from it. In the first place, by prayer; but this means we have already considered. In the second place, by avoiding any opportunities of sin; and this we desire now to consider thoroughly.

S. Bernardine of Sienna says, "That, amongst the precepts of Christ, one of the most celebrated, which is as it were the foundation of religion, is to flee from the opportunities of sin." If the devil did converse with us, he would tell us that the most hateful exhortations to him, are those which counsel, the flying from sinful opportunities; that he laughs at the resolutions and promises of a repentant sinner who does not avoid the temptations to sin. These opportunities, in reference to sensual pleasures especially, are as a bandage which is placed over the eyes, and which prevents any person from further seeing the resolutions he has made, the lights he has received, and the eternal truths; in short, it makes him to forget all things, and renders him like one blind. This was the cause of the ruin of our first parents—their not fleeing from the opportunity of sin. God had prohibited them even to touch the forbidden fruit; for Eve said to the serpent, "God hath said, Ye shall not eat of it, neither shall ye touch it, lest ye die." (Gen. iii. 3.) But the incautious one "saw," "took," and "did eat." First she began to admire the apple; then she took it in her hand; then she ate it: "He that loveth danger shall perish therein." (Ecclus. iii. 27.) S. Peter says that "your adversary the devil, as a roaring lion, walketh about, seeking whom he may devour." (1 S. Peter v. 8.) Hence, says S. Cyprian, what does he do when he seeks to enter a soul from whence he has been cast out? He bides the opportunity. "He explores what may be that part of it through the opening in which, it may be entered." If the soul suffer herself to be led with the sinful opportunity, the enemy truly will enter it again, and will devour it. The Abbot Guerric says, that Lazarus from the dead "came forth bound hand and foot with the grave-clothes," (S. John xi. 43); and rising so, returned tc die. The author would express, the unhappiness of him who rises from sin, but rises bound with the opportunities of sinning; that such an one, though he rise, nevertheless will turn back and die. He who desires to be saved must leave not only the sin, but even the opportunities of sinning.

But you will say, I have now changed my life, and I have no longer any evil design with that person; not even any temptation to sin. I answer—It is related that there are in Africa certain bears who hunt apes which save themselves upon the trees. The bears then feign death; the apes descend and become their prey. The devil acts thus; he makes the temptation appear to be dead, but when the person has descended, he then quickens the temptation, which devours him. Oh, how many miserable souls who frequented prayer, Holy Communion, and who might have been called Christians, but who, by throwing themselves into temptation, have remained the prey of hell.

Isaiah was bidden to "Cry, ... All flesh is grass." (Isa. xl. 6.) Upon which S. Chrysostom reflects and says, Is it possible that grass should not burn when placed in the fire? "Place a lamp amidst hay, and then dare to deny that it is consumed." S. Cyprian says likewise, "It is impossible to be surrounded with flames and not to burn." The prophet warns us that our strength is as tow in the flames. "The strong shall be as tow." (Isa. i. 31.) Solomon likewise says that he is a fool who would pretend to walk upon red-hot coals and not be burned. "Can one go upon hot coals, and his feet not be burned?" (Prov. vi. 28.) Such also is the fool who pretends that he can place himself in the temptations of sin without falling. There is the command given, "Flee from sins as from the face of a serpent." (Ecclus. xxi. 2.) Gualfridus says that we must not avoid its bite only, but that we should avoid even the touch and the approach of it.

But you say, that house and that friendship are to my interest; but if you really see that that house is for you the way of hell—"Her house is the way to hell, (Prov. vii. 27)—there is no remedy; you must leave it, if you would be saved. Our Blessed Lord goes beyond this, saying that "If thy right eye offend thee, pluck it out, and cast it from thee." (S. Matt. v. 29.) Mark the words "from thee." You must cast it, not near, but far from you, which is saying, that you ought to remove afar every temptation to sin. S. Francis of Assisi said, that the devil tempts spiritual persons who have given themselves to God in a different way from that in which he tempts the wicked; and first, he does not seek to bind them with a cord, he is content with a hair; then he binds them with a thread; then with a string; afterwards with a cord, and so finally he draws them into sin. He who wishes, therefore, to be liberated from this danger, it behoves from the first to despise all those hairs, all those sinful opportunities, such as salutations, presents, notes, and the like. And, speaking particularly of those who have the habit of the sin of impurity, it will not suffice to avoid the proximate temptations only, the remote must be shunned, to save from falling back again into sin.

It is necessary for him who desires earnestly to save his soul, to strengthen and renew continually his resolution, never to separate himself from God, to repeat frequently the saying of the saints, "Let all be lost, and God not be lost." But it is not enough to resolve alone not to lose Him more, he must adopt means also, so as not to lose Him. The first means, is to avoid the temptations to sin, of which already mention has been made; the second, is to frequent the Sacraments of Confession and Holy Communion. In that house which is often swept, dirt does not reign; so by confession the soul is kept pure, and it not only obtains remission of sins, but even help to resist the temptations. The Communion, then, is called Heavenly Bread, because as the body cannot live without earthly food, so the mind cannot live without heavenly food. "Except ye eat the Flesh of the Son of man, and drink His Blood, ye have no life in you." (S. John vi. 53.) On the other hand, to him who often eats of this Bread it is promised, "If any man eat of this Bread, he shall live for ever." (S. John vi. 51.) Wherefore the ancient Fathers called the Communion "The medicine by which we are freed from our daily sins and are preserved from deadly sins." The third means, is mental prayer. "Remember the end, and thou shalt never do amiss."

(Ecclus. vii. 26.) He who keeps before his eyes the eternal truths, death, judgment, eternity, will not fall into sin. God enlightens us by meditations, "They had an eye unto Him, and were lightened." (Ps. xxxiv. 5.) In meditation, He speaks to us and causes us to understand what we ought to fly from, and what we ought to do. "I will allure her, and bring her into the wilderness, and speak comfortably unto her." (Hos. ii. 14.) Meditation, then, is that blessed furnace in which is enkindled Divine love. "While I was thus musing, the fire kindled." (Ps. xxxix. 4.) Moreover, as it has been often shown, to be preserved in the grace of God, it is absolutely necessary to "continue instant in prayer," and to ask for the graces which we need. He who does not use mental prayer, hardly prays, and he who does not pray, will certainly be lost.

We ought therefore to use the means of working out our salvation, and of leading a well-regulated life. In the morning, on rising, make the Christian acts of thanksgiving, love, offering, and good resolution with prayer to our Blessed Lord, that He would preserve us for that day from sin. After meditation, go to Holy Communion. Practise some spiritual reading during the day, and in the evening make an examination of conscience. Ask of God always the gift of holy perseverance, and especially in the time of temptations, invoking then more frequently the holy Name of Jesus as long as the temptation lasts. So doing you will certainly be saved, and if you do it not, you will as certainly be lost.

Affections and Prayers.

My dear Redeemer, I thank Thee for the lights which Thou hast given to me, and the means which enable to work out my salvation, and I promise Thee that I will firmly follow them. Give me Thy help, that I may be faithful; I see that Thou willest to save me, and I desire to be saved, principally to please Thy heart—Thou Who hast so greatly desired my salvation. I do not wish, no, my God, to resist any more the love Thou bearest for me: which made Thee bear with me with so great long suffering whilst I had offended Thee. Thou callest me to

Thy love, and I desire nothing more than to love Thee. I love Thee, O Infinite Good! Alas! I pray Thee, by the merits of Jesus Christ, never more to suffer me to be ungrateful; either make my ingratitude to cease, or end my life. Lord, Thou hast begun the work, now complete it. "Stablish the thing, O God, that Thou hast wrought in us." (Ps. lxviii. 28.) Give me light, give me strength, give me love.

CONSIDERATION XXXII

The Love of God

"We love Him because He first loved us." 1 S. John iv. 19.

FIRST POINT.

CONSIDER, in the first place, that God deserves to be loved by you, since He loved you first, that you might love Him, and He has been the first of all to love you. "I have loved thee with an everlasting love." (Jer. xxxi. 3.) The first to love you on earth, were your parents, but they did not love you before they knew you; but God loved you before you had any being. When neither your father nor your mother were in the world, God loved you; when the world was not even created, God loved you. And how long before the creation of the world did God love you? Perhaps a thousand years or ages. There is no need to reckon years and ages. Know, that God has loved you from eternity. "I have loved thee with an everlasting love, therefore, with loving kindness have I drawn Thee." (Jer. xxxi. 3.) In short, God has loved you since He has been God; as long as He has loved Himself, He has loved you. Therefore S. Agnes had good reason to say, "I am prevented by another love." When the world and the creature demanded her love, she answered, "No, O world; no, O creature, I cannot love you. My God has been the first to love me, and it is therefore right that I should consecrate my love to God alone."

Thus, my brother, from eternity has thy God loved you, and from love alone, has selected you from the number of many men that He could have created, and has given you being and a position in the world. For your love even, He has made many other beautiful creatures, that they might serve you, and might remind you of the love which He has for you, and which you owe to Him. S. Augustine writes, "Heaven, and earth, and all things, tell me that I ought to love Thee." Whence, the Saint observed, the sun, the moon, the stars, the mountains, the rivers, they seemed as if they would all speak and say to him, "Augustine, love God, since He has created us for you, in order that you might love Him." The Abbot de Rancé, when he admired the hills, fountains, and flowers, said they recalled the love that God had towards him. S. Teresa said that creation reproached her own ingratitude towards God. S. Mary Magdalene of Pazzi, whenever she held in her hand any beautiful flower or fruit, felt as if wounded with a certain arrow in her heart, with the love towards God, saying within herself, Thou, my God, hast planned from eternity to create a certain flower or fruit, in order that I might love Him.

Consider further the especial love that God had towards you in causing you to be born in a Christian land, and in the bosom of the true Church. How many are born amongst idolaters, Jews, Mahometans, or heretics, and are lost! How few have it their lot to be born amongst men, where the true faith reigns, and of the number of those few, the Lord has elected you. How many millions of persons are deprived of the Sacraments, of sermons, of the example of good companions, and of all the other helps to salvation, which are in the true Church! And God has willed to grant you all these great helps, without any merit on your part, even seeing beforehand your demerits; for, whilst He thought of creating you and of procuring for you all these favours, He already foreknew the injuries which you would do to Him.

Affections and Prayers.

O Sovereign Lord of heaven and earth, Infinite Good, Infinite Majesty, Who hast so loved men, how is it then that Thou art so disregarded of men? But amongst these men, Thou, my God, hast so particularly loved me and bestowed upon me such special grace, that Thou hast not granted to others, and I seem to have despised Thee more than others. But I throw myself at Thy feet, O Jesus, my Saviour. "Cast me not away from Thy presence." (Ps. li. 11.) I should deserve to be cast away, for the ingratitude which I have committed, but Thou hast said that Thou knowest not how to cast away a penitent heart that returns to Thee. "Him that cometh to Me, I will in no wise cast out." (S. John vi. 37.) My Jesus, I repent of having offended Thee. In the time past I have been ungrateful to Thee; now I own Thee for my Saviour and my Redeemer, Who died to save me, and to be loved by me. When shall I cease, my Jesus, to be ungrateful to Thee? When shall I begin to love Thee truly? Behold, this day I resolve to love Thee with all my heart, and to love none other than Thee. O Infinite Goodness, I adore Thee for all those who adore Thee not; and I love Thee for all those who love Thee not. I believe in Thee, I hope in Thee, I love Thee, I offer Thee my all; aid me with Thy grace. Thou knowest indeed my weakness. But if when I did not desire Thee, nor loved Thee, Thou bestowedst so many favours upon me, how much more should I hope in Thy mercy, now that I love and desire but to love Thee? My Lord, give me Thy love; but so fervent a love, that it may compel me to forget every creature; a strong love, that it may enable me to overcome all difficulty in pleasing Thee; a perpetual love, that may ever abide between me and Thee. All these things I hope for, O my Jesus, through Thy merits.

Second Point.

But God has not only given to us so many beautiful creatures, He cannot be said to be satisfied until He has arrived at the giving us, even Himself. "Who loved me, and gave Himself for me." (Gal. ii. 20.) Accursed sin has caused us to lose the Divine grace and heaven, and to become the slaves of hell; but the Son of God, to the wonder of heaven and nature, willed to come on earth and become Man, to redeem us from eternal death, and to enable us to obtain that grace and that heaven which we had lost. What a marvel would it not be to see a king become a worm for the love of worms! But it should excite in us an infinitely greater wonder, to see a God become man for the love of men. "Made Himself of no reputation, and took upon Him the form of a servant, and was made in the likeness of men," (Phil. ii. 7), or clothed with flesh—"The Word was made flesh." (S. John i. 14.) But this wonder increases, when we see that which this Son of God, both did and suffered for our sakes. A single drop of His Blood, one tear, one single prayer of His was sufficient to save us; since this being the prayer of a Divine Person was of infinite value, and was sufficient not only to save the whole world, but an infinite number of worlds. But no, says S. Chrysostom, "that which was sufficient for our redemption was not sufficient for His love." He did not will to save us only, but since He loved us so much, He desired to be much loved by us; and therefore He willed to choose for Himself a whole life, fully laden with pains and insults, and a death the most bitter of all deaths, that we might understand the infinite love with which He burned towards us. "He humbled Himself and became obedient unto death, even the death of the cross." (Phil. ii. 8.) Oh, the excess of Divine love which neither men nor angels will ever be able to comprehend! S. Bonaventure calls it "Excess of sorrow, excess of love." If the Redeemer had not been God, but our simple friend or parent, what greater proof of affection would He be able to give us than to die for us? "Greater love hath no man than this, that a man lay down his life for his friends." (S. John xv. 13.) If our Blessed Lord had had to save His own Father, what more could He have done by His love? If, my brother, thou hadst been God and the creator of Jesus Christ, what more could He have done for you than to have sacrificed His life in the midst of taunts and sorrows? If the vilest man on earth had done for you that which Jesus Christ has done, could you live without loving Him?

But what say you? Do you believe in the incarnation and death of Jesus Christ? Do you believe in Him, and yet not love Him? And can you think of loving anything else save Jesus Christ? Perhaps you doubt whether He loves you? But S. Augustine says, "It was on this account that Christ came, that man might know how much God loved him." Before the Incarnation, man could doubt whether God loved him with tenderness; but after the incarnation and death of our blessed Lord, who can longer doubt? And what greater tenderness of His affection was He able to show to you, than in sacrificing His Divine life for you? We have had an ear to hear the words—creation, redemption, a God in a manger, a God upon a Cross. O holy faith, enlighten us!

Affections and Prayers.

O my Jesus, I see that Thou hast had nothing more Thou couldst do to place me in the necessity of loving Thee; and I see that I have procured by my ingratitude the placing of Thee under an obligation to abandon me. Yet for ever blessed be Thy patience, which has borne with me so long. I should merit a hell expressly for myself, but Thy death gives me confidence. Ah! teach me to know well the grounds which Thou hast for being loved, O Highest Good! and compel me to love Thee. I well knew that Thou, my Jesus, didst die for me; and after knowing this, how have I been able to live for so many years forgetful of Thee? Oh, were I able to turn back again, and live over again those past years, my Lord, I would give them all to Thee. But these years return not. Ah, grant that for the rest of life which remains to me, I may spend the whole of it in loving Thee, and giving Thee pleasure. My dear Redeemer, I love Thee with all my heart; but do Thou increase this love in me; make me ever to remember what Thou hast done for me, and permit me not to live any more ungrateful to Thee. No, I will no longer resist the lights which Thou hast given me. Thou desirest to be loved by me, and I desire to love Thee. And whom should I wish to love, if I do not love God, Who is infinite beauty, infinite goodness? a God Who died for me, Who suffered with so great patience, and Who, in place of punishing me as I deserved, has changed the punishment into grace and favour. Yes, I love Thee, O God, worthy of infinite love; and I sigh and seek for nothing else than to live wholly occupied in loving Thee, and forgetful of everything which is not Thee, O Infinite Love of my soul; succour Thou a soul that desires to be wholly Thine.

Third Point.

The marvel increases when we see then the desire which our blessed Lord had to suffer and to die for us. Whilst living, He said, "I have a baptism to be baptized with; and how am I straitened till it be accomplished!" (S. Luke xii. 50.) I must be baptized with the baptism of My own Blood; and I feel Myself dying with the desire that My passion and death may speedily come, since by this, man may quickly know the love that I bear to him. It was this feeling which made Him say, on the night preceding His Passion, "With desire I have desired to eat this Passover with you." (S. Luke xxii. 15.) Therefore S. Basil of Seleucia writes, "God cannot be satiated by His love for men."

Ah, my Jesus, men do not love Thee, because they do not consider the love that Thou hast borne for them. O God, a mind that reflects that God died for this, and had such a desire to die, that He might show His affection, how can such a mind live without loving Him? "The love of Christ constraineth us." (2 Cor. v. 14.) S. Paul says, that it is not only that which our blessed Lord has done and suffered, but the love which He has shown in the suffering for us that obliges us, and, as it were, forces us to love Him. Considering this, S. Laurence Justinian exclaimed, "We see the wise infatuated through excess of love." Who could ever believe, had not faith assured us, that the Creator had willed to die for His creatures? When the death of Jesus Christ was preached to the heathen, they regarded it as folly, which they could never believe, as the Apostle testifies, "We preach Christ crucified, unto the Jews a stumbling block, and unto the Greeks foolishness." (1 Cor. i. 23.) And how could it be, they would say, that a God, most happy in Himself, Who has no need of anything, should have come down to earth, should have become man, and should have died for the love of men, His own creatures. But yet it is an article of faith, that Jesus Christ, the true Son of God, for His love to us, was given to death. "Christ . . . . loved us, and hath given Himself for us." (Eph. v. 2.)

And wherefore has He done this? That we should live no longer to the world, but to that Lord alone that willed to die for us. "He died for all, that they which live, should not henceforth live unto themselves, but unto Him Which died for them." (2 Cor. v. 15.) He has done this, that by the love which He has shown for us, He may gain every affection of our hearts. "To this end Christ both died and rose, and revived, that He might be Lord both of the dead and living." (Rom. xiv. 9.) Hence the saints, considering the death of Jesus Christ, have thought that it was little to do, to give life and all things for the love of a God so loving. How many nobles and princes have left parents, riches, country, and even kingdoms, to seclude themselves in the cloister, and to live for the love of Jesus Christ alone! How many martyrs have sacrificed their lives! How many virgins, renouncing splendid nuptials, have gone rejoicing to death, so to render some recompence of affection to the God who died for their sakes! And you, my brother! what have you done yet for the love of Jesus Christ? As He died for the saints, so He died even for you. What, at least, do you think of doing with the remainder of your life, which God grants to you, that you may love Him? Henceforth, look intently at and often upon, your crucified Lord; and beholding Him, recall the love that He had borne for you, and say to yourself, Then, hast Thou my God died for me? Do this at least often, still so doing, that you may be unable to do less than to feel yourself sweetly constrained to love a God Who has so greatly loved you.

Affections and Prayers.

O my Redeemer, it is true that I have not loved Thee, because I have not considered Thy love to me. Ah, my Jesus, I have been very ungrateful; Thou hast given Thy life for a death the most bitter of all, and I have been so forgetful, that I have not willingly thought about it. Pardon me, and I promise that henceforth, my crucified Love, Thou shalt be the one object of my thoughts, and of all my affections. Also, when the devil and the world shall offer me some forbidden fruit, recall Thyself to me, my loved Saviour—the pains which

Thou hast suffered for my sake—that I may love Thee, and never more offend Thee. If my servant had done for me that which Thou hast done, I should not have had the heart to wound him; and I have often turned away from Thee, Who died for me. O beautiful flame of love, which compellest Thee, a God, to give a life for me; come, inflame, fill my whole heart, and destroy in it every affection towards the creature. Ah, my loved Redeemer, how is it possible to think of Thee in the manger of Bethlehem, on the Cross at Calvary, or in the Sacrament on our altars, without loving Thee? My Jesus, I love Thee with my whole soul. During the remaining years of my life, Thou shalt be my only Good, my only Love. The unhappy years are sufficient for me, during which I lived miserably forgetful of Thy Passion and Thy love. I give myself entirely to Thee; and if I do not give myself as I ought, take hold of me, and reign in all my heart. "Thy kingdom come." (S. Matt. vi. 10.) Let it serve no other than Thy love; speak of no other; treat of no other; think of no other; sigh for nothing, but Thy love and Thy pleasure. Aid me ever with Thy grace, that I may be faithful to Thee. I confide in Thy merits, O my Jesus!

CONSIDERATION XXXIII

The Holy Communion

"Take, eat; This is My Body." S. Matt. xxvi. 26.

FIRST POINT.

LET us observe how great a gift is this Holy Sacrament; how great is the love that Jesus has shown to us in this gift, and how great is His desire that we should receive this His gift.

Let us consider, in the first place, the GREAT GIFT which Jesus Christ procured for us, in giving Himself to be wholly food for us in the Holy Communion. S. Augustine says that our Blessed Lord, "although He is omnipotent, was not able to give us more than this." S. Bernardine of Sienna asks, "What greater treasure can the heart of man possess, than the most holy Body of Christ?" The prophet Isaiah cries, "Declare His doings among the people." (Isaiah xii. 4.) Publish, O men, the loving inventions of our good God. If our Redeemer had not given us this gift, who ever would have been able to ask for it, who would ever have dared to say to Him, Lord, if Thou desiredst to make us know Thy love, conceal Thyself under the form of Bread, and permit us to feed on Thee? It would have been esteemed madness even to think of this. S. Augustine asks, "Would it not seem madness to say, Eat My Flesh and drink My Blood?" When our Blessed Lord revealed to His disciples this gift of the Holy Sacrament which He wished to leave them, many of them could not attain to the belief of it, and they parted from Him, saying, "How can this Man give us His Flesh to eat? . . . . This is an hard saying; who can hear it? (S. John vi. 52, 60.) But what men were not able at any time to conceive, the great love of our Lord Jesus Christ, both intended and wrought.

S. Bernardine says that our Blessed Lord left us "this Sacrament to be a memorial of His love," and the record which S. Luke has left us of our Lord's words, agrees with this statement, "This do in remembrance of Me." (S. Luke xxii. 19.) S. Bernardine adds that the love of our Lord was not satisfied with sacrificing His life for us: "In that excess of fervour, when He was ready to die for us, He was impelled by this ocean of love to do a greater work than ever had been wrought, to give to us His Body for food." Abbot Guerric says, that in this Sacrament Jesus "poured out upon His friends the last strength of His love;" and the same sentiment is expressed more forcibly, when it was said of old that in the Eucharist our Blessed Lord, "as it were, poured out upon men the riches of His love."

S. Francis of Sales says, What a refinement of love it would be deemed, if a prince at table were to send to a poor man a portion of his own dish! How much more if he sent to him his whole dinner, if finally he sent him a piece of his own flesh that he might eat it? Our Blessed Lord in the Holy Communion gives us for food not only a part of His own table, not only a part of His own body, but His whole Body: "Take, eat; this is My Body," and together with His Body He gives us even His Soul and His Divinity. In short, says S. Chrysostom, in the Holy Communion Jesus Christ "gave Himself to thee wholly, and left nothing for Himself." S. Thomas Aquinas adds, that "God in the Eucharist has given to us all that He is, and all that He has." S. Bonaventure exclaims with wonder of our Blessed Lord's presence in the Eucharist, "Behold He Whom the world cannot contain, is our prisoner." And if the Lord in the Eucharist gives us His whole Self, how can we fear that He will deny us any grace that we ask of Him: "How shall He not with Him, freely give us all things?" (Rom. viii. 32.)

Affections and Prayers.

O my Jesus, and what has ever led Thee to give Thy whole Self for our food? And what remains, after Thou hast given us this gift, to compel us to love Thee? Oh! Lord, give us light, and make us to feel how excessive is the love which caused Thee to reduce Thyself to food, to unite Thyself with us poor sinners. But if Thou givest Thyself wholly to us, it is a reason that we also should give ourselves wholly to Thee. O my Redeemer, how have I been able to offend Thee, Who hast so loved me, and Who hast had nothing more that Thou couldst do to gain my love? Thou hadst become Man for me; Thou didst die for me; Thou hast made Thyself my food; tell me what more it remains for Thee to do? I love Thee, O Infinite Goodness; I love Thee, O Infinite Love! Lord, come often into my soul: inflame me wholly with Thy holy love, and cause me to forget all else, so that I may neither think of, nor love any other than Thee.

SECOND POINT.

Let us consider, in the second place, the GREAT LOVE of Jesus Christ, which He has shown to us by such a gift. The Holy Sacrament is a gift which is given from love alone. It was needful for our salvation, according to the Divine decree, that the Redeemer should have died, and by the sacrifice of His life should have made satisfaction to Divine Justice for our sins; but what necessity was there, that after having died, He should leave Himself to us as food? But thus love willed. "For no other reason," says S. Laurence Justinian, did our Lord institute the Eucharist, "than as a token of His exceeding love." And this is exactly what S. John wrote: "When Jesus knew that His hour was come that He should depart out of this world unto the Father, having loved His own, ... He loved them unto the end." (S. John xiii. 1.) Jesus, knowing that the hour had come for Him to depart from this earth, wished to leave a most marked proof of His love, which was this gift of the Holy Sacrament, as is signified particularly in the words, "He loved them unto the end;" that is, with the highest love, as both S. Chrysostom and Theophylact explain it.

And it should be remarked, that the Apostle records the time in which our blessed Lord wished to leave this gift, which was at the hour of His death—"The same night in which He was betrayed took Bread; and when He had given thanks, He Brake It, and said, Take, eat: THIS is My Body." (1 Cor. xi. 24.) At the very time whilst the men were preparing the scourges, the thorns, and the Cross, to kill Him, did He, the loving Saviour, wish to leave this last proof of His love. Wherefore in death, and not during life, did He institute this Sacrament? S. Bernardine answers, that "the things which are celebrated at the hour of death for marks of friendship are the more firmly impressed upon the heart, and are the more lovingly treasured up in the memory." He continues, that our blessed Lord had before this given Himself to us in many ways. He had given Himself to us to be a Companion, a Master, a Father, a Light, an Example, a Victim. "It was the last degree of love, when He gave Himself to us for food; since He gave Himself to us in the most perfect union, as the food and the eaters of it are in every way united into one." So our Blessed Lord was not content to unite Himself to our human nature only, but He willed by this Sacrament, to find a means of uniting Himself even to each one of us in particular.

S. Francis of Sales says, that in no other action, can the Saviour be thought of as being more tender, more loving, than in this, in which He so annihilates Himself, so to speak, and so reduces Himself to food, that He may penetrate our souls, and may unite Himself with the hearts of His faithful ones. As S. Chrysostom writes, that upon which the angels do not dare to fix their eyes, "to this we are united, and we are made with IT one Body and one Flesh." He continues: "What shepherd feeds the sheep with his own blood? And wherefore do I say a shepherd? There are many mothers who deliver up their children to other nurses; but this He permitted not, but He feeds us Himself with His own Blood." But wherefore does He make Himself our food? S. Chrysostom answers: "He mingled Himself with us, that we might be one with Him; for this is the desire of those who love ardently." Therefore it was, that our Blessed Lord willed to perform this most wonderful of all miracles—that "The merciful and gracious Lord hath so done His marvellous works, that they ought to be had in remembrance, He hath given meat unto them that fear Him," (Ps. cxi. 4, 5)—that He might satisfy the desire that He had, of remaining with us and of uniting in one, our own with His most Sacred Heart. S. Laurence Justinian exclaims, "O Lord Jesus, how wonderful is Thy love, Who so willed to incorporate us with Thy Body, that we might have with Thee one heart and one mind inseparably bound together."

Father de la Colombiére said, "That if anything could shake my faith in the mystery of the Eucharist, I should not be able to doubt the power, but rather the love of God, which He has revealed to us in this Sacrament." How can the bread become the Body of Jesus? How can Jesus be found in more than one place? I answer, that God can do all things. But if you ask me how God can love man to such an extent as to be willing to become his food, I can only answer, that I do not understand it, and that the love of Jesus cannot be more fully comprehended. But Lord, this excess of affection, in reducing Thyself into food, is not agreeable to Thy majesty! But S. Bernard replies, "Love is conscious of no dignity;" and S. Chrysostom says, that love is bound by no consideration of convenience, when it seeks to make itself known to the loved one: "Love lacks reason, it goes whither it is led, not whither it ought." S. Thomas Aquinas rightly calls the Holy Communion "a Sacrament and pledge of love;" and S. Bernard the "love of loves;" and S. Mary Magdalene of Pazzi styled, Holy Thursday, the day of its institution, "The day of love."

Affections and Prayers.

O infinite love of Jesus, worthy of infinite love! Alas! when, my Jesus, shall I love Thee as Thou hast loved me? Thou couldst do no more to make Thyself loved by me, and I have had the heart to leave Thee, O Infinite Good, and to turn myself back to vile and miserable riches. Oh, enlighten me, O my God, discover to me evermore the glories of Thy goodness, so that I may be altogether enamoured of Thee, and weary myself to give Thee pleasure. I love Thee, my Jesus, my Love, my All; and I desire very often to be united with Thee in this Sacrament, that I may separate myself from all things, and love Thee alone, my Life. Succour me, O my Redeemer, through the merits of Thy Passion.

THIRD POINT.

Let us consider, in the third place, the GREAT DESIRE of our Lord Jesus Christ, that we should receive Him in the Holy Communion. "Jesus knew that His hour was come." (S. John xiii. 1.) But how was our Blessed Lord able to call *His hour* that night in which He was to experience, the beginning of His bitter Passion? Yes! He called it *His hour*, since in that night He was about to leave us, that Divine Sacrament for the perfect union of Himself with His beloved souls. And this longing made Him say, "With desire, I have desired to eat this passover with you." (S. Luke xxii. 15.) Words, by which our Redeemer wished to make us understand the desire that He had of uniting Himself with each one of us in this Sacrament. "With desire, I have desired:" it is thus that the great love which He bears us, forces Him to speak. S. Laurence Justinian calls it "a voice of the most burning love." And he willed to leave Himself under the form of bread, so that all might be able to receive Him; for, if He had placed Himself under the form of any precious food, the poor would not have had the power to receive it, and even if He had left Himself under the form of any other food not precious, it might perhaps not have been found in every part of the world; therefore, it was that Jesus willed to leave Himself under the form of bread, since bread is of small cost; it is found everywhere, so that in every place it can be obtained and received.

Through the great desire that the Redeemer had to be received by us, not only did He exhort us to receive Him with such invitations as, "Come, eat of My Bread, and drink of the Wine which I have mingled," (Prov. ix. 5); "Eat, O friends; drink, yea, drink abundantly, O beloved, (Sol. Song v. 1); but He imposed the reception of Himself by positive command, "Take, eat;

THIS is My Body," (S. Matt. xxvi. 26.) So that we may come to Him to receive Him, He allures us with the promise of eternal life: "Whoso eateth My Flesh . . . . hath eternal life." (S. John vi. 54.) "He that eateth of this Bread shall live for ever." (Ib. 58.) And if we do not thus, He threatens us with exclusion from heaven: "Except ye eat the Flesh of the Son of Man . . . . ye have no life in you." (Ib. 53.) These invitations, promises, and threats, all come from the desire which our Blessed Lord has of uniting Himself with us in this Sacrament, and His desire flows from the great love which He bears us. As S. Francis of Sales observes, The end of this love is no other, than that it may unite itself to the beloved object; and so in this Sacrament, our Blessed Lord wholly unites Himself with the mind: "He that eateth My Flesh and drinketh My Blood, dwelleth in Me, and I in Him. (S. John vi. 56.) Hence it is, that He so greatly desires that we should receive Him. A bee could not be found that, with so great impetus of love, darts upon the flowers to extract the honey, as our Blessed Lord comes to the souls who desire Him.

Oh, that the faithful would understand the great good, that Holy Communion brings to the soul. Jesus is the Lord of all riches, since the Father has made Him Lord of all things. "The Father had given all things into His hands." (S. John xiii. 3.) Hence, when Jesus Christ comes into a soul in the Holy Communion, He carries with Him the infinite treasures of grace; as Solomon says, speaking of eternal Wisdom, "All good things together came to me together with her, and innumerable riches in her hands." (Wisd. vii. 11.)

S. Dionysius says, that "the Eucharist has the highest power of perfecting holiness." S. Vincent Ferrer recorded, that the soul profits more by one communion than by a week of fasting on bread and water. The holy Fathers have declared the Sacrament to be "the antidote by which we are freed from daily sins, and preserved from those which are deadly." Hence, S. Ignatius calls it "the medicine of immortality." Innocent III. said, that our Blessed Lord, "through the mystery of the cross, liberated us from the power of sin; through the sacrament of the Eucharist, He liberates us from the power of sinning."

Besides, this Sacrament kindles the Divine love. "He brought me to the banqueting house, and his banner over me was love; stay me with flagons, comfort me with apples; for I am sick of love." (Sol. Song ii. 4, 5.) S. Gregory Nyssen says, that the Communion is precisely that "banqueting house," where the soul is in such a way inebriated by Divine love, that it becomes forgetful of the earth and all created things, and that this is really to languish with Divine love. Father Olympio says, that nothing so inflames with love towards God as the Holy Communion. "God is love." (1 S. John iv. 8.) And He is the fire of love: "God is a consuming fire." (Deut. iv. 24.) The Eternal Word came to kindle this fire of love in the world. "I am come to send fire on the earth, and what will I, if it be already kindled?" (S. Luke xii. 49.) And Oh, what bright flames of sacred love does Jesus kindle in souls, which with such a desire, receive Him in this Sacrament! S. Chrysostom says that "the Eucharist is a coal which inflames us; that, like lions breathing fire, we depart from that Table, being made terrible to the devil.

But some will say, I do not often communicate, for the reason that I seem cold in Divine love; but this, says Gerson, would be the same, as if a person were unwilling to go near the fire because he felt cold. By how much the more we feel cold, by so much the more, we ought to approach frequently the holy sacrament, that we may ever desire to love God. S. Francis of Sales writes, If they ask you "why you communicate so often?" tell them that two classes of persons ought to communicate often; the perfect and the imperfect; the former to preserve their perfection, the latter to attain to perfection." S. Bonaventure said also, "Although thou art cold, yet approach, trusting in the mercy of God; he so much the more needs a physician, as he feels himself to be the more ill." S. Mechtildes adds, "When thou art about to communicate, desire to have all the love that any heart ever had for Jesus Christ, and He will receive it, that thou mayest have the love thou desirest."

Affections and Prayers.

O Beloved of souls, my Jesus! there remains no further proof of love by which to show us that Thou dost love us; and what more is there that Thou canst think of to make us love Thee? Also, grant me, O Infinite Goodness, to love Thee, from this day forward, with all strength, and with all tenderness. Than Thou, my Redeemer, who can love my soul with more tenderness, Who, after having given Thy life for me, dost give me Thy entire Self in this Sacrament. Ah, my Lord, may I ever remember Thy love, by my forgetfulness of all else, and so love Thee only, without interruption, and without reserve. I love Thee, my Jesus, above all things; and I desire to love Thee only, I beseech Thee to sever from my heart all affections which are not for Thee. I thank Thee that Thou hast given me time to love Thee, and to bewail the offences which I have committed against Thee. My Jesus, I desire that Thou shouldst be the sole object of all my affections; succour me, save me; and let it be my salvation to love Thee with all my heart, and for ever, in this life, and in the life to come.

CONSIDERATION XXXIV

Conformity to the Will of God

"In His pleasure is life." Ps. xxx. 5.

FIRST POINT.

ALL our salvation and all our perfection, consist in loving God. "He that loveth not . . . . abideth in death." (1 S. John iii. 14.) "Charity, which is the bond of perfectness." (Col. iii. 14.) But the perfection of love consists, then, in the uniformity of our will with the Divine will. Since this is the chief effect of love, according to S. Dionysius, to unite the wills of those who love, so that they have but one heart and one will. So therefore our repentances, our communions, our alms-deeds, please God in proportion as they correspond with the Divine will, since otherwise they are not virtues but defects, and worthy of correction.

It was principally to teach us this truth by His example, that our Blessed Lord came down from heaven. Mark what He said on coming into the world, as the Apostle writes, "Sacrifice and offering Thou wouldst not, but a Body hast thou prepared Me. . . . Then said I, Lo, I come to do Thy will, O God." (Heb. x. 5, 7.) "Thou, My Father, hast refused the victims offered by men, Thou willed that I should sacrifice to Thee by death that Body which Thou hast given Me. Behold Me ready to do Thy will." And this He expressed frequently, saying, "I came down from heaven, not to do Mine own will, but the will of Him that sent Me." (S. John vi. 38.) And by this He desires that we should know His great love to His Father, when we see that He died in obedience to His will. "But that the world may know that I love the Father; and as the Father gave Me commandment, even so I do." (S. John xiv. 31.) He says afterwards, that He acknowledges for His own, those alone, who do the Divine will. "Whosoever shall do the will of My Father Which is in heaven, the same is My brother, and sister, and mother." (S. Matt. xii. 50.) This, then, is the one scope and desire of all the saints in all their works—the fulfilment of the Divine will. Henry Suso said, "I would much rather be the vilest worm on earth, according to the will of God, than a seraph according to my own." S. Teresa wrote, "All that he ought to try to procure, who exercises himself in prayer, is to conform his own to the Divine will, and he may be assured that in this conformation the highest perfection consists; he who most aims at such conformity, will receive from God the choicest gifts, and will make most progress in the spiritual life." The blessed in heaven, love God perfectly from their entire conformity to the Divine will. Hence it was that our Blessed Lord taught us to pray, that by us "Thy will be done on earth, as it is in heaven." (S. Matt. vi. 10.) He who performs the Divine will, becomes a man after the Lord's "own heart," just as the Lord called David, "I have found David, the son of Jesse, a man after Mine own heart, which shall fulfil all My will." (Acts xiii. 22.) And why? Because David was always prepared to follow the Divine will—"O God, my heart is ready, my heart is ready." (Ps. cviii. 1.) And He desired nothing further of the Lord than that he might be taught to do His will, "Teach me to do the thing that pleaseth Thee." (Ps. cxliii. 10.)

Oh, of what great value is the act of perfect resignation to the will of God! It is sufficient in itself to make a saint. Whilst S. Paul was persecuting the Church, our Blessed Lord appeared to him, enlightened him, and converted him; the Saint immediately desired to do the Divine will: "Lord, what wilt Thou have me to do?" (Acts ix. 6.) And then our Lord said at once, "He is a chosen vessel unto Me, to bear My name before the Gentiles." (Acts ix. 15.) He who fasts, gives alms, mortifies himself for God, gives Him a part of himself—but he who gives God his will, gives Him his entire self, and this is that whole which God demands of us—the heart, that is, the will. "My son, give me thine heart." (Prov. xxiii. 26.) To fulfil the Divine will, in short, is the aim of all our desires, devotions, meditations, communions—it expresses the scope of all our prayers—the seeking for grace, that we may follow all that God would have us do; the asking for light and strength, to conform ourselves in all things to His will, but especially in the embracing of these things which are opposed to our self love, as Venerable Avila said, that a single "Blessed be God," for things contrary to us, was of more avail than an infinity of thanksgiving for such things as please us.

Affections and Prayers.

Oh, my God! my entire ruin in time past has been through my being unwilling to conform myself to Thy holy will. I hate and abjure many times, those days and moments in which, by doing my own will, I have opposed Thine, O God of my soul. Now I give it all to Thee; receive it, O my Lord, and bind it so closely to Thy love that it may never be able again to rebel against Thee. I love Thee, Infinite Goodness, and for the love that I bear Thee I offer myself wholly to Thee. Dispose of me, and of all that belongs to me, as it may please Thee, so that I in all things may resign myself to Thy holy will. Free me from the disgrace of having done that which was contrary to Thy will, and then do with me as Thou wilt. Eternal Father, hear me, for the love of Jesus Christ. My Jesus, hear me through the merits of Thy Passion.

Second Point.

We must conform ourselves to the will of God, not only in things contrary to us which come directly from God, such as loss of health, desolation of spirit, loss of relatives or possessions; but even in those ills which come from Him indirectly, such as slanders, slights, injustices, and all other kinds of persecution. And we should remember, that when we are injured by any one, in our goods or our honour, that God does not will the sin of him who injures us, but that He rightly wills our poverty and our humiliation. It is certain that whatever happens, does so by the Divine will. "I form the light, and create darkness: I make peace, and create evil." (Isa. xlv. 7.) The Preacher had said before, "Prosperity and adversity, life and death, poverty and riches, come of the Lord." (Ecclus. xi. 14.) In short, all things come from God, those that are good and those that are evil.

We call them evil, since we think and make them evil to us; but if we would accept them with resignation as coming from the hands of God, they would become to us, not evils, but blessings. The jewels which makes the crown of the saints so rich, are the tribulations, accepted from God, considering that all things came from His hands.

The holy Job, when he was told that the Sabeans had seized his goods, replied, "The Lord gave, and the Lord hath taken away." (Job i. 21.) He did not say that the Lord gave me these goods, and the Sabeans have taken them away; but "the Lord hath taken away;" and therefore Job blessed Him, considering, that all had happened after His will: "Blessed be the Name of the Lord." (Job i. 21.) The holy martyrs, Epictetus and Ato, when they were tortured with iron hooks and burning torches, only said, "Lord, fulfil Thy will in us!" When dying, these were their last words, "Be Thou blessed, O Eternal God, since Thou hast given us grace to fulfil Thy good pleasure."

This should be our frame of mind when adverse things befall us. Let us accept them all from the Divine hand, not only with patience, but with readiness, after the example of the Apostles, who "departed from the presence of the council, rejoicing that they were counted worthy to suffer shame for His Name." (Acts v. 41.) And what greater happiness can there be, than to endure some cross, and to know that by embracing it, we give pleasure to God?

If we desire, then, to live in uninterrupted peace, let us strive from henceforth to embrace the Divine will, saying ever of all things which may happen to us, "Even so, Father: for so it seemed good in Thy sight." (S. Matt. xi. 26.) O Lord, so hath it pleased Thee: so let it be. To this end we should direct all our meditations, communions, and prayers, ever imploring God that He would conform us to His will. Let us offer ourselves to Him, saying always, "My God, behold us! do with us as pleaseth Thee.

Affections and Prayers.

Oh, my Divine King! my beloved Redeemer, come Thou and reign from this day forward alone in my soul, and take entire possession of my will, since I desire nothing more, than to will as Thou willest. My Jesus, in the time past I have so often displeased Thee by opposing myself to Thy holy will, this thought gives me greater pain than if I had suffered every kind of punishment. I repent of it; it makes me sorry in my whole heart. I have deserved punishment. I do not refuse, but I accept it. Save me only from the punishment, of being deprived of Thy love, and then do with me as Thou pleasest. I love Thee, my dear Redeemer; I love Thee, my God; and because I love, I desire to do all things as Thou wilt. O Will of God! Thou art my love. O Blood of my Jesus, Thou art my hope; through Thee I hope to be henceforth united to the Divine will. This will shall be my guide, my desire, my love, and my peace; in which I desire ever to live and rest. "I will lay me down in peace, and take my rest." (Ps. iv. 9.) I will ever say, in all things that may happen to me, "My God, Thou hast thus willed, and so I will. My God, I will only as Thou hast willed; in me ever let "Thy will be done in me." (S. Matt. vi. 10.) My Jesus, by Thy merits grant me grace that I may ever repeat this sweet saying of love—"Thy will be done."

Third Point.

He who is united to the Divine will, enjoys even in this life, perpetual peace. "There shall no evil happen to the just." (Prov. xii. 21.) Yes; since the mind cannot have a greater contentment, than to see its every wish fulfilled, and if it does not will otherwise than the will of God, it has whatever it wishes for, —since whatever happens does so, entirely by the will of God. Resigned souls, says Salvian, if they are humbled, have what they desire; if they suffer poverty, they wish to be poor; in short, they will all things just as they happen, and therefore they lead a blessed life. Let come what will, cold or heat, or loss, or persecution, or sickness, or death, he who is united to God's will says, "I wish for this." He who rests upon the Divine will, and who is pleased with whatsoever the Lord may do, is like one placed above the clouds, who sees the tempests roll with so great rage below: but they do not touch him, neither hurt nor disturb him. It is of this peace that the Apostle says that it "passeth all understanding," (Phil. iv. 7,) which exceeds all the joys of the world, and is moreover such firm peace, that it allows of no change. "The discourse of a godly man is always with wisdom; but a fool changeth as the moon." (Ecclus. xxvii. 11.) The fool, that is to say, the sinner, "is changed as the moon;" he increases to-day, he lessens to-morrow; to-day he laughs, to-morrow he cries; to-day he is bright and altogether cheerful, to-morrow he is afflicted and morose; in short, he changes as things prosperous or adverse happen to him. But the righteous, like the sun, is ever equal and uniform in his tranquillity in all things that may happen, for his peace rests in his conforming himself to the Divine will.

We cannot fail to feel, in the inferior part of our soul, some stings from adverse things; but in the superior part, peace will ever reign, when our will is united with that of God. "Your joy no man taketh from you." (S. John xvi. 22.) But how great is the foolishness of those who resist the will of God, since what He wills must without fail be fulfilled. "Who hath resisted His will?" (Rom. ix. 19.) Whence these miserable ones have to suffer indeed the cross, but without fruit and without peace. "Who hath hardened himself against Him, and hath prospered?" (Job ix. 4.)

What else does God will, if not your good? "This is the will of God, even your sanctification." (1 Thess. iv. 3.) He wills to see us holy, by seeing us happy in this life, and blessed in the next. Let us consider that all the crosses which come to us from God "work together for good." (Rom. viii. 28.) Punishments even are not sent for our destruction, but that we may amend, and thus gain eternal happiness. God so loves us, that He not only desires, but is solicitous of the salvation of each one of us. "The Lord careth for me." (Ps. xl. 20.) And what will the Lord deny us, for, on our behalf He has given His Son Himself. "He that spared not His own Son, but delivered Him up for us all, how shall He not also with Him freely give us all things?" (Rom. viii. 32.) Let us then always abandon ourselves into the hands of that God, Who ever has concern in our good whilst we are in this life; "Casting all your care upon Him, for He careth for you." (1 S. Pet. v. 7.) Let us say with the sacred Spouse, "I am my Beloved's, and my Beloved is mine." (Cant. vi. 2.) My Beloved thinks of my good, and I desire to think of nought, but how I may please Him, and be uniting myself to His holy will. The Abbot Nilus says that we should never pray that God would do as we wish, but that we may do as He wills.

He who so acts, will lead a happy life, will die a holy death; and he who dies, wholly resigned to the Divine will, leaves behind him a moral certainty of his salvation. He who has not in life been united to the Divine will, cannot be so in death, and will not be saved. Let us endeavour, then, to render ourselves familiar with certain passages of Holy Scripture, which may help ever to keep us united with the Divine will. "Lord, what wilt Thou have me to do?" (Acts ix. 6.) Tell me, O Lord, what Thou willest me to do, that I may do it with all my will. "Behold the handmaid of the Lord." (S. Luke i. 38.) Save me, O Lord, and then do with me as pleaseth Thee; I am Thine—I am no longer my own. When any more considerable trouble happens to us, let us say, at once, "Even so, Father, for so it seemed good in Thy sight." (S. Matt. xi. 26.) So let it be, my God, as it pleases Thee. In addition to these, hold as sweet, the third petition of the Lord's Prayer, "Thy will be done in earth, as it is in heaven." (S. Matt. vi. 10.) Let us say it often with affection, and repeat it many times over. Happy are we, if we live and die, saying, "Thy will be done."

Affections and Prayers.

O Jesus, my Redeemer, Thou didst consume Thy life on the Cross in an agony of grief, to render Thyself the cause of my salvation; have pity then on me, and save me; and suffer not that soul, redeemed by Thee at so great a price, and by so much love, to hate Thee for ever in hell. Thou art not able to do more than oblige me to love Thee; and this Thou gavest me to understand when, before the death on Calvary, Thou saidst those loving words, "It is finished." (S. John xix. 30.) But how have I since, recognised Thy love? For the time past, I can say truly that I have done nothing, save offend Thee, and oblige Thee to hate me. I thank Thee for having borne with me with so much patience, and for now giving me time to remedy my ingratitude, and to love Thee before I die. Yes, I desire to love Thee, and to do everything that may please Thee; and I give to Thee, my will, my liberty, all that I have. I sacrifice to Thee from this time, my life; and I accept that death which Thou mayest send me, with all its pains and its attendant circumstances. I unite this sacrifice, from this time, with that great sacrifice which Thou, my Jesus, didst make for me, of Thy life upon the Cross. I desire to die that I may obey Thy will. Ah, through the merits of Thy Passion, grant me grace, that I may be in life ever resigned to Thy ordering of events; and when death shall come, grant that I may embrace it with a like submission to Thy holy good pleasure. I am willing to die, my Jesus, to please Thee; I would die saying, "Thy will be done."

www.ingramcontent.com/pod-product-compliance
Lightning Source LLC
Chambersburg PA
CBHW032108230426
43672CB00009B/1669
9783742814722